Contemporary Indian Diaspora

Contemporary Indian Diaspora

Literary and Cultural Representations

Edited by
Angshuman Kar

RAWAT PUBLICATIONS
Jaipur • New Delhi • Bangalore • Hyderabad • Guwahati • Kolkata

ISBN 978-81-316-0708-4

© Contributors, 2015

No part of this book may be reproduced or transmitted in any form or by any means, electronic or mechanical, including photocopying, recording or by any information storage and retrieval system, without permission in writing from the publishers.

Published by
Prem Rawat for **Rawat Publications**
Satyam Apts, Sector 3, Jawahar Nagar, Jaipur 302 004 (India)
Phone: 0141 265 1748 / 7006 Fax: 0141 265 1748
E-mail: info@rawatbooks.com
Website: www.rawatbooks.com

New Delhi Office
4858/24, Ansari Road, Daryaganj, New Delhi 110 002
Phone: 011 2326 3290

Also at *Bangalore, Hyderabad, Guwahati* and *Kolkata*

Typeset by Rawat Computers, Jaipur
Printed at Chaman Enterprises, New Delhi

Contents

Acknowledgements   vii

Contributors   ix

Literary and Cultural Representations of Indian Diaspora: New Perspectives   1
Angshuman Kar

Part 1
Theorizing Contemporary Indian Diaspora: Literary and Social Perspectives

1. Overwriting Memory: The Diaspora and Its Present   13
Jasbir Jain

2. That Third Space: Interrogating the Diasporic Paradigm   29
K. Satchidanandan

3. Diasporic Meditations   37
Mohan Ramanan

4. Globalization, Diaspora, and Transnationalism: Challenges and Opportunities for the Indian Diaspora   43
Ajaya K. Sahoo

Part 2
Contemporary Indian Diaspora in Fiction

5. Globalization, Diaspora, and the Dynamics of Genre: 'Imaginative Realism' in M.G. Vassanji's *The Assassin's Song*   67
Krishna Sen

6	Known Stranger: The 'Asian' in African Writing **T. Vijay Kumar**	81
7	Interrogating the 'Other' in Contemporary Indian Diaspora Fiction **Angshuman Kar**	90
8	Contextualizing *The Lowland* **Nilanjana Chatterjee**	102
9	Remapping the Fiction of Indian Diaspora: Zadie Smith's *White Teeth* and the Conundrums of Multiculturalism **Ashok K. Mohapatra**	113

Part 3
Contemporary Indian Diaspora in Films

10	Indian Diasporic Films: Tone, Tenor, and Accents **Himadri Lahiri**	139
11	Evolution, Manifestation, and Future Trends of Indian Diasporic Cinema in Britain **Somdatta Mandal**	158
12	Hybridity, Humour, and Resistance: The Case of Meera Syal MBE and the British Asian Diaspora **Vimal Mohan John and Aysha Iqbal Viswamohan**	184

Part 4
Contemporary Indian Diaspora in Plays and Poems

13	Why the Play *The Black Album*?: Hanif Kureishi, the Playwright and the Publishing Industry **Arnab Kumar Sinha**	199
14	Meena Alexander: A New Poetics of Dislocation **Subodh Sarkar**	213
15	Imtiaz Dharker's Responses to 9/11 and 7/7: A Study **Sanjoy Malik**	227

Index	238

Acknowledgements

The editor and the publisher thank the following publishing houses for granting permission to reprint material in this book:

Routledge for allowing us to reprint 'Globalization, Diaspora, and Transnationalism: Challenges and Opportunities for Indian Diaspora' by Ajaya K. Sahoo, which was originally published in *The Multicultural Dilemma: Migration, Ethnic Politics, and State Intermediation* (London: Routledge, 2012, 30–46), edited by Michelle Williams.

Pencraft International for allowing us to reprint 'The Third Space: Interrogating the Diasporic Paradigm' by K. Satchidanandan, which was originally published in K. Satchidanandan's *Authors, Texts, Issues: Essays on Indian Literature* (New Delhi: Pencraft, 2003).

The editor acknowledges his indebtedness to Professor Rama Kundu and Professor Himadri Lahiri for their invaluable suggestions for this project.

Contributors

Ajaya K. Sahoo is Assistant Professor and Director of the Centre for the Study of Indian Diaspora, University of Hyderabad. His areas of research interests comprise international migration, South Asian diaspora, transnationalism, religion, and ageing. Some of his recent publications include *Indian Transnationalism Online: New Perspectives on Diaspora*, co-edited with Johannes Kruijf (Ashgate, 2014); and *Indian Diaspora and Transnationalism*, co-edited with Michiel Baas and Thomas Faist (Rawat, 2012).

Angshuman Kar is Associate Professor and former Head, Department of English and Culture Studies, The University of Burdwan, West Bengal. He has also served the Sahitya Akademi as the Secretary of the Eastern Region. He has been widely published in India and abroad and has co-edited *The Politics of Social Exclusion in India: Democracy at the Cross-roads* (Routledge, 2010). Kar is also the recipient of the Australia-India Council Fellowship (2006) and a well-known Bengali poet.

Arnab Kumar Sinha is Assistant Professor in the Department of English and Culture Studies, The University of Burdwan, West Bengal. He has done his PhD on Chinua Achebe. He has co-edited *Indian Fiction in English: Mapping the Contemporary Literary Landscape* (2013). His areas of interests include African literature, South Asian literature, and diaspora studies.

Ashok K. Mohapatra is Professor of English at Sambalpur University, Odisha. He has published books and research papers both in India and abroad in the areas of postcolonial studies, cultural studies, translation studies, and stylistics. He is the editor of *Sambalpur Studies in Literatures and Cultures*. He has also guest edited *Global South* for Indiana University Press. Currently he is translating ancient Odia poetry.

Aysha Iqbal Viswamohan is Professor of Film Studies, Drama, and Popular culture in the Department of Humanities and Social Sciences, IIT Madras. She has published six books and over 30 papers in Indian and international journals. Her most recent work is *Postliberalization Indian Novels in English: Global Reception and Politics of Award* (Anthem, 2013).

Himadri Lahiri is Professor in the Department of English and Culture Studies, The University of Burdwan, West Bengal. He has published *Asians in America: Diasporic Perspectives in Literature* (2011) and edited *Literary Transactions in a Globalized Context: Multi-Ethnicity, Gender and the Market Place* (2011). His articles have been published in national and international journals and anthologies. He is now writing, along with Dr Ananda Mohan Kar, a book on the representations of the Chinese in India.

Jasbir Jain, Director, IRIS and a KK Birla Fellow in Comparative Literature, has written extensively on cultural and literary issues with a special focus on narratology, gender, and Indian literatures. Amongst her most recent publications are *Theorizing Resistance* and the forthcoming *Forgiveness: Between Memory and History*.

K. Satchidanandan, a well-known Malayalam poet, has won 27 literary awards including the Sahitya Akademi Award. He has more than 20 collections of poetry besides several books of travel, plays, and criticism including five books in English on Indian literature. He has represented India in many Literary Festivals and Book Fairs across the world including those held in London, Paris, Berlin, New York, Lahore, Abu Dhabi, Sharjah, Moscow, Montreal, Medellin, Delhi, and Jaipur. He was a Professor of English, the editor of *Indian Literature* and later the Secretary of the Sahitya Akademi and the Director of the

School of Translation Studies, Indira Gandhi Open University, Delhi.

Krishna Sen is former Head of the Department of English, University of Calcutta, and Visiting Professor at the University's Women's Studies Research Centre. She was Leverhulme Professor at the University of Leeds in 2008; Visiting Professor at the University of Vermont and Nippon Fellow at the Salzburg Seminar, both in 2002; and has delivered invited lectures at several universities including Stanford, Berkeley, and SOAS. She has several publications to her credit, the most recent being an edited volume, *Writing India Anew: Indian English Fiction 2000–2010* (Amsterdam University Press, 2013).

Mohan Ramanan is Professor of English at the University of Hyderabad and has been teaching since 1971. He has published widely in forums both in India and abroad and has enjoyed most of the fellowships usually available for English teachers. He has also taught abroad and is a published poet and a musician.

Nilanjana Chatterjee is Assistant Professor, Department of English, Durgapur Government College, West Bengal. She is working on the diasporic fiction of the women writers of the Indian subcontinent for her PhD. Her areas of interests are Indian English literature, diaspora studies, gender studies, and cultural theories.

Sanjoy Malik is Assistant Professor of English in the Department of English and Culture Studies at The University of Burdwan, West Bengal. He is currently working on the poetry of Imtiaz Dharker for his PhD. He has presented papers in several national and international conferences. His areas of interests include gender studies, diaspora studies, and postcolonial studies.

Somdatta Mandal is Professor of English and former Chairperson at the Department of English and Other Modern European Languages, Visva-Bharati, Santiniketan. Her areas of interest are contemporary fiction, film and culture studies, diaspora studies and translation. A recipient of several prestigious awards and fellowships like the Fulbright – Pre-doctoral

Fellowship, Fulbright Visiting Teaching Fellowship, Charles Wallace Trust and British Council Fellowship, Rockefeller Residency Fellowship at Bellagio, Salzburg Seminar Fellowship, Shastri Indo-Canadian Faculty Enrichment Fellowship, she has been published both nationally and internationally.

Subodh Sarkar is an eminent Bengali poet. He has received many literary awards including the Sahitya Akademi Award. He has been invited to read his poems in many prestigious literary festivals in India and abroad including those held in the USA, the UK, Greece, and Germany. He was also the editor of *Indian Literature*. Sarkar is now an Associate Professor of English at City College, Kolkata.

T. Vijay Kumar is Professor of English at Osmania University, Hyderabad. His research interests include postcolonial literatures, the Indian literary diaspora, translation, and educational television. His co-edited volumes include *Globalisation: Australian-Asian Perspectives* and *Focus India: Postcolonial Narratives of the Nation*.

Vimal Mohan John did his PhD from the Department of Humanities and Social Sciences, IIT Madras, where currently he is pursuing postdoctoral research on an extended fellowship in the area of film studies. He has published several papers in national journals and presented papers in various national and international conferences.

Literary and Cultural Representations of Indian Diaspora
New Perspectives

ANGSHUMAN KAR

Beyond the Borders: Diaspora in a Transnational World

After Khachig Tölölyan's famous statement in the first issue of *Diaspora* (1991), 'diaspora' has emerged as an umbrella term which includes not only community dispersal but also any form of migration. The term 'diaspora', Tölölyan argues, 'shares meanings with a larger semantic domain that includes words like immigrant, expatriate, refugee, guest-worker, exile community, overseas community, ethnic community' (4). In fact, at a conference in 1998 in Paris, Tölölyan even reported that the authors who had written in *Diaspora* had used the term 'diaspora' for 38 diverse groups.[1] As a result of this shift in the paradigm, certain significant changes have taken place in diaspora criticism. Undermining more rooted forms of belongings to regions and nations and sidelining the issues of persecution and oppression [highlighted by critics like Dabag and Platt (*Identität in der Fremde*) and Safran ('Diasporas in Modern Societies: Myths of Homeland and Return')], some diaspora critics have started focusing more on the 'constructive potential' of diaspora by viewing it as 'mediating cultures' (Clifford) wherein migrants try to come to terms with hybridized identity and multiple belongings (Tölölyan, K., 'Rethinking Diaspora(s)'). But this is only one side of the coin, as indiscriminate use of the term 'diaspora' and an uncritical celebration of fluidity have been contested by several other critics. In a 2004 essay, 'Deconstructing and Comparing Diasporas', William Safran, for instance, objected to the indiscriminate use of the term diaspora by arguing that 'the indiscriminate extension of the label to almost any group of expatriates, or even to individual migrants, has denuded the concept of much of its historical meaning and led to a conflation of the term, which has made it difficult, if not impossible, to distinguish diasporas from other kinds of minority communities and to reduce the concept to a useless metaphor' (9–10). I do not see reasons for objecting to the use of the term for individual migration which has almost become the norm of this globalized, transnational world and is as frequent as, if not more, the communal dispersal. Neither do I find anything wrong in the denuding of the term of its historical meaning, as history is always dynamic and never fixed and static; terms do have their histories of development. In this radical statement of Safran what concerns me is the possibility of the conversion of the term into a useless metaphor because of its indiscriminate use and overuse. I do agree with Safran when he asserts that diaspora communities have to be distinguished from other minority groups. We need to remember that all diaspora communities are minority groups but all minority groups are not diaspora communities.

What then constitutes diaspora, or, to be more specific, constitutes diaspora identity? Safran writes: 'diasporas comprise special kinds of immigrants because they have retained a memory of, a cultural connection with, and a general orientation toward their homeland culture and/or religion; they relate in some (symbolic or practical) way to their homeland; they harbor doubts about their full acceptance by the hostland; they are committed to their survival as a distinct community; and many of them have retained a myth of return' ('Deconstructing and Comparing Diasporas' 10). A definition like this might raise many eyebrows. It could be argued that in the new transnational constellation, routes have become more important than roots and flux than fixity. Increase in the ease of air travel and the worldwide connectivity that the cyberspace offers have jeopardized the older notions of home and belonging highlighting flux and fluidity of the diaspora experience. The world in recent years has seen immigrants who have one ancestral country, were born in another, had education in another and have temporarily settled down in yet another. What is the homeland for one such immigrant? A very pertinent question and very difficult to answer. But despite this fluidity of the identity of a diasporan, in critical and practical discourses, a diasporan is seldom dissociated from his/her homeland. We do talk about Indian diaspora, Greek diaspora, Irish diaspora and the like. Of course, along with homeland, Safran has also talked about religion, which is a very important parameter of diaspora identity. A lot has indeed been written on Sikh or Hindu or Muslim diaspora. Safran has not talked about ethnicity or language, but these two are also two other important parameters (think of Bengali diaspora or Punjabi diaspora or Khasi diaspora in the Indian context) of diaspora identity. One of these multiple parameters unquestionably intersects with the other but does not negate it. A Bengali diasporan in the US might well think of himself or herself – simultaneously or as and when required – as a part of South Asian diaspora, Indian diaspora and Hindu/Muslim diaspora. True that the homeland is conceived no more in the way it was used to be some 30 years back. True that transnational movements and the fracture in the diaspora identity along the religious/ethnic/linguistic lines have complicated the notion of 'home' and 'homeland'. But 'home' or 'homeland', for a diasporan, has not completely disappeared. Jhumpa Lahiri, who was born in England and then spent a significant time of her life in the US, and now has moved with her family to Rome, might think that she belongs nowhere. But she is very much considered an Indian (and perhaps, a Bengali too!) diaspora writer. One's identity is not only determined by the way one thinks of oneself, but also very much by how one is seen by others.

The relationship between transnationalism and diaspora also needs to be examined seriously. While some have argued in favour of using the two terms synonymously, some like Braziel and Mannur have tried to distinguish diaspora from transnationalism arguing that while transnationalism implies 'the flow of people, ideas, goods, and capital across national territories in a way that undermines nationality and nationalism as discrete categories of identification, economic organization, and political constitution', diaspora 'refers specifically to the movement – forced or voluntary – of people from one or more nation-states to another' (8). The flow of people is indeed often the result of, or at least connected with, the flow of goods and capital across national boundaries, but perhaps is never synonymous with it. Since even while on the move, people – unlike goods and, in particular, finance capital – carry the baggage of memory, the fluidity of capital and goods is different from the fluidity of the people on the move, though one usually intersects with the other. Braziel and Mannur, thus, have argued that though diaspora could be regarded as 'concomitant with transnationalism, or even in some cases consequent of transnationalist forces', it should not be 'reduced to such macroeconomic and technological flows' (8). Diaspora conditions, therefore, despite the present-day focus on routes and flux, are never free from the ever-present traces of roots.

The Book and Its Issues

Re-situating Indian Diaspora

Indian diaspora is, perhaps, one of the most diverse diasporas of the world. It has never been homogeneous and is divided along the lines of religion, region, and language. Migration of the Indians to different parts of the world has also not been uniform and consistent. Causes and consequences of migration have varied with the variation in time and space. Based on the six categories of Indian emigration historicized by Landy et al.[2] William Safran, Ajaya K. Sahoo, and Brij V. Lal have mapped the history of Indian diaspora through four distinct phases:

- Pre-colonial emigration;
- Colonial emigration that began in the 1830s to the British, French, and Dutch colonies;
- Post-colonial emigration to the industrially developed countries; and
- Recent emigration to West Asia. (xv)

These four phases, again, are often viewed in terms of the difference between the old diaspora and the new diaspora. It has been argued that the old diaspora could not maintain regular and close contact with the homeland, while the new diaspora, thanks to the revolution in transport and communication, is in continuous touch with the homeland and kins. However, like the old, the new diaspora is not a homogenous category and is fractured in terms of not only religion, region, and language but also class and caste. These are some of the issues dealt with[3] by K. Satchidanandan and Krishna Sen in their essays in this book. In an earlier essay, Sen has even used the terms 'subaltern migrants' or 'submigrants' to suggest the growing importance of class, particularly in the context of Indian diaspora.

Apart from caste and class, religion has always been important in Indian diaspora and it has acquired new meanings and dimensions in the post-9/11 context. Hate crimes and state suspicion have redefined religious affiliations which, in turn, have not only altered the old dynamics of relations between the natives of the hostland and the Indian diasporans but also between the Indians and other diaspora communities as also between one Indian diaspora community and another. Affiliations are being mediated, fashioned and re-fashioned by anxieties and trauma of different kinds. Three essays of this book, those of Arnab Kumar Sinha, Subodh Sarkar, and Sanjoy Malik, have treated some of these issues. My small piece in the book is also a continuation of their attempt at mapping the changing dynamics of relations between different communities within Indian diaspora and their negotiations with other non-Indian diaspora communities as well as with the natives. The slash in the binary that was earlier thought to be the marker of separation and association between the natives and the Indian diasporans only has now shifted itself to many new and un-thought-of positions. Problems of acculturation are no more the only problems for an Indian diasporan. S/he has to negotiate with problems of other kinds at other levels, beyond the old binary of the native/diasporan. Overcoming all these difficulties, it is interesting to note, as a collective force, Indian diaspora, as is shown in Ajaya K. Sahoo's essay in this book, is gradually becoming an economic and political asset to India.

Indian Diaspora within India?

Indian diaspora is not only conceived as situated outside India, beyond the geographical boundary of the nation-state, but very much within India. I attended a national seminar on diaspora and folklore this March in NEHU where most of the papers were on internal diaspora in India. Young scholars enthusiastically spoke on Garo diaspora in Assam or Khasi diaspora in Kolkata. In this book, Mohan Ramanan has also talked extensively on his diasporic experiences of living as a Tamil Brahmin in Kolkata. Ramanan's essay makes me think aloud about some issues, which, perhaps, we can no more avoid. Can internal migration be diasporic? Is there a homeland within a homeland? Will the use of the term 'diaspora' for the internal migrants turn it into a useless metaphor? Is a Northeast Indian in Delhi simply a member of a minority group or a diasporan? Could the killings of the Northeast Indians in the capital of our country be considered hate crimes? It is difficult to give 'yes/no' type of answers to these questions. The questions themselves are much more important than the answers. India is a huge and diverse country; if someone migrates from the Northeast to the South, it means a dislocation in the real sense of the term. But that could not be the case for someone migrating from Bengal to Odisha. History of India – both pre- and/or postcolonial – have brought some parts of the country so close to and have kept some other parts so separated from each other that the context – both historical and geographical – of migration has to be considered before using the term 'diaspora' for internal migration. Mohan Ramanan has argued that nobody is at home, everybody is abroad. True, in a sense. In a sense, everybody is in exile. But the context and the degree matter.

Diasporic Writing and Diaspora Studies

What is diasporic writing, or, what defines diasporic writing? I use the word 'writing' in a broad sense to include all forms of scripting; the term covers literature and performance, fiction and film. Some of the essays in this book – those of Somdatta Mandal and Himadri Lahiri – have raised direct or oblique questions about the nomenclature 'diasporic writing' and argued for the need for redefining and remapping the terrain of diaspora. Lahiri, for instance, has questioned if a diasporic director comes back to India and makes a film based on India – will that be enough to call such a film diasporic? If a non-diasporic director makes a film on, say, Indian diaspora in the UK – will that be a diasporic film? What makes a film diasporic? Location? Story? Characters? Cast? Or, the identity of the director? These are pertinent questions and are important in the context of diasporic 'writings' in general. Lahiri argues that a film that has no apparent connection with diaspora, might have diasporic dimensions. True. But can such a film be called diasporic? I doubt. To me, for diasporic writing, the most important thing is the identity of the author and then comes the story and the location. I would even like to propose that we should distinguish diasporic writing from diaspora studies. Diasporic writing must be on diaspora experiences and the author must be a diasporan. If an Indian diaspora filmmaker makes a film on India, I would not call it a diasporic film. Similarly, if an Indian director, who does not live in diaspora, makes a film on diaspora experiences, I would also not call it a diasporic film. I, however, agree with Lahiri that these films might have diasporic dimensions and also buy his argument that we need to critically look at a diasporan's take on India and an Indian's take on diaspora. That is exactly why, I would like to argue, we need to study these films (and writings like these) under the broad rubric of 'diaspora studies'. Diasporic writing, of course, is a part of – and has to be situated in the context of – diaspora studies. This book is also a book on diaspora studies and not on diasporic writings. That is why I have included Ashok K. Mohapatra's essay on Zadie Smith, as it offers a counter perspective on Indian diasporic writings.

Who is a Writer of the Indian Diaspora?

What makes one a writer of Indian diaspora? Some 30 or 40 years back, different terms were used to describe different Indian diaspora writers. For instance, to mark Raja Rao's visits to the homeland at regular intervals, the term 'expatriate writer' was used for Rao. Such terms have ceased to exist in contemporary critical discourses. Disappearance of such terms, however, has not been able to homogenize the heterogeneity of the Indian diaspora writers. Old questions and debates have been replaced by new ones. Should we call writers like V.S. Naipaul and Bharati Mukherjee – who have insisted on not considering them as 'Indian' writers – writers of the Indian diaspora? Is it just to consider someone like Neil Bissoondath (who is very remotely connected to India) or Meena Alexander (who, as is often pointed out by critics, left India for the US in her middle age in search of a better academic career) as a writer of Indian diaspora? Yes. I have already argued that individual migrants, irrespective of the causes of migration – have very much become part of the Indian diaspora. Again, for a writer of the Indian diaspora what matters is not the 'remoteness' or 'closeness' of the connection with India but the cultural association. Naipaul and Mukherjee – despite their own preferences respectively for the British and the American identities – are very much writers of the Indian diaspora, so are Bissoondath and Alexander. I have rather reservations about the use of the term 'Indian diaspora writer' for certain other authors. Is it just to call those authors Indian diaspora writers who live six months of a year abroad? Is such a writer also Indian diaspora writer who stayed for two to three years abroad and then has permanently relocated to India? Is Anurag Mathur an Indian diaspora writer? What about

Amitav Ghosh? Why should, again, 'Indian diaspora writer' be used as a tag only for those who write in English? What about the diaspora *bhasha* or language writers? One of the major Bengali poets, Alokeranjan Dasgupta, is in Germany for decades now. Very few Indian English diaspora poets' works can match the excellence of Alokeranjan's poetry, but he is seldom mentioned alongside them and is considered simply as a 'Bengali' poet or, at best, an Indian poet, but never a diaspora poet! It seems that to be a diaspora writer, one has to write in English. The angst, the trauma and the alienation that an Indian English diaspora writer experiences are also experienced by a *bhasha* writer of Indian diaspora. Indian diaspora studies must focus more and more on *bhasha* literatures of Indian diaspora. This is a point justly underlined by Jasbir Jain in her essay in this book and I fully agree with her claim that the *bhasha* writers are in constant touch with the homeland and that is why, perhaps, they are more specific than the Indian English diaspora writers in portraying the cultural nuances. To the critics, what should matter is not the medium but the honesty of expression.

Why Study the Cultural Representations of Indian Diaspora and How?

Indian diaspora is globally recognized as one of the most influential diaspora communities. Politically and economically it has become important to India too. *Pravasi Bharatiya Divas*, the day on which Indian diaspora is celebrated officially by the Indian government, is itself a proof of the governmental recognition that Indian diaspora has received. This, however, is not the only reason for studying the cultural representations of Indian diaspora. We, the Indian academics, should study the cultural representations of Indian diaspora for reasons more important than this. We are defined by our gaze at others and others' gaze at us, and none of these two gazes is more important than the other. Cultural representations of Indian diaspora offer a site – and perhaps this is the only site – where these two gazes meet and intersect. An Indian diasporan is both an Indian and a non-Indian. His/her take on India is both our take and others' take as is his/her take on the hostland, and both are important to us. Both Indian diasporic writings and Indian writings with diasporic dimensions, therefore, have to be studied not only to understand Indian diaspora writers' negotiations with globalized and transnational forces but also to situate ourselves on a global map. We cannot and should not even reject a text that offers nothing other than India-bashing as the reasons for the bashing – and the mentality that produces the bashing – needs to be studied. This should not mean an invitation to an uncritical celebration of Indian diaspora and its cultural representations. Neither does it mean that the cultural representations of Indian diaspora are important only as culture sites and are above aesthetic judgement. I would rather like to argue that we need to critically celebrate[4] Indian diaspora and its cultural representations. The very uneven character of the cultural representations of Indian diaspora requires our critical appreciation. The cultural representations of Indian diaspora are important, but importance, as we know, does not always guarantee excellence.

Notes

1. See Safran's essay 'Deconstructing and Comparing Diasporas' in *Diaspora, Identity and Religion: New Directions in Theory and Research*.
2. Landy et al. have divided the history of Indian migration into six phases:

    '(a) merchants who went to East Africa or Southeast Asia before the 16th century; (b) migration of various groups (traders, farmers) to neighbouring countries (Sri Lanka, Nepal); (c) indentured labourers to colonial empires like the Caribbean, Fiji, Mauritius, or Natal; as well as migration through middleman (*kangani, maistry*) to Southeast Asia; (d) migration of skilled workers after the Second World War towards the developed countries (UK); (e) migration of contract workers to the Gulf countries; and (f) recent migration of knowledge workers to developed countries (USA)' (quoted in Safran, Sahoo and Lal xv).

3. So many other scholars like Makarand Paranjape, Jasbir Jain, and Avadhesh Kumar Singh have written on this. See Paranjape's *In Diaspora: Theories, Histories, Texts*. See also Paranjape's 'Interrogating Diasporic Creativity: The Patan Initiative', Jain's 'Memory, History and Homeland: The Indian Diasporic Experience' and Singh's 'From Gunny Sack to Ruck Sack: Proposals Pertaining to Indian English Diasporean Discourse' in *Theorizing and Critiquing Indian Diaspora*.
4. For this term, I am indebted to Avadhesh Kumar Singh and Makarand Paranjape. Singh first used the term in his presentation in an international seminar on Indian diaspora in Patan and Singh's use of the term was underlined by Paranjape in his 'Interrogating Diasporic Creativity: The Patan Initiative'.

References

Braziel, Jana Evans and Anita Mannur. 'Nation, Migration, Globalization: Points of Contention in Diaspora Studies'. *Theorizing Diaspora*. (eds) Braziel and Mannur. Oxford: Blackwell, 2003. 1–22.

Clifford, J. 'Diasporas'. *Cultural Anthropology* 9.3 (1994): 302–338.

Dabag, Mihran and Kristin Platt, (eds). *Identität in der Fremde*. Bochum: Brockmeyer, 1993.

Jain, Jasbir. 'Memory, History and Homeland: The Indian Diasporic Experience'. *Theorizing and Critiquing Indian Diaspora*. (eds) Kavita A. Sharma, Adesh Pal, and Tapas Chakrabarti. New Delhi: Creative Books, 2004. 74–81.

Kokot, Waltraud, Khachig Tölölyan and Carolin Alfonso (eds). *Diaspora, Identity and Religion: New Directions in Theory and Research*. London: Routledge, 2004.

Paranjape, Makarand, (ed.). *In Diaspora: Theories, Histories, Texts*. New Delhi: Indialog, 2001.

———. 'Interrogating Diasporic Creativity: The Patan Initiative'. *Theorizing and Critiquing Indian Diaspora*. (eds) Kavita A. Sharma, Adesh Pal, and Tapas Chakrabarti. New Delhi: Creative Books, 2004. 42–73.

Safran, William, Ajaya Kumar Sahoo, and Brij V. Lal. 'Indian Diaspora in Transnational Contexts'. Introduction. *Transnational Migration: The Indian Diaspora*. (eds) Safran, Sahoo and Lal. London: Routledge, 2009. vii-xxxv.

Safran, William. 'Deconstructing and Comparing Diasporas'. *Diaspora, Identity and Religion: New Directions in Theory and Research*. (eds) Waltraud Kokot, Khachig Tölölyan and Carolin Alfonso. London: Routledge, 2004. 9–29.

———. 'Diasporas in Modern Societies: Myths of Homeland and Return'. *Diaspora* 1.1 (1991): 83–99.

Sharma, Kavita A., Adesh Pal, and Tapas Chakrabarti, (eds). *Theorizing and Critiquing Indian Diaspora*, New Delhi: Creative Books, 2004.

Singh, Avadhesh Kumar. 'From Gunny Sack to Ruck Sack: Proposals Pertaining to Indian English Diasporean Discourse'. *Theorizing and Critiquing Indian Diaspora*. (eds) Kavita A. Sharma, Adesh Pal, and Tapas Chakrabarti. New Delhi: Creative Books, 2004. 224–249.

Tölölyan, K. 'The Nation-state and Its Others: In Lieu of a Preface'. *Diaspora* 1.1 (1991): 3–7.

———. 'Rethinking Diaspora(s): Stateless Power in the Transnational Moment'. *Diaspora* 5.1 (1996): 3–36.

Part 1

Theorizing Contemporary Indian Diaspora

Literary and Social Perspectives

Chapter 1

Overwriting Memory

The Diaspora and Its Present

JASBIR JAIN

> ... the life one has lived is unknowable except in the most superficial of ways, that one is somehow doomed to be a tourist in the landscape of one's past – and the tourist's landscape is one that exists only in imagination, its objectivity suspect, its reality fluid.
> — Neil Bissoondath[1]

> All it took then in Trinidad was looking for Indians, all it took now in Canada was skin colour. We had not moved one inch.
> — Ramabai Espinet[2]

> Son, I am glad you left. We too backward here.
> — Cyril Dabydeen[3]

Who is the diaspora? The reader may notice that all the three epigraphs I have selected are from writings of the children of the indentured labourers, the third, fourth, or fifth generation. Additionally all of them are twice migrants, the second migration taking place voluntarily to a new land, away from the land of their birth and upbringing. The second migration at once provides them with two homelands – one they have known and experienced physically, the other remembered through cultural artefacts, fractured narratives, twice or thrice removed tales and the words that are present in their everyday discourse echoing a faraway past.

The South Asian diaspora, especially with histories of indenture, has been amply theorized and theory, as is expected, is constantly shifting and evolving as frameworks, approaches and locations change. It is important to ask the question: what is it that enters the theoretical discourse to change the direction? Is it just newness, some unexplored area, a new psychological or philosophical approach or a new piece of writing that challenges existing theories? I am convinced that writing goes ahead of theory and refuses to be framed by it; we theorize in order to locate our own perceptions and responses, and at times adopt a framework which appears to offer space, meaning, and newness.

Migrations are in themselves as ancient as known histories – whether we refer to the Biblical journeys or the travels motivated by adventure, lure of wealth, search for land or power. Migrancy and dislocation have always been there but what makes the diaspora significant is that the early journeys were not guided by any of the above motives – not even pure exile. They were out of compulsion and need, and brought with them a denial of a human condition. Today diaspora is an umbrella term which fails to make any distinction between exiles, indenture, slaves, expatriates, or employment dislocations. Concepts such as nation, citizenship, and human rights have entered the discourse. In fact, the change in the all-inclusive meaning of diaspora, in itself, partly narrates the reason why Vijay Mishra makes a general distinction between the 'old diaspora of exclusiveness ... and the new diaspora of the border ...' (27), but Makarand Paranjape holds a different view. Bringing travel, rural-urban divide and relationships between the two diasporas, he is of the view, 'The diaspora, then, must involve a cross-cultural or cross-civilization passage ... . Also, the crossing must be forced, not voluntary; otherwise the passage will amount to an enactment of desire-fulfilment' (6). In such a case there would necessarily be a little mourning and a mild cultural shock, if any, at the first encounter.

No matter which method we adopt toward defining or un-defining it, no definition will hold all diasporic journeys together whether imperial migrations, settler communities, adoption of a country other than a homeland and tenures of employment in unfamiliar terrains. The last is applicable to the British in India and meets most of the requirements of Paranjape, including language and religion. William Arnold's novel, *Oakfield; or Fellowship in the East*,[4] written while in India is a testimony to the loneliness and trauma. Perhaps an important distinction one could make is between linear and non-linear. In actuality the early South

Asian diaspora as contract employees, for whom the dream of return was neither feasible, and later, not even promising made linear journeys. Today's intellectual and technological migrations are also largely linear with the money power and the dubious mixture of visibility/invisibility. In Canada and elsewhere, racial differences make the immigrants a visible minority but for all else, in terms of agency and power, there is an anonymity attached to the majority. But as Uma Parameswaran once pointed out that the power (and recognition), which the Indian diaspora experiences on a return visit to home is like a heady wine. The exchange rate of the dollar and the pound gives them an additional advantage.[5]

Another subdivision comes into being through the writing in languages, when Punjabi, Gujarati or Marathi writers abroad write in their mother tongues. Associated with this is also a sense of parochialism created both in their homeland as well as hostland. In the latter it builds up a sense of community as magazines, plays and performances knit people together. Even those who write in English often build a sense of belonging on the basis of the language they learnt as their first language.[6] These are some of the ways of belonging, hoarding memory, preserving the past, and in one way putting the traumatic incidents such as Komagata Maru in the past.

I have in mind three other solitary categories – those who remember and those who forget. During a visit to South Africa, I picked up a collection of short stories by Ronnie Govender, *At the Edge and Other Cato Minor Stories* (1996),[7] which as they dealt with apartheid in South Africa also carried an Indian past in names and customs. I wrote to him and he responded, not really admitting an Indian past but apparently reflecting it in his writing. I presume he has not visited India. Another work *Black Chin, White Chin* is a novel, which is described as an evocative portrait of five generations of descendants of former indentured Indian labourers and their struggle to build an identity in an emerging South Africa.[8] But the diasporic criticism from India and about India does not engage with these writers who have not migrated a second time or moved to the west, and have not fallen into the role of a victim, despite their success in intellectual terms. Why? The second of these neglected categories is one of exiles unless they or we have the ability to romanticize them. My reference is to the well-known artist, M.F. Husain, who was also a filmmaker, and had finally to leave India when it became impossible for him to express himself in his chosen mediums due to right-wing opposition, a general hostility and vandalization of his paintings. Where lay his trauma – here or there? He migrated at the age of 91 and later when an honorary citizenship was offered to him by the government of Qatar, he accepted it. Husain died in 2006 in a foreign land. His death can be mourned by Zafar's ghazal '*Do gaz zameen bhi na mili kuye yaar mein*' (Not even two yards of land was available in the abode of my beloved).[9] For Husain, exile was one-way, a rejection by his country and without the possibility of return, leading to a sense of betrayal and loneliness and hard to live with. Does a Husain need a collectivity to claim diaspora attention?

My third category is the global soul, who has adapted himself to new technologies and globalization and is a nomad, who makes no claims and belongs nowhere. In fact, Pico Iyer uses an epigraph from Simone Weil's poem, which ends with the line, 'We must be rooted in the absence of a place'. This is a willed otherness, a willed deracination inhabiting spaces which simultaneously expand and shrink. One word Iyer uses frequently is nowarian, embodying within it a sense of constant replacement and perhaps renewal. Iyer is unable to read his native language, has had a travelling childhood, a habit which has persisted in adulthood. He records a meeting with Kazuo Ishiguro, who was a child migratory at age five and part neither of Japan, nor of Britain and labelled by his looks as a foreigner in the western world. These experiences of removal and distinction are shared alike by diaspora and global soul. The global soul draws its freedom from a sense of non-affiliation of being 'loosed from time as much as from space'. Iyer writes 'I had no history, I could feel, and lived under the burden of no home ...' (23). He admits that unable to pronounce his given name, he goes by an Italian name. Never been in a position to vote, he has ended up renouncing all democratic participation and locating nation, nationality and rootedness of belonging in a no man's land. Where does one place the global soul in terms of identity and subjectivity, in terms of long term relationships and the archives of memory?

Having listed the categories that defy collective definitions, I have now to ask myself two questions: why should we, located in India, theorize the diaspora? And if there is enough cause for doing so, how should we set about it? There is reason enough to theorize the diaspora, especially the expressions of relatedness and remembrance, their affiliations with the mother country and the audiences and admirers they find here as also for the recognition at the international level by award deciding juries on cultural or anti-cultural grounds. We need to theorize and evaluate them for more reasons than the one stated above: especially the language writers who have a constant communication with their homeland and are more specific in their treatment of cultural nuances than the writers writing in English, but the latter get a wider academic attention. The fact that a fair amount of academic effort is spent on diasporic studies, obviously by encroaching on the space of the writing in English by the non-diasporic ones, is another fact that needs to be examined in terms of academic worth and justification. There is sufficient cause to theorize the diaspora if for naught else, in order to get our bearings straight. Now the other significant question remains: *how*?

Sudesh Mishra in his work *Diaspora Criticism* has given a detailed account of the major theoretical approaches up till the beginning of the present century. The work appeared in 2006; one can safely assume that the period till 2004 has been covered including that of Paul Gilroy (*Black Atlantic*, 1993), Homi Bhabha, Vijay Mishra, Dipesh Chakrabarty, and Stuart Hall. There is also another work, Sam Durant's *Postcolonial Narrative and the Work of Mourning* (2004) which like Vijay Mishra's asks the question of remembering: what do we remember and what forget and how are the two processes interlinked? The work draws attention not only to the selective nature of memory but also its counterpart of forgetting and amnesia – willed or not willed. When territorial expanses change and language becomes distant, how does one inhabit a vacuum and make it habitable? I will, however, not go into these aspects, especially not at this point but would like to respond to Vijay Mishra's 'Diaspora and the Art of Impossible Mourning' and Shiva Kumar Srinivasan's 'Diaspora and its Discontents' both of which work with and reconstruct theoretical issues.

Vijay Mishra takes up the Derridean reference to mourning, signifying a total finality and the impossibility of retrieval. Derrida's *Work of Mourning* is about the loss of his friends and consists of addresses delivered in their memory, mostly as *mémoires* and are adieus and recollections: as such the finality of death is what is considered. Mishra by using 'Impossible Mourning' also indicates a definite finality of the past which can never be recovered either physically or emotionally or kept alive through an unchanged memory. It is a loss which has to be remembered as a loss; the journey has been a linear one, in this case the indenture workers' sea journeys. But there is another word in Mishra's title, which calls for attention – 'Art' in the 'Art of Impossible Mourning'. This can have several connotations – art as a practice, as that of professional mourners, a repetitive act, a constant presence which through externalization and repetition, works as a therapy, and art as a narrative, the telling or imagining of an event otherwise inaccessible, to keep the memory alive for future generations, as a recording. In this connection, it would be relevant to explore the dimensions of memory in Paul Ricoeur's work, *Memory, History and Forgetting* (2004). Ricoeur draws our attention to the finality which a narrative confers on the real (276). He goes on to add that even in historical recounting the past is overlaid, 'the historian's representation is indeed a present image of an absent thing, but the absent thing itself gets split into disappearance, into existence in the past' (280). The past is over but not done with. It is still there in its ghostly existence, caught in the moment, incapable of any flexibility or shift or renewal.

Does this account for the diaspora's constant return to the past, to a history known only through fragmentary accounts and incomplete and rough-edged, half remembered and half forgotten customs, practices and rituals, almost like a distant archives, now in ruins? Caryl Phillips in his *Crossing the Bar*[10] has captured the past through imagined lives, memories of three siblings placed in different spaces and living in the fluidity of time. One part of the jig-saw puzzle is supplied by the diary of the slave ship's captain, an unwilling slave of his compulsions, locked up in the memories of his family. This too is a kind of mourning, an externalization of an inherited past. It is also a 'resistance to history' in its sidelining of statistics and in travelling back to the point of the beginning after its journey of over nearly two centuries. Recounting imagining and narrating are acts which simultaneously turn to the past and the future and attempt to construct a bridge. Vijay Mishra, himself, a *jahazi bhai*, dislocated from Fiji and presently in Australia, commands a certain authority in his glance back. He insists on the work of mourning as a necessary prelude to setting the 'ego free'. Mishra's reference inevitably travels back to the Freudian melancholia, distinguishing between the two – mourning and melancholia. While the first sets the ego free the second possesses it through its failure to objectify the loss.

But as we look at the progeny of the indentured workers, is it not that the 'trauma' is now distantly realized in the form of a displacement and not as an experienced act, that identification with the hostland is more or less complete with the Caribbean past surfacing more often than their ancestors' India, as part of their lives? I have in mind writers like Neil Bissoondath.[11] This gives rise to other related questions such as: why does diaspora writing dwell on the past and what significance does ancestral history have for the recovery of a lost identity? In contrast to the displaced categories, why do writers like Bharati Mukherjee, Salman Rushdie, and Rohinton Mistry turn to history, when each writer is so different from the other? And *how* do they remember history? The older diaspora and their generation foreground space – houses, rooms, attics before moving on to landscapes, rituals, customs, practices, the bamboo marriage, while voluntary diaspora circles around cities, Kolkata, Mumbai, Bangalore which in themselves are expansive and non-definable forces that resist possession. Moreover, if we wish to problematize nation and homeland, how does one surmount the factor of citizenship, divided loyalties and long distance nationalism?

Vijay Mishra, in the essay under discussion, expands on the idea of the proxy newly fabricated homelands (37) constructed on the basis of narrow loyalties, religious histories, and new identity formation. Significant factors in this reconstruction are money power and the desire of political power. Sudesh Mishra, likewise refers to this and views it as a resistance to hybridity, and listing a whole lot of works embodying the idea writes, '... all testify to diaspora as the smithy where menacing forms of ethnonationalisms are ritually hammered out. Such reactionary positions, if not openly then covertly, rely on the *political disavowal of an ethical future* based on recognising the asymmetry of race, ethnicity, nation and culture' (Sudesh Mishra 76, emphasis mine). I deliberately emphasize the loss of the ethical as well as the underlying anti-modern and pro-feudal position. Do we not have the right to resist and question this? The participants in these moves are mostly the voluntary diaspora, not the ones who left under compulsion. Long distance nationalism is disruptive and has strong links with terrorism and is frightening both in its appropriation of our democratic rights and its hidden hand in fostering a fragmentation of our national psyches. The recent election scenario, the lobbying based on right wing ideologies, new split identities coming into being through divided diasporic selves into a pro-native culture and, on the other hand, a pro-western code of living marked with a certain disdain for the homeland. There is an obvious need to question the nature of the impossible mourning, its truth and fiction. Do we locate it somewhere near Lacan's *real* and *imaginary*, both of which are in the long run unreal, or accept a certain degree of homelessness as an unacknowledged reality? Zizek while commenting on the Lacanian concept of the real also comments on the melancholic and writes 'the melancholic is not primarily the subject fixated on the lost object, unable to perform the work of mourning on it; he is, rather, the subject who possesses the object, but has lost his desire for it, because the cause which made him desire the object has withdrawn, lost its efficiency'. Hence melancholy has come to stand 'for the presence of the object'. Again, Kate McGowan in 'The Real' talks about the Wachowski brothers film trilogy *The Matrix* and referring to it as an interrogation of the real, locates the idea of freedom in the act of thinking and willing, not memory. The real is also a recall, hence a representation and as such is not real.

The second essay, I wish to consider is Srinivasan's 'Diaspora and Its Discontents'. Srinivasan works with the Freudian concept of 'discontent', the 'irremediable antagonism between the demands of the instinct and the restrictions of civilization' (Freud, quoted in Srinivasan 52). Moving on to the extension of repression to Marxist critics, he finally arrives, inevitably as it were, at the Lacanian approach to the relationship between the order of the imaginary and the institution of aggressivity, a correlate of narcissism in the human subject.[12] Srinivasan then proceeds to make a valuable distinction between historical and structural as also between a material interpretation of repression and the more intrinsic response in terms of negotiating narcissism and alienation. Repeatedly he uses the combined term 'imaginary aggressivity', by which his emphasis is on identity formation leading to a more stable self and subjectivity. Srinivasan doesn't use the terms which I have, but the moment we disconnect the imaginary aggressivity from the inequity in society the origin of the new emancipatory narrative has to lie somewhere in the individual, especially if, at some point, the Lacanian mirror stage is to be recognized. This supplements Vijay Mishra's view that mourning 'sets the ego free' (36). Except Srinivasan, linking the same imaginary to aggressivity, foregrounds the latter and attributes to it a positive action, rather than an indulgence in historical narratives and traumatic mourning. Trauma in itself is a difficult experience to reconstruct or relive. What we remember of it, except for a sense of loss which lies buried deep down within us, is an imagined recollection of the conscious memory.

Again, when we review the history of visits home vis-à-vis return, the anger and hatred often displayed by the diaspora, the emotional moving away, unable to participate at any existential level, there is an acknowledgement that the return home will fail to reinstate.[13] It is through this psychoanalytical approach the compulsive act of reliving or recreating the past of diasporic writers writing about India is explained by several critics including Mishra and Srinivasan.[14] Srinivasan's query as to why does the subject repeat, voices what many of us have asked: why do they come back to India (emotionally, not necessarily physically), in search of their raw material? Is it a 'pure' renegotiation of memory and space? Or is there some other motive? Because all histories that are imagined do not necessarily rest on known narratives. This is a larger question and the answer will vary from writer to writer, work to work and I'll refrain from taking it up here as it requires expansion beyond the present concern.[15]

Placing the theoretical positions of Vijay Mishra and Srinivasan side by side one is conscious of a difference in their positions and the directions they wish to indicate. Mishra moves through a position of mourning of recall to the emancipation of the ego, while Srinivasan's structural approach is a psychoanalytic analysis (I was initially going to use the word dissection, which is appropriate in its own right). But none of the two critics provides the answer to my question: *Why* do we, located in India, a distanced memory of a forgotten and an abandoned home, feel the compulsion to theorize their work? I can see two reasons both overlapping with the *how*. True, diaspora writing is uneven: some of it merely exotic, a formula put together, some other more seriously and inwardly involved, close to the heart and echoing Trilling's concept of authenticity, with the relationship to India, both a personal and an intellectual engagement, capable of transcending the one to one communication and reaching out to express more existential concerns, but some is only an exercise in India-bashing. The reasons for return are very different in each case. It is not necessarily a search for raw material in the writing which speaks from personal involvement, exploration or historical engagement or a deep-rooted need to know the past, while the exotic, formula writing is a search for newness and difference, an easy-at-hand accessibility where myth, violence or stagnancy can be woven into the narrative. There is an urgent need to examine the writing of the diaspora and their impulse to come back in their memory or imagination to Indian themes in a more critical way, than we have done so far.

The celebratory status yielded to all alike, and more especially the virulent ones and exotic manufactured histories, leads us to ask the question how do they relate to us at home? And this is not merely an ideological question; it is more concerned with intention, direction, and purpose. Do they appropriate and encroach upon the creativity at home? They are more visible, more easily accessible to the western reader with their own distant eye which dilutes cultural ethos while the writing in Indian languages, with its unfamiliar cultural nuances, is not so easily accessible to them. Arun Mukherjee has accepted this in *Oppositional Aesthetics* and Gayatri Spivak justifies it in her introductions to Mahasweta Devi's stories on similar grounds. My own experience of unfolding Indian and Indian diasporic writing abroad confirms me in this view. Ismat Chugtai's 'Chauth Ka Jora' is difficult for the western reader and Ananthamurthy's *Samskara* requires a greater involvement from the reader, while Bharati Mukherjee's melodramatization of the Kali image in *Jasmine* is so obvious, and any formula narrative about sati, dowry death or the outline of the *Ramayana* narrative or of the *Mahabharata* gets accepted fairly easily. The literary and critical space they initially claim because of their Indianness, appropriates the native space reducing the relationship between us and them to that of *id* and *ego*. I use the Freudian concepts here. The problem is not entirely with the writing but with the uncritical critical reception which has shifted from aesthetics to origins and is often, in the writing in English, already governed by the recognition abroad. Is there no qualitative difference between how we read and how the other culture reads? Is a literary text totally self contained and has no connection with the outside or with cultural receptions or locations?

I intend to focus on some Caribbean writers who have migrated, a second migration, to Canada or England, writers who have an ancestral history of indenture, in order to address the question of their relationship to India and the manner in which their writings reflect their inherited memories of the past – Naipaul, Bissoondath, Dabydeen, and Espinet. Naipaul's writing is virulent and full of condescension, except for *A House for Mr Biswas*. His travelogues are journeys already performed in his mind or framed by his readings, except for *India: A Million Mutinies Now*, where he identifies with the rising religious aggression and comments upon this vitality. Lacking the space to elaborate further I refer the reader to his *Letters Between a Father and Son* which includes several written to his sister.[16] His choices for escape, he feels, are limited: not Trinidad which has no history, not India which has only a historical past, hence another island, Britain where he lovingly relates to the landscape.[17]

Naipaul's *The Mimic Men* is a most revealing text, which recalled even in his Nobel Lecture, described it as a book about colonial men mimicking the conditions of manhood, men who had grown to distrust everything about themselves (2001). It is here that the Freudian relationship between *id* and *ego* applies to him. The truth is that we carry the past with us, though we never visit it (*Mimic Men* 185). I draw the reader's attention also to a reference to *Asvamedha*, the horse sacrifice (152–153). Naipaul has always carried his double origin uneasily, hating both, resisting and resenting both but returning to them over and over again. The Naipaulian view is that all revolutions are futile. In his two later novels about India, both of which received unfavourable reviews, *Half-a-Life* and *The Magic Seeds*, Willie is a failure. His involvement in the revolution leads to nothing and a subsequent move to Africa, stresses the same. There is no cause worth fighting for and thus Willie is doomed to sponging on others in England. Nowhere is there any move on Willie's part towards self reflection, no questioning of the individual's role. The title of the second novel *Magic Seeds* is obvious in its reference to genetically modified, terminator seeds which do not propagate and are sterile.

In contrast to Naipaul, Bissoondath, his own sister's son, opts out the Naipaulian inheritance as does Cyril Dabydeen.[19] The other

Dabydeen – David – in England also lovingly explores his past. But what is it they remember from the land of their ancestors? I'll take up only two examples: Bissoondath's first collection of short stories and his non-fiction *Selling Illusions*. The latter is an identification with Canada and a questioning of the official multicultural policy, but the first *Digging Up the Mountains* offers rich narrative experiments with personas, landscapes and imagined constructs, working at several levels of migrations, of belonging and alienation and constructing the self bit by bit by being buffeted about rather than defining it through location in the idea of race, a distant past or an alienated self. The scenes of his childhood memories are from West Indies – not India. Dabydeen, likewise, roots himself in the West Indies, and when he refers to India, it is through picked up symbols. In the story 'Jet Lag' in *My Brahmin Days,* where he negotiates the Naipaulian fear of India, as the flight lands he reminds himself, 'I was a Canadian entering a foreign land. This was no mere defence mechanism. History dispensed with, Kala Pani vanished. The flux of time and change only .... I was a Canadian in a vast new land' (82–83). (But ironically the officer at the airport includes him in his sweeping statement, 'We are all Indian here'). The problem of belonging is at both levels – race and emotion. India is not a nightmare, people here are as normal and well-meaning and hospitable as elsewhere (refer *My Brahmin Days*). But all the while he is conscious and accepts the possibility of realizing fully well that it is not possible to return to the past and aware that he doesn't belong there. Dabydeen, like Bissoondath, transmutes history through selected events and creates a childhood past in the Caribbean home of plantations. Ramabai Espinet, who is another Caribbean who has migrated to Canada, in her novel *The Swinging Bridge*, weaves both her past – the immediate and the ancestral – together in the history and its recordings in a family narrative where houses and land symbolize belonging, where the approaching end of her brother Kelly does not make the novel pessimistic or Kelly a passive character.

Coming back to the initial premise – how do we theorize and why do we theorize, it is obvious that there is a need to question existing theories, if our relationships are not to end up in myth-making and generalities, and if we are to capture the changing shifts in diasporic writing, a psychoanalytic approach is most significant, whether it is trauma or discontent or the uncovering of the subconscious. I have used location along with the

Freudian *id* and *ego*. We need to recognize and critique, diasporic writing not as an ego evolving itself on our presence but as a different category, calling for judgement on its own. Similarly, we need to free ourselves of the easy subordination based on affiliation rather than aesthetics, and recognize our own subjectivity, across our different languages, including English as one of them and bring them together not as a purely academic exercise but as an aesthetic and a historical reality. And this I feel allows us to be objectively perceptive, to evaluate aesthetically and to locate them in history and oeuvre. No work of art is truly independent or self-contained. Exile or forced migration is a 'space-time continuum' that has not been chosen, but once placed in such a situation the constructing of a new society or community is an ethical responsibility, which the writer cannot abandon.

Notes

1. See Neil Bissoondath's *Doing the Heart Good*, 13. Bissoondath's novel and Rohinton Mistry's *Family Matters* (2003) stand the comparison favourably. Mistry, a migrant, returns to India for his location, recreates and relives it with love, while Bissoondath chooses Canada, writes a narrative equally powerful dealing with relationships between generations.
2. See Ramabai Espinet's *The Swinging Bridge*, 78.
3. See Cyril Dabydeen's 'Berbice Crossing' in *Berbice Crossing and Other Stories*, 111.
4. William Arnold (1828–1859) was Matthew Arnold's younger brother who worked in the British administration in India. He wrote several articles and one novel, *Oakfield; or, Fellowship in the East* (1853), exploring spiritual meeting points between East and West. Critical of the unfriendly and unchristian attitude of his British colleagues, the novel is sad and lonely. William died young at the age of 31.
5. In fact, most of the upper class diaspora buy their furnishings and jewellery from India and plan exotic holidays to Goa, Kerala, or Ladakh. This is for two reasons – the less expensive material compared to that of the West, and also to escape as much of home stay as possible. Some even go to the extent of staying in hotels instead of the family homes. Intellectuals seek more visibility here;

writers wish to capture a large reading public. Justifiable reasons but hardly any different from the outsiders.

6. For more details, refer my essay, 'The New Parochialism: Homeland in the Writing of the Indian Diaspora'. *In Diaspora: Theories, Histories, Texts.* (ed.) Makarand Paranjape. New Delhi: Indialog Publications, 2001. 79–92.
7. Ronnie Govender is an established writer – short story writer, novelist and playwright. This collection of short stories published by Manx in 1996 is about the lives of the indentured community.
8. Description on the back cover of the novel (New Delhi: Harper Collins, 2007).
9. Bahudar Shah Zafar, the last Mughal Emperor, was imprisoned in Rangoon after the Indian defeat in 1857. The grave is of utmost significance to the Muslims – his own and those of his ancestors. Intizar Husain in his novel *Basti* and several of his short stories points out this importance. Refer *Basti*, 139.
10. Caryl Phillips is also a child migrant like Pico Iyer, but unlike him is rooted in the historical past.
11. Neil Bissoondath, a Caribbean-Canadian, lives in the present and is directed towards the future. Refer especially his *Selling Illusions: The Cult of Multiculturalism in Canada* where he insists on recognition as a Canadian. The same year another work came out *If You Love This Country: Fifteen Voices for a United Canada*.
12. Srinivasan, see footnotes 6 and 7, 65.
13. Ibid.: 56–57.
14. Ibid.: 57. Though it is equally true that while part of the reason is this, somewhere also is the autobiographical impulse, a past which imparts them a distinct identity and which for reasons of its being different happens to be highly marketable. Naipaul was one of the first to realize this.
15. Srinivasan anticipates me in his reference to the Partition of India as a traumatic event and the need to explore the psychological traumas of refuges, exiles, *muhajirs*, and the dislocated.
16. *Letters between a Father and Son* with an Introduction and notes by Gillon Aitken (Little, Brown and Company, 1999). He advises his sister in a letter dated 24 November 1949, to look at India as a dead country still running with the momentum of hey day (9).
17. Refer *The Enigma of Arrival.*
18. Both *Half-a-Life* and *The Magic Seeds* are histories of Willie's travels, non-commitment and continued failures.

19. The direct inheritor of Naipaul's version of relationships and recollections through memory surprisingly is Kiran Desai, a first generation immigrant, who with her very title *The Inheritance of Loss* (2006), dons a negative mantle and ends up with three static characters and an illegal immigrant, and introduces the Gurkha Land Movement as a strategic intervention in the family saga. But the Indian reception was both feverish and frenzied with a flood of amateur critical papers on the novel.

References

Bissoondath, Neil. *Digging Up the Mountains: Selected Stories.* Toronto: Macmillan, 1985.
——. *Doing the Heart Good.* Toronto: Cormorant Books Inc., 2002.
——. *Selling Illusions: The Cult of Multiculturalism in Canada.* Toronto: Penguin Books, 1995.
Dabydeen, Cyril. *Berbice Crossing and Other Stories.* Yorkshire, England: Peepal Tree, 1990.
——. *My Brahmin Days and Other Stories.* Toronto: Tsar Publications, 2000.
Derrida, Jacques. *The Work of Mourning.* (eds) Pascale-Anne Brault and Michael Haas. Chicago: Chicago University Press, 2001.
Espinet, Ramabai. *The Swinging Bridge.* 2003. New Delhi: Penguin, 2004.
Husain, Intizar. *Basti.* 1979. Trans. Frances Pritchet. New Delhi: Harper Collins, 1995.
Iyer, Pico. *The Global Soul.* London: Bloomsbury, 2000.
McGowan, Kate. *Key Issues in Critical and Cultural Theory.* Jaipur: Rawat Publications, 2008. 102–119.
Mishra, Sudesh. *Diaspora Criticism.* Edinburgh: Edinburgh University Press, 2006.
Mishra, Vijay. 'Diasporas and the Art of Impossible Mourning.' *In Diaspora: Theories, Histories, Texts.* (ed.) Makarand Paranjape. New Delhi: Indialog Publications, 2001. 24–51.
Mukherjee, Arun. *Oppositional Aesthetics: Readings from a Hyphenated Space.* Toronto: Tsar Publications, 1994.
Naipaul, V.S. *The Enigma of Arrival.* London: Picador, 2002.
——. *Half-a-Life.* London: Picador, 2001.
——. *Magic Seeds.* New York: Vintage, 2004.
——. *The Mimic Men.* 1967. London: Picador, 2002.
Paranjape, Makarand. Introduction. *In Diaspora: Theories, Histories, Texts.* (ed.) Paranjape. New Delhi: Indialog Publications, 2001. 1–14.

Phillips, Caryl. *Crossing the Bar*. London: Pan Macmillan, 1994.
Ricoeur, Paul. *Memory, History and Forgetting*. Trans. Kathleen Blamey and David Pallauer. Chicago: Chicago University Press, 2004.
Srinivasan, Shiva Kumar. 'Diaspora and its Discontents'. *In Diaspora: Theories, Histories, Texts*. (ed.) Makarand Paranjape. New Delhi: Indialog Publications, 2001. 52–67.
Zizek, Slavoj. 'How to Read Lacan: Troubles with the Real.' Web. 12 June 2014. <www/lacan.com/zizalien.atm.referred>

Chapter 2

That Third Space

Interrogating the Diasporic Paradigm

K. SATCHIDANANDAN

> I reorganise my living room
> asking each piece
> Where it would like to be placed.
> I give a new spot to the sofa and the lamp,
> Change the drapes, and
> Replace the old rug with a wall-to-wall carpet.
> When everything is just right
> I begin to wonder:
> Where among these
> Should I place myself?
>
> — Panna Naik, 'The Living Room'

> (If the exile's) body cannot appropriate its given landscape ... the substantial body dwindles into phantasm ... Language ... degenerates Into a dead script when the bodily power of a people no longer instils it with particularity, no longer appropriates it in the expression of a emergent selfhood ... . In the battle between the body and the spirit, the outworn script of English as we find it here must be made to open its maw and swallow, swallow huge chaoses, the chaoses of uninterpreted actuality.
>
> — Meena Alexander, 'Exiled by a Dead Script'

> ... It is from those who have suffered the sentence of history – subjugation, domination; diaspora, displacement – that we learn our most enduring lessons.
>
> — Homi K. Bhabha, 'Post-Colonial Criticism'

While one does not doubt the enduring value of the diasporic experience as a spring of agonized inspiration, multiple identities, new subjectivities, creative memories and fresh perspectives on language and life, a stage seems to have come when one should problematize the concept of the diaspora, not to deny to it its authenticity as a state of experience but to qualify, complexify, and interrogate it in order to understand it better. For one thing, there has been a tremendous quantitative and qualitative change in the phenomenon of diaspora owing to the great demographic upheavals of the last century, especially its last decades, and to the unprecedented growth of the technologies of communication including the maturing of the multimedia communication systems and cyber technologies. Even though the word 'exile' continues to be fashionable and is not yet entirely devoid of significance, the new speed, reach and dimension of communication networks including the dimensions of vision, sound and movement, and the increased possibilities of forming a little real – not 'imagined' – community of one's own people who are from the same country and perhaps even speak the same language have definitely changed the nature of the experience of exile: it is no more solitary in most cases; it is a shared experience. One may well argue that it is only like shifting your confinement from a closed solitary cell to a more open prison with a few jailmates who share the anxieties of return: but those who think it is the same have never experienced the pangs of sequestration in the maddening darkness of a closed prison. Arjun Appadurai and Anthony Smith have also pointed out how large communication networks erode national boundaries even as they promote intense interaction between members of diasporic communities: but these communities remain local and provincial even as they acquire transnational characteristics. The homeland becomes at once remote and accessible due to the contradictory phenomena of migration and cyber communication. Consequently, as Nalini Natarajan points out, the contemporary episteme is ruled not by experience but by images that by their sheer proliferation and scope have become more real than anyone could have anticipated even a few decades ago. These images, verbal, auditory, and visual play a crucial role in shaping diasporic subjectivities. She points out how the impact of these images unites the sartorial, culinary, literary, cinematic and religious, for instance in the video channels for Indian diasporic viewers. It has also been noted how these images combine memory, experience, and desire in suggestive ways juxtaposing mythological images with those of advertisement, thus creating new discourses that bring together religion, consumerism, cosmopolitanism, and national identity. While challenging the media hegemony in the metropolis, they also reinforce other hegemonies within the community: of religion, class, or caste.

Questioning the Assumptions

While the word 'diaspora' may be used as umbrella-term for immigrant writers, it also conceals the differences in their backgrounds as well as contexts. The first general assumption is that the diaspora refers to those who write in English as presumed by Emmanuel S. Nelson in his bio-bibliographical source book, *Writers of the Indian Diaspora*. Where does a Malayalam writer in Oman, a Tamil writer in Singapore, a Bengali writer in Paris, or a Hindi writer in Mauritius figure? Or is writing in English, which paradoxically enough is international writing at least by aspiration, the inevitable precondition for being qualified as 'diasporic'?

The second general assumption is that the diasporic writer occupies a kind of second space, of exile and cultural solitude. But may be Homi Bhabha is right when he calls it a third space (*Location of Culture*), a hybrid location of antagonism, perpetual tension, and pregnant chaos. The reality of the body, a material production of one local culture, and the abstraction of the mind, a cultural sub-text of a global experience, provide the intertwining threads of the diasporic existence of a writer: this is a neither/nor condition that Sura P. Rath calls 'Trishanku' in his article 'Home(s) Abroad: Diasporic Identities in Third Spaces'. 'The products of this hybrid location are results of a long history of confrontations between unequal cultures and forces, in which the stronger culture struggles to control, remake, or eliminate the subordinate partner' (Lavie and Swedenburg. Bhabha sees individual and local experiences of diasporic writers as a part of the larger processes of historical change. The inter-subjective and collective experiences of nationness, community interest or cultural values are negotiated in the emergence of the interstices, the overlap and displacement of domains of difference. 'The negotiation of cultural identity,' he says, 'involves the continual interface and exchange of cultural performances that in turn produce a mutual and mutable recognition (or representation) of cultural difference'. The representation of difference, as he warns is not to be hastily read as the reflection of pre-given ethnic or cultural traits set in the fixed tablet of tradition. 'The social articulation of difference, from the minority perspective, is a complex on-going negotiation that seeks to authorise cultural hybridities that emerge in moments of historical transformation.'

Forms of Othering

The context of immigration also can alter the nature of the diasporic experience. The earlier diasporas of the neo-colonial and postcolonial world were often a product of forced immigration, of people running away from religious and other political or social persecution. But several Indians who migrated to America in the mid-1970s and afterwards were going in search of a better life, greater promises of prosperity and material success. They did not have to burn the bridges with their past, at times, especially in the case of many academics, who had to strengthen those connections since they had to teach in South Asian departments. The new immigrant was a new kind of colonizer, taking full advantage of the war-time labour market, at the same time having no intention of ruling over the land. They had a home to go back to and an identity to protect; they were 'resident aliens' who kept up their citizenship and indulged in and even theorized a politics of identity, say, like Gayatri Spivak or Amartya Sen, thus taking full advantage of their status. I would suggest that one may have to look more closely at the class component of the diasporic experience: and there one can hardly ignore the difference between a refugee Bangladeshi or Philippine worker in Saudi Arabia and an academic capitalizing on his/her scholarship in his/her language or literature in an American University. One can hardly compare their state to the pagan Indian, Chinese, or Mexican immigrants of the 19th century, or worse still, the African immigrant workers who were treated as filthy, uncivilized slaves and beasts.

Like the class factor, the language factor also counts, as the experience of someone writing in English from England, USA, Canada or Australia, especially in terms of accommodation, negotiation and reception, is certain to be different from that of a writer writing in English in France or Gujarati in England. Again there is the gender factor. The diasporic experience is also a gendered experience when it comes to the writing of Indian women abroad, say Meena Alexander, Panna Naik, Malati Rao, Sudha Chandola, Sujata Bhatt, Anita Desai, Kamala Markandaya, Bharati Mukherjee, Suniti Namjoshi, Jhumpa Lahiri, and others.

The minority-majority status too contributes to the intensity or otherwise of the felt alienation. A Tamil in Ceylon or an Indian in Mauritius is even perceived as a threat by the dominant community there because of the size and confidence of these migrant populations. Again, the experience of the second generation or third generation migrant is very different from that of the first generation migrant: home becomes unreal to them, just a space of imagination rather than of nostalgic recollection. I have seen this transposition of Kerala from memory to imagination in the second generation American immigrants from my state. They reconstruct their homeland from fragments of information gathered from hearsay or from the internet. For them, home is not a place to return to, but a place to fantasize about, or may be to visit some time as a guest or a tourist.

One has, in short, to take into account different forms of 'othering' experienced within the diaspora, as also different levels of identity. Imagining the other is not necessarily a crippling experience; it also defines one's Self and reassures one about one's own distinct identity. The narrative production of home assumes many strategies according to one's relation to the place one came from, the place one came to, and the place one belongs to. The idea of home is also related to time that transforms it into history or myth. Post-colonialism seems to come full circle in those writers who inhabit the third space, live the third culture, and shape the third history.

The Diaspora Within

We are living at a time when the idea of 'Indianness' is being interrogated from different perspectives of Dalits, tribals, women, gays, lesbians, and minorities for example. The essentialist, often Orientalist, conception of India derived from Colonial-Indological and nationalist discourses is beginning to give way to a more federal democratic perspective of a polyphonic India, a mosaic of cultures, languages and literatures, and worldviews. But the critical discourse on the diaspora still seems to swear by that exotic, eternal India which is also at times woven into the diasporic writer's own perception of the country, while several Indian writers writing in the languages today are engaged in projecting different imagined communities, alternative nationhoods.

According to Homi Bhabha, the discourse of the wandering peoples of the diaspora marks a 'shifting boundary that alienates the frontiers of the modern nation'. Thus it interrupts the monologic discourses of modern metropolises with their imperial memories. It is a moment of the disinherited unsettling imperial inheritance and thus challenging the monolith of the modern Western nation; but it can also foster cultural nationalism by suggesting, say, a Hindu hegemony while pulling down another. Patriarchy, class structure and ethnic conflicts too can well be reproduced and reinforced by diasporic ideologies. I have seen sections of Indians in the United States practising a kind of apartheid worse than that of the Whites against the Coloured, while they should by normal logic and just politics have identified themselves with them. Distinctions of class and sect and patriarchal norms within the family are also often reproduced by the diaspora as part of the reproduction of structures at home, often viewed as the structures of the lost golden past, and hence also of the Promised Future. Fortunately more and more diasporic writers are becoming aware of the relativity of the concept of the diaspora, its inherent contradictions, with its multiple possibilities of alienation and assimilation, retreat into remembered patterns and revolt against them, of being the colonizer and the colonized, marginal and central.

Finally, I would like to point to the diaspora within. Now that the old concept of a unisonant nation with a single unified culture is being challenged, it may be possible to extend the concept of the 'diaspora' at least in relative, linguistic and regional-cultural terms, within the country: the Malayali diaspora in Delhi, the Tamil diaspora in Bangalore, the Bengali diaspora in Bombay, or a Santhali diaspora in Calcutta, for example: mostly these populations, of migrant workers, officers, media-persons, businessmen, and academics, are concentrated in cities giving them a cosmopolitan character, and in turn finding a kind of solace in these many-tongued, multicultural milieu. I can speak with some authenticity about the Malayali diaspora that has made significant contribution to Malayalam literature especially since the 1960s. Even some genres of writing have entirely been products of diasporic consciousness: for example, the 'military fiction' (*Pattalakkatha*) came from writers like Kovilan, Parappurath, Vinayan, and Nandanar who were in the army and thus got exposed to people and languages from different parts of the country. These are stories and novels that depict the life in the barracks in all its complexity. Many of the stories and novels of the diasporic writers are marked by the presence of non-Malayali characters who are even protagonists at times. Significant novels like M. Mukundan's *Delhi*, O.V. Vijayan's *Pravachakante Vazhi* (The Way of the Prophet), V.K.N.'s *Arohanam* (The Ascent) and Anand's *Alkkoottam* (The Crowd) and *Marubhoomikal Undakunnathu* ('How Deserts are Made' published by Penguin in English under the title *Desert Shadows*) are pan-Indian in the range of their experience and the spread of their characters and at times reflect this cosmopolitanism even in their style and linguistic structure. Words and even sentences in other languages, particularly Hindi, are interwoven with Malayalam in the texts of some of these novels. Modernism in Malayalam, fiction in particular, is entirely a creation of diasporic Malayali writers living in Delhi, Bombay, and Calcutta. O.V. Vijayan, V.K.N., M. Mukundan, Kakkanadan, M.P. Narayana Pillai, Sethu, Kamala Das, Punathil Kunhabdulla, Paul Zacharia: all these pioneers of the new fiction lived, at least in their formative years as writers, in cities outside Kerala, experiencing an alienation, a solitude, a torment of the absurd and the irrational and an existential angst as intense and as creative as that of say, Kafka, Beckett, Sartre, or Albut Camus whom many of them identified with in the early 1960s of the last century. Some of the pioneers of modern poetry, like M.N. Paloor, Madhavan Ayyappath, and Kadammanitta Ramakrishnan also lived in the cities outside Kerala. However, urban life affected them in a different way and appears in their poetry as distrust in the system, fear of the crowd, the experience of boredom, philosophic detachment, fragmentariness of expression, and a kind of nostalgia for their lost villages in Kerala that get transformed in their poetry into emerald green imagined spaces of pristine purity and simplicity.

References

Alexander, Meena. 'Exiled by a Dead Script'. *Contemporary Indian English Verse: An Evaluation.* (ed.) Kulshrestha Chirantan. New Delhi: Arnold, 1980. 16–23.

Bhabha, Homi K. *Location of Culture*. London: Routledge, 1994.

———. 'Post-Colonial Criticism'. *Redrawing the Boundaries: The Transformation of English and American Literary Studies.* (eds) Stephen Greenblatt and Giles B. Gann. New York: Modern Language Association of America, 1992. 437–457.

Lavie, Smadar and Ted Swedenburg, eds. *Displacement, Diaspora, and the Geographies of Identity*. Durham: Duke University Press, 1996.

Naik, Panna. 'The Living Room'. *Journal of South Asian Literature* 21.1 (1986): 9.

Natarajan, Nalini. 'Introduction: Reading Diaspora'. *Writers of the Indian Diaspora*. 1993. (ed.) Emmanuel S. Nelson. Jaipur: Rawat Publications, 2010. xiii–xix.

Rath, Sura P. 'Home(s) Abroad: Diasporic Identities in Third Spaces'. *Journal of Contemporary Thought* (1999): 7–23.

Chapter 3

Diasporic Meditations

MOHAN RAMANAN

We are all, I am convinced, Diasporic in one way or the other. It has to do with the shrinking of the world and the effects of globalization. No one really lives at home, everyone is abroad, even if abroad is the next town or city. I myself grew up in Kolkata and the Tamil Brahmin community, to which I belong, did feel keenly its difference from the larger Bengali community out there. The Bengali boys would bully us and tease our girls, make fun of our Idli and Sambar (tetulpani, they called it), but think nothing of swilling a great quantity of Sambar for a happorth of Idli or Dosa, with tears streaming down their faces, because it was tangy and spicy. To their credit, however, I must acknowledge that if our girls were teased by Bengalis of other Paras or localities there would be hell to pay but teasing is teasing and we did feel alienated. This almost ghetto like mentality had another aspect to it. To the extent that you felt different you also clung to your cultural symbols. For the Tamilian it was Maneka Cinema where I saw 'Veerapandiya Kattabomman' with Sivaji Ganesan playing the hero, or MGR and M.R. Radha in their various roles. Our Tamil was built on the dialogues we heard and in cultural events at the South India Club or at Vijay Sports Club or Excelsiors, exclusively Tamil clubs, these dialogues would be the stuff from which members regaled their audiences. South India Club at the intersection of Lansdowne Road and Rash Behari was iconic and so were these clubs with their various tournaments organized either in their premises or in the Dhakuria lakes. My fondest memories are of various Mamas (uncles) who played ball badminton or showed their prowess in the waters. My father could float on the Dhakuria waters for minutes on end, something I have found even professional swimmers are unable to do. Then there was the Ayappa Sangam and the festivities in the winter months when the pilgrimage to Sabarimalai would be undertaken with myself looking with wide eyed admiration at the trance-like state to which many devotees would transport themselves. There was the Rasika Ranjana Sabha in Lake Road, I believe, where religious activities and great concerts of Carnatic Music would be held. On Sundays these concerts always began at 4:25 pm to beat Rahukalam which is between 4:30 and 6 pm on Sundays and these concerts went on till 10 pm. These gargantuan musical feasts are a thing of the past but we heard Semmangudi, Chembai, M.D. Ramanathan, Madurai Mani Iyer and yes even the great Ustad Bade Ghulam Ali Khan. Occasionally the organizer had to convince unmusical neighbours that they would switch off mikes or finish the concert before 10 pm and occasionally there would be arguments about our right to hold such events. It did not matter if Durga Puja or Saraswati Puja took up the late hours but our Rama Navami procession had to be curtailed to meet the unreasonable objections of our Bengali masters, because that is how they behaved or even if they did not, that is how we kowtowed to them and enslaved ourselves. The situation now in Kolkata is different. My cousins are all married to Bengali spouses and the Komala Vilas (the natural retreat of Tamils passing through Kolkata which offered the best coffee, filtered if you please), Banana Leaf, and other South Indian eateries are frequented by Bengalis and there is much comraderie. I understand that *Chanda* for Pujas is still collected by aggressive methods but that is a Kolkata problem, not a Tamil difficulty it used to be when I grew up in Kolkata in the 1950s.

In 1961, I went to Bangalore to study in a Public School and to live in a boarding house. My father, worried about the political situation in Kolkata and fearing that his irrepressible son would become a Naxalite packed me off to a five-year exile. Now home is where your parents are and the Bangalore exile was felt keenly by me not the least because I was not getting the Brahminical food I was accustomed to – its mix of Tamil and Kerala cuisine – the Maltam lingo I spoke at home (Mal from Malayalam and Tam from Tamil) – and the generally good middle class Hindu values. I resented in this Christian school having to say Amen at Grace (I would say Narayana) and I was upset that the Anglo Indian boys generally and the Coorgi boys in particular got at me for my Hinduness and Brahmin background respectively. If we were 'Under Punders' in Kolkata we were Bommans in Cottons, Bommans a derogatory abbreviation for Brahman. I did not mind chapel which was compulsory for boarders and I saw prayer in chapel as private space where I could communicate my innermost thoughts and intimate desires to an unseen God whom I called Krishna or Guruvayurappa after the Lord of Guruvayur. But education has its purposes and the English education I had in Cottons has had a remarkable impact on me. At one level I am a child of Macaulay, steeped in English values because you can't separate a literature and a language from the values of the native speakers of that language and in Bishop Cottons we got not only English but also Englishness. We were, for example, forbidden to speak any language except English, on pain of punishment, and we were fed on a diet of English – Christian values, so much so I could boast that I knew more about the Bible than some Christians. English education, has had the influence any teacher of English knows and which s\he has tried to remedy through a variety of means. It has, at its worst, left one deracinated and even superior to native values. How often in my salad days when I was green in judgement I have cocked a snook at examples of unenglishness, whether it was in dress habits or cuisine or accent. I now know better but the impact of school is still with me and what your parents have not done for you or missed by not educating you in your mother tongue, cannot be made up for by the substitutes one tries out and certainly not by English education. Some connection is indeed lost and that has made all the difference. In School, by the way, my Kolkata origins also led to my being called a Bengali Babu which is ironic when the Bengalis were not accepting of me. Thus the alienation and exile of Bangalore made for a deepening of what undoubtedly is my diasporic status and a diasporic state of mind.

From Bangalore, on my father's transfer from Kolkata, we lived in Madras, now Chennai. Incidentally the renaming of cities where I have lived as Kolkata from good old Calcutta, Chennai from Madras with all its historical associations, Bengaluru from the anglicized Bangalore which conjures up visions of Generals Cariappa and Thimmayya, of Colin Cowdrey, the Madras Engineering Group, the Coffee House and Lake View Bar in Parade

Grounds, also shows up the difference between your past and present and is a contributory factor in the destabilizing process which is a key aspect of diasporic consciousness. Madras, which for the diasporic Tamil community in Kolkata, was an imagined centre of culture proved to be, in its own way, alienating. The Mylapore super dooper is snobbish and does not easily take to the Maltam Brahmin, imagining that the language he speaks is pristine while Maltam is a fusion of two languages. The fact is that he is ignorant because his own language is after all the present version of several mutations of the Tamil, and his Tamil itself with its Brahminical inflexions, is unlikely to please a Karunanidhi or a Nedunchezhian or a Mathiazhagan who in their dravidian pride look upon all Brahmins, diasporic or no, as intruders. But for me there were so many jeopardies – being a Kolkatan and a Bangalorean in Chennai, being Maltam, being Brahmin. If this does not make for some form of alienation, what will?

It is mainly a question of language as I see it in this respect. The pride people have in their language (in the Telugu area I now live in, it is rife and usually at the cost of Tamil which is a bête noir for Telugus), I have seen is only acceptable if it is a question of one's identity but to assert your identity at the cost of everyone else is wrong. It is somewhat like the Jews who were oppressed now repaying their oppressors, by oppressing the Palestinians who have as much right to the land as the Jews. Pride of language is not a bad thing but it must not deteriorate into hatred for other languages and the desire to put them down. A sure cause of alienation then in my case was this defensive position into which I found myself repeatedly thrown in because my dear Maltam was seen as infected in relation to mainland Tamil and this linguistic superiority of the Mylaporean was accompanied by a perception of his being a superior being to the Kerala Tamilian who was neither here nor there. There was the further alienation of being Brahmin in Dravida Desha and the ill effects of this caste prejudice have been felt by me because I am an exile from Tamil Nadu where in spite of my PhD I could get no job either in Madras Christian College or in Loyola, both colleges in which I studied, where the spectre of reservation, then not so pronounced, was already in operation, ever so slightly. I lost out because I was not Christian and not Dalit. Is this not alienating?

From Madras where I secured my degrees I went to Pilani in Rajasthan. This is one place where I never felt alienated. I have tried to understand why. For one thing I knew enough Hindi to pass muster and for another I never saw local Rajasthani chauvinism in any of my dealings with the people there. Admittedly I was in a University and the atmosphere there is usually liberal but even when I walked the ten miles to nearby Chirawa or went on a camel's back to 40 mile distant Jhunjhunu, I felt at home even though I was abroad. I say abroad but I have said enough to suggest that I really had no home. So here is another pattern of the diasporic consciousness. One learns to live abroad and treat it as home. So give or take occasional human frailties and instances of unpleasantness, I have both in Pilani and my present home in Hyderabad, erstwhile of Andhra Pradesh and now of Telengana, felt absolutely at home. It has much to do with Rajasthani and Hyderabadi Tehseeb. As far as Hyderabad is concerned the welcoming nature of these peoples and the cosmopolitan nature of the city I love and live in is a fact and I trust will be preserved carefully. Admittedly there is in the Telengana sentiment a nativism which is coarse and insensitive but if you talk only of Hyderabad it is different and Telengana or no Telengana there is a Hyderabadiat which transcends linguistic, caste, and communal passions. It is this Hyderabad, the site of Urdu and Telugu coexisting, the place where politeness has been made into a fine art and where secularism in the true sense of the term has been the ideal, where I may say that though I may be a Tamil diasporean, I am still at home.

Tagore wrote *Ghare Baire* (*Home and the World*) and he provides us a metaphor for an explanation of aspects of the diasporic. The airport is another metaphor for this coming and going of people who apparently are in a perpetual state of travel, the Modern Odysseuses, journeying perpetually and finding home wherever they go. In my frequent foreign sojourns, I have often keenly felt the absence of my cultural symbols and the loss of the familiar rhythms of my life in India with its early morning rising, the elaborate Brahminical rituals and prayers and the choice food, eaten as a family. Abroad some of these rituals are disrupted and one does feel the loss keenly, but with time even abroad has begun to look like home, but with a difference. For example the sun rises early in Amercia and sets late, even as late as 8.30 pm and for me sensitive to the idea of Sandhya and the sacredness of the hour this is off putting. But I have grown to accept it as my children have accepted it because they have no way out but to stay there. There are Indian stores and Indian cultural symbols and Indians live Indianly most of the time in America and we have learnt to be comfortable there even though we may be in a state of out-standingness. This out-standingness is a term used with respect to exile and homelessness and I believe it was Kahlil Gibran who used it first to describe his standing outside the American mainstream while still being American. In these days of multiculturalism outstandingness, where you give equal importance to your hyphenated self – Asian-American, Latin-American, and so on, is a crucial marker of identity.

It is surely noteworthy that out of every three Indian writers in the Indian English tradition at least one or two live in one of the world's metropolitan centres and like Vikram Chandra feel obliged to use terms like Karma and Dharma to assert their Indianness. Meenakshi Mukherjee and Rajeswari Sunder Rajan objected to the use of these loaded terms arguing that it betrayed a diasporic writer's anxiety of Indianness and Vikram Chandra responded convincingly that he had as much right to the use of these terms as any native Indian might. I believe this controversy puts paid to notions of exclusiveness or essential Indianness. There is no such thing and all of us are diasporic in that we all have several identities and we have several selves and these interpenetrate to create a palimpsest and this hybridity is felt not only by people who live outside their native spaces but equally by those so called purist nativists. On this showing Tagore's formulation that we should live locally and think globally is an apt description of our and my own existential condition.

CHAPTER 4

Globalization, Diaspora, and Transnationalism

Challenges and Opportunities for the Indian Diaspora

AJAYA K. SAHOO

> One of the most characteristic, indeed essential, aspects of diasporas is their transpolitical linkage to the homeland. This includes cultural, economic, and demographic imports and exports and reciprocal influences. (Safran, 'Jewish Diaspora' 45)

Diasporas exist because of their transpolitical linkages with the homeland. My argument here is that diasporas cannot exist without a homeland and the homeland benefits by recognizing its diaspora, especially in an era of increased globalization. As long as the homeland recognizes, patronizes, and praises its diasporans, the diaspora not only remains connected with the homeland socially and culturally but also becomes an economic and political asset. There have been several discussions on the topic of globalization and diaspora over the last three decades. The diaspora debate, since then, has taken many twists and turns by recognizing many of the old and lost diasporas along with 'new ethno-national diasporas' (Sheffer). Additionally, many diasporas have now become so powerful that they influence the economy and polity of the host society and homeland simultaneously. This nexus between diaspora and homeland has become more pronounced in this age of globalization. Many of the global diasporas have played a crucial role in the political and economic development of their homeland. One may cite the examples of the Jewish diaspora, Armenian diaspora, Chinese diaspora, Indian diaspora, or any other diaspora at a global level. Although there is now a proliferation of literature dealing with how diasporas played a crucial role in the development of their homeland, the contribution of the homeland in successful restoration of diasporas has been largely neglected. The question arises, why do diasporas become so important for the homeland and vice versa? How does globalization facilitate the diaspora and homeland nexus? Diasporic groups are often considered as 'outsiders' by the host societies and are also, by definition, 'outsiders' in their homeland or ancestral land.

In any case they are vulnerable to discrimination and exploitation in the land of their settlement and not infrequently many of them have also remained outside the concerns of nation-states of their origin until recently. After examining the much-debated concepts of diaspora, globalization and transnationalism, this chapter examines the challenges and opportunities before the Indian diaspora in the present context of global economic and political changes.

Delineating a Diaspora

Although diasporas are formed as a result of migration flows, not all migrations lead to diaspora formation. In his definitive model of diaspora, William Safran ('Diasporas in Modern Societies' 83–84) analyses a variety of collective experiences to define diasporas as follows:

- They, or their ancestors, have been dispersed from a specific original 'center' to two or more peripheral, or foreign, regions.
- They retain a collective memory, vision, or myth about their original homeland – its physical location, history, achievements, and, often enough, sufferings.
- Their relationship with the dominant element of society in the hostland is complicated and often uneasy. They believe that they are not, and perhaps cannot be, fully accepted by their host society and therefore feel partly alienated and insulated from it.
- They regard their ancestral homeland as their true, ideal home and as the place to which they or their descendants would (or should) eventually return – if and when conditions are appropriate.
- They continue to relate, personally or vicariously, to that homeland in one way or another, and their ethnocommunal

consciousness and solidarity, which reach across political boundaries, are importantly defined in terms of the existence of such a relationship. That relationship may include a collective commitment to the maintenance or restoration of their original homeland and to its independence, safety, and prosperity. The absence of such a relationship makes it difficult to speak of transnationalism.

- They wish to survive as a distinct community – in most instances as a minority – by maintaining and transmitting a cultural and/or religious heritage derived from their ancestral home and the symbols based on it. In so doing, they adapt to hostland conditions and experiences to become themselves centers of cultural creation and elaboration.
- Their cultural, religious, economic, and/or political relationships with the homeland are reflected in a significant way in their communal institutions.

Another scholar, Rogers Brubaker, identified three core elements 'that remain widely understood to be constitutive of diaspora. The first is dispersion in space; the second, orientation to a homeland; and the third, boundary-maintenance' (5). While the concept of diaspora has been subject to various interpretations, its geographical and territorial dimensions are clear. According to Steven Vertovec the term 'diaspora' is often applied to 'describe practically any population that is considered 'deterritorialized' or 'transnational' – that is, which has originated in land other than that in which it currently resides, and whose social, economic, and political networks cross the borders of nation-states or, indeed, span the globe' ('Three Meanings of "Diaspora"' 277). Diasporas, although by definition are scattered apart geographically, are held together by factors such as a common ethnic identity and a collective relation toward the original homeland. For Khachig Tölölyan, the editor of the journal Diaspora, the concept refers to the entire 'semantic domain that includes words like immigrant, expatriate, refugees, guest workers, exile community, overseas community, ethnic community' (4).

Globalization and Diaspora

By the end of the 20th century, the concept of globalization had come to be associated with the liberalization of markets and the growth of multinational corporations (MNCs) or transnational corporations (TNCs) spread over several nation-states. It has given rise to 'worldwide diffusion of practices, expansion of relations across continents, organization of social life on a global scale and growth of shared global consciousness' (Lechner 330). There is greater interdependence between nation-states across borders, not merely in trade and commerce but in almost all aspects of life. With the revolutionary advancement in technologies of information, communication and travel during the 1980s and 1990s, there has been a steep increase in the global transfer of people, capital, technology, media and ideologies across several nations, as discussed in terms of 'scapes'[1] by Arjun Appadurai.

One of the major constituent effects of globalization has been the uncontrollable, large volume of international migration necessitated by the very process itself. The revolution in information and communication technology combined with global economic integration, and changes in production systems and labour markets have significantly affected international migration. Robin Cohen uses the term 'diasporization' as a concept akin to globalization, suggesting that the two are inseparably enmeshed. Though not the same, they mutually reinforce each other. According to Cohen, 'globalization has enhanced the practical, economic and affective roles of diasporas, showing them to be particularly adaptive forms of social organization. As diasporas become more integrated into the cosmopoli, their power and importance are enhanced' (155).

Diasporic globalization, a term used by Michel Laguerre refers to 'human migration, voluntary or involuntary, the dispersion of the emigrants to more than one site, the connection of the various sites to each other through various forms of social interaction, and the maintenance of transnational relations between the homeland and the resettled émigrés ... these border-crossing practices are symbolic of the expansion of the nation beyond its jurisdictional boundaries' (5). In many respects 'borders breed uneven geographies of power and status' (Hyndman 1). The movement of millions across borders is often associated with the emergence of ethnic minority communities.

Thomas Faist argues that 'while the impact of globalization is often assumed to be universal and worldwide, approaches linked to the concepts of diaspora and transnationalism refer to phenomena that occur within the limited social and geographic spaces of a particular set of regions or states'. According to him, globalization approaches and world theories differ from diasporic and trans-nationalist approaches in at least three respects:

First, all cross-border concepts refer to the importance of cross-border or even 'deterritorialized' politics, economics and culture .... Second, there is also no claim that a global or world consciousness is evolving in a linear way .... Third, terms such as 'diaspora' and 'transnationalism' or 'transnationalisation' do not suggest a (linear) progression of the universalisation of rights, as world approaches do. ('Diaspora and Transnationalism' 14–15)

The International Organization for Migration (IOM) estimated that in 1990 there were over 80 million migrants who had moved out of the country of their origin. Among them 30 million were said to be irregular migrants and another 15 million were refugees or asylum seekers. By 1992, the number of migrants increased to 100 million, of whom 20 million were refugees and asylum seekers (Castles and Miller). The United Nations estimated in July 2002 that there were 185 million people living for 12 months or more outside their country of birth or citizenship (UN Population Division). A majority of them are international migrants who are potential immigrants in their destination countries and who often integrate into the society by becoming permanent residents.[2] These international migrants bring not only their skills and expertize but also their culture and lifestyles with them. In contemporary times, the internet, affordable airfare, and comparatively cheap overseas communication facilities have helped to maintain a strong relationship with the homeland for most of the people who live outside their country of origin.

Diaspora and Transnationalism

The relationship of any diaspora with the homeland/motherland falls under the broader domain of international relations as it involves at least two countries that formally permit their subjects to interact with each other. Even in the absence of such formal understanding and other constraints, relations of an imaginary kind could exist through building structures and institutions that recreate the places of origin by diaspora communities. Today the diasporic communities go beyond the host nation-state and motherland to network with their communities dispersed around the globe. The emergence of such networking, cutting across several countries, is most appropriately described by the term 'transnationalism'.

Transnationalism generally implies migration of people across the borders of one or more nations. It also refers to the deterritorialization of population along with their material and non-material cultural commodities. Portes et al. argues that 'in other areas of human activity, transnationalism involves individuals, their networks of social relations, their communities, and broader institutionalized structures such as local and national governments' (220). In the field of international migration, the term transnationalism developed rapidly during the late 1990s. In fact, the terms such as transnational networks, transnational communities and diasporas are often used interchangeably in many of the contemporary studies. For instance, Caroline Knowles argues that the concepts of diasporas and transnationals are 'not distinct but blend into each other in describing similar sets of people, circumstances and social processes' (155). Transnational networks form a precondition to the emergence of transnational communities and the process of this transformation is generally designated by transnationalism. A transnational community, as Michel Bruneau writes, 'links the global to the whole range of greatly different local, networking places, without hierarchy between these different hubs' (43).

According to Faist, transnational communities encompass diasporas, but not all transnational communities are diasporas (21). Diaspora communities, like the Chinese in Chinatowns or Indians in their ethnic enclaves of 'Little India' the world over, have built homes away from home, but the transnational networks of the contemporary era have facilitated members of these communities to be here and there. The above-mentioned processes of globalization and technological advancement have given rise to networking among the diaspora communities dispersed across the world (Bhat and Sahoo). Hence, there is an urgent need to re-examine and capture the emerging phenomenon in the transnational social spaces.

Transnational social spaces (Basch et al.; Faist, 'Transnationalization in International Migration') or social fields (Levitt and Schiller) are constructed from the transnational networks, which in turn are built upon transnational family networks (interactions between members of a family living in different countries) as well as upon the networking of community organizations (caste associations, religious institutions, for instance). These networks enable immigrants to maintain simultaneous connections with two or more nation-states. Further, these networks are intensified as a result of globalization, deterritorialization, continuous circulation of people (such as labour), capital (especially the role of the World Bank, the International Monetary Fund, and the World Trade Organization), and information (through the internet and other means of rapid communication) across countries. Such intensified transnational networks constitute a single community with global spread. As Peter Kivisto writes, 'transnational immigrant social spaces require the creation of a new form of ethnic community. What makes a diaspora different from the more familiar form that typified immigrant enclaves in industrializing nations a century ago is that it is located in a space that encompasses two or more nation-states, a situation made possible by time-space compression' (568). According to Faist, 'whether we talk of transnational social spaces, transnational social fields, transnationalism or transnational social formations in international migration systems, we usually refer to sustained ties of persons, networks and organizations across the borders across multiple nation-states, ranging from little to highly institutionalized forms' ('Transnationalization in International Migration' 189).

Transnational networks have significant socio-economic, cultural, and political impacts on migrants themselves, the host society and the homeland. The remittances and investments that flow between transnational migrants to their families back home as well as the socio-cultural networks with the homeland, as in the case of the Jewish, Chinese, and Indian diasporas, are interesting examples of transnational networks. This sustained transnationalization of migrant ties is currently on a steep increase. Further, the global economy, along with international business operations and the acceptance of dual nationality by hostland governments, offers opportunities for promotion of transnational interactions. Like the economic impacts of transnational migrations, the social, cultural, and political impacts too are considerable. As Vertovec points out, 'many migrant communities maintain intense linkages and exchanges between sending and receiving contexts including marriage alliances, religious activity, media and commodity consumption .... The political impact of transnational phenomena takes many forms especially with regard to "questions of citizenship" and "homeland politics"' ('Transnationalism and Identity' 575).

As mentioned earlier, revolutionary developments in the spheres of transport and communications during the past three decades has introduced far-reaching changes in all societies, including the diasporic communities dispersed in different countries away from their countries of origin. Insofar as the diasporic communities are concerned, not only are the ties with the homeland reinforced and intensified but they are extended to reach the members of their community settled in many other parts of the world. Unlike the earlier motherland-centred, dyadic diasporic relations, diaspora communities today have multiple centers of interaction. This is perhaps best captured by Milton Esman:

> Most, but not all diasporas maintain a sympathetic attachment to their former homeland. They remit funds to family members and frequently to their former communities and to causes they favor. They frequently contribute to political changes to economic development in their former homeland. They may support or they may oppose its present government, extending moral and financial assistance to the side they favor. The diaspora may split into factions, supporting competing parties in their former homeland. (18–19)

It is clear from the above discussion that diaspora and transnationalism are simultaneous effects of globalization, in other words, it is globalization that is making diaspora and transnationalism possible. In the next section, I will discuss the causal connection between globalization and transnationalism in the case of the Indian diaspora.

Evaluating the Indian Diaspora

The Indian diaspora is considered as one of the most modern[3] and largest diasporas in the world. It has grown apace in the past three decades to comprise more than 25 million people spread over all continents. Although that figure is small compared to the more than a billion inhabitants in the homeland, it has reached a critical mass in various host countries. It has developed institutions, orientations, and patterns of living specific to the institutional structures and socio-political contexts of different hostlands. These patterns have been marked not only by the influences of the hostland culture but by relations with the homeland (Safran et al. vii). People of Indian origin today represent a significant proportion of the population of some countries such as Mauritius, Trinidad and Tobago, Guyana, Surinam, Fiji, South Africa, and Malaysia. They are a visible and respectable minority in multicultural countries like United Kingdom (UK), the United States (US), Canada, and Singapore.

Much of the history of early migrations of cosmopolitan traders and merchants from India before the 18th century hardly produced any significant diasporas,[4] though they have played important role in globalizing the Indian economic products and thereby the Indian culture (see Kaur). As Amartya Sen notes, 'ideas as well as people have moved across India's borders over thousands of years, enriching India as well as the rest of the world' (86). The Indian trading diaspora that formed as a result of the longstanding business networks is different from the other global diasporas that formed as a result of religious and political persecutions (see Levi). In some of the countries where Indians settled permanently before the 16th century, they held dominant economic and political positions. This was not only because of their demographic composition but also because of their hard labour and economic success. This dominance persisted for them for quite some time until the European powers took over their trading ports in the 16th and 17th centuries.[5] This is the period when Indian international migration began to take shape. By the end of 18th century, Indians were found in all countries of Southeast Asia. By the beginning of the 19th century into the mid-20th century, they slowly moved into the Caribbean and African countries. This migration expansion resulted from the growth of capitalism and transportation on the one hand and economic and political problems at home coinciding with India's incorporation into the British Empire on the other hand. According to Judith Brown:

> As the British economy led the way in industrialization, world trade and international finance, it dominated a new world economic order, drawing in raw materials to feed its industries and its people .... India was at the heart of this deepening global

interconnection, and became increasingly significant for Britain as a source of raw materials, as market for manufactured goods, a destination for capital investment, and a source of labor for other parts of the Empire. (14)

The history of the modern Indian diaspora is broadly comprised of three major streams following the diverse situations under which Indians have immigrated to different countries. The first stream includes third to fifth generation descendants of the early immigrants during the mid-19th century, to the British and other European colonies in Africa, Southeast Asia, Fiji, and the Caribbean as plantation labourers and railway workers under the 'indenture system'.[6] Under this system, some 1.5 million persons migrated to the above destinations (Clarke et al.). Although they have played significant roles in different spheres of the host economy and society, their contributions were hardly recognized. For instance, 'in an environment where a number of races were closely juxtapositioned, Indian diasporics often occupied an in-between space between the colonizer and the territorially-based colonized. They formed a middle stratum between the British and the Black Africans in many parts of Africa' (Raghuram and Sahoo 8). Different scholars have highlighted the indentured Indian diasporas in their works and even categorized them either on the basis of their migration history or functions they perform in the host society, e.g. while Cohen uses the word 'labour/service diaspora' (178) in his typologies of global diasporas,[7] Esman uses the word 'middleman minorities' (15) a sub-class of entrepreneurial diasporas in his three classes of diasporas.[8] The second phase of migration consists of professionally trained and skilled emigrants, referred to in the literature as the brain drain, to the developed countries of the West during the second half of the 20th century (see Khadria). However, with the onset of globalization and the internationalization of the labour force, migration today is no longer associated with brain drain. The migration of Indian labour, semi-skilled and unskilled, to the countries of the Gulf (mainly to the six countries Saudi Arabia, United Arab Emirates, Qatar, Kuwait, Bahrain, and Oman) following the oil boom form the third stream. Many of them have left behind their families in India and remit savings towards family maintenance and investments. They form the majority among the expatriate Indians and are denied any citizenship rights in the countries of their work.

Out of the above three streams, the first two streams of migrations produced two distinctive diasporas who may be termed respectively as the old diaspora and the new diaspora (Mishra). Their distinctions may be observed from the contexts of their emigration and destinations, socio-economic background and the degree of interaction with the motherland. While the new diaspora have retained vibrant relationship with their family and community in India, the majority of the old diaspora have lost their contact with the motherland. In the course of their long journey by ship to distant destinations, the unknown co-passengers became 'jahaji bhai' (literally meaning 'ship brother', a brotherly affinity owed to travelling together). The Indian diaspora communities formed during the colonial era were totally denied access even to their own folk attached to different plantations under 'a new system of slavery' (Tinker) invented by the British colonialists, let alone any access to means of transportation and communication to engage with the motherland. The postcolonial emigrants on the other hand not only enjoyed the advantage of being professionally trained, middle-class, Anglophone Indians having high levels of success and integration in the industrialized countries of the West but also earned adequate income that could facilitate frequent communication and a vibrant relationship with the places of their origins. These relationships range from personal ties with friends and relatives, through informal linkages with the associations, organizations and institutions of caste, religion, region, and language, to official interactions at the state and national levels.

Globalization, Diaspora, and Homeland

As mentioned earlier, globalization associated with recent advancement in technologies of transportation, communication, information, and the internet has contributed immensely to the growth of transnational networks – connecting diaspora with the homeland. There is revival of the local at the global context with the shrinking of time and space. As Pires-Hester has rightly pointed out, 'studies of diaspora populations have usually focused on either the sending or receiving side of the migration cycle. Diaspora relations with the ancestral homeland have been of relatively recent concern' (485). Diasporic communities in the world consider the ancestral homeland according to several factors: '(a) the conditions under which its ancestors left the homeland, (b) the distance at which their community is now in relation to that homeland, (c) the duration of settlement in the host country, and (d) the socio-economic and political conditions in the host country' (Jayaram 48). Since going back to the original homeland is a natural desire of many diasporans, many instances of reverse migration are taking place from diaspora towards homeland, creating a circular migration or permanent return migration (Chacko; Harvey).

One of the important dimensions of globalization today is the flow of capital from the diaspora to the homeland as a result of several factors like the affluence of diasporic Indians in the host economy and influence in the host politics, the increasing hostility of being an ethnic minority in the wake of political and religious factors, or the growth and development of India's economy and society. In the last two decades, India has developed from a poor underdeveloped economy to one of the most successful and prosperous economies in the world, thanks in part to globalization and the diasporic contribution. The networks that take place between India and the Indian diaspora today are manifold, ranging from micro-level networks such as transfer of money/remittances and consumer goods to families and relatives back home, constructive ideas for community development to that of macro-level networks such as the trade and investment in real estate, industries, institutions, corporations, and influence in homeland politics. In his book *Diaspora, Development, and Democracy*, Devesh Kapur talks about Indian diasporic networks and their role in facilitating global trade. He focuses on two important sectors of the economy where India shone in the recent past: the information and technology (IT) sector and the diamond-cutting and polishing industry. He argues that the success of Indian IT professionals in Silicon Valley in the United States has positively impacted the growth of the domestic Indian IT sector. And, in dealing with the growth of India's diamond-cutting industry, he traces the 'historical trajectory of Indian émigrés and India's involvement in the global diamond trade since the early 1960s' by providing two important case studies (the largest Jain-owned diamond companies in Antwerp – Eurostar and Rosy Blue) that 'illustrate the linkages between the success of the Indian diaspora and India's place in the global diamond trade' (100–101).

It is now a fact that, in the wake of globalization and in response to global demands, India has extended support to its diasporic communities and in return the diasporic communities have participated fully in the development initiatives of the homeland. For a long time, India has neglected the issues and concerns of its diaspora because of its own internal problems and inadequate government policies. However, with the emergence of a nationalist consciousness among Indian political elites in the early 20th century, there was a shift in the nature of the relationship between India and the Indian diaspora. As Mani and Varadarajan rightly observe: 'beginning with attempts to pressure the British Indian government to ban recruitment of unskilled labor and appoint commissions to investigate charges of abuse against plantation and mill owners, nationalist involvement in causes pertaining to overseas 'Indian' communities soon took on distinct political overtones' (58–59). During the first five decades of India's independence, the diaspora had limited linkages with the places of its origin, most of which were familial and religious. In a few cases, remittances were also sent to the parents or relatives. Diasporic interactions were individually promoted through home visits, marriage alliances, pilgrimage to sacred places, and overseas family reunions. There were hardly any significant economic and political engagements with the Indian diaspora at the national level (Ray; Mani and Varadarajan). However, this has changed since the 1990s, especially after liberalization – a period when India gained its 'economic confidence' and at the same time the 'Indian diaspora became successful in the United States' (Kapur 190). Vinay Lal argues that the success of the Indian diaspora in the US was 'intrinsically related to India's standing in the world, the country's economic progress, and its geopolitical alliances' (63).

Under the economic liberalization of the early 1990s, a series of reforms affecting the industrial, trade, and financial sectors aimed to make the Indian economy fast growing and globally competitive. Efforts were made to attract foreign direct investment by providing facilities to foreign companies to invest in different fields of economic activity, encouraging investment in the country by Non-Resident Indians (NRIs), and removing obstacles to the entry of MNCs in India. These measures allowed Indian companies to enter into foreign collaborations and also encouraged them to set up joint ventures abroad. Thus, liberalization and the new industrial policy in the 1990s sought involvement of overseas Indians in investing both in terms of capital and technology (Jain).

There are mainly three mechanisms – remittances, bank deposits, and foreign direct investment (FDI) – through which the Indian diaspora became the source of large financial flows into India (Kapur). India is one of the world's largest receivers of remittances in absolute terms, with almost $12.9 billion received in 2000, rising to $52 billion in 2008. Similarly the FDI into India has increased considerably; between 2000 and 2005 FDI in India averaged around $5 billion annually but jumped to about $19 billion in 2006 to 2007. The third source of financial flows, NRI bank deposits, also increased from $12.4 billion in 1990 to $32.5 billion in 2003 (Kapur 104–112).

Further, the Government of India (GOI) made several new policies to strengthen the linkages with its diaspora. One such policy was the introduction of the People of Indian Origin (PIO) Card. The PIO Card was launched by the Ministry of Home Affairs in March 1999 to reinforce the emotional bonds between India and the Indian diaspora. Persons of Indian origin up to the fourth generation settled anywhere in the world, except for a few specified countries, are eligible to apply for this card. Under the PIO Card scheme, there is no need for a visa to visit India or to register with the Foreigner's Registration Office if the continuous stay does not exceed 180 days. Thus, the PIO Card made the journey of people of Indian origin back to their homeland much more simple, easy, flexible, and hassle-free.

In addition to the PIO Card, the government policy facilitated diasporic engagement when the High Level Committee (HLC) on Indian Diaspora[9] was formed by the Ministry of External Affairs in September 2000 to assess the status, needs and roles of NRIs and PIOs. The Committee submitted its report to the Prime Minister in January 2002, recommending measures to revise country-specific plans for forging a mutually beneficial relationship with diaspora. In its interim report (MEA, 2001), the HLC recommended that the government address some of the following important issues: (a) charging a lower fee for the PIO Card but for a decreased validity of 10 years (rather than 20 years of validity for a fee of $ 1,000), (b) observation of Pravasi Bharatiya Divas on 9 January (the day Mahatma Gandhi returned to India from South Africa) of every year, in India and abroad, to recognize and appreciate the role of Indian diaspora in the promotion of India's interest, (c) the institution of the Pravasi Bharatiya Samman Award for eminent PIOs and NRIs, and

(d) granting of dual citizenship. In fact, all of these suggestions were implemented with immediate effect, except the dual citizenship.

The first global meeting of the Indian diaspora and the Indian government – the Pravasi Bharatiya Divas (PBD) – was organized on 9 January 2003 and subsequent conventions are held every year on the same day. This glamour and glitz event not only serves as a venue recognizing the Indian diaspora, it also showcases diasporic achievements in science and technology in attempts to convince the diaspora either to return or to invest more in the homeland. Mani and Varadarajan have emphasized that the 'PBD is a striking example of the new historical, political, and cultural relationship between the Indian state and diasporic populations in the early 21st century. Marking a radical departure from previous government policies toward NRI and PIO populations, the conference signals the commitment of the Indian state to the welfare of diasporic populations' (45).

The GOI introduced another scheme in 2005, the Overseas Citizenship of India (OCI) policy essentially providing for dual citizenship.[10] Certain PIOs who migrated from India and acquired citizenship in a foreign country other than Pakistan and Bangladesh are eligible for OCI as long as their home countries allow dual citizenship (Ministry of Home Affairs, Government of India 2005). This has raised many debates in India and has become a matter of concern for the Indian diaspora. Recognizing the advantage of conferring dual citizenship, on grounds similar to many other Western countries who have already offered it, Jagdish Bhagwati, an eminent American economist of Indian origin, appealed to the GOI in his inaugural address in the 2010 PBD conference:

> It is time for us to recognize that, in the modern world, where people move from one jurisdiction to another while retaining loyalty to both, it makes sense to offer dual citizenship … . Alongside, we must also open up ways in which the Diaspora's right to vote is also made possible. There are several ways in which this can be done: e.g. by providing a limited number of seats in the Lok Sabha which all NRIs can vote for as a bloc; or by allowing NRIs to register to vote in the States from which they originate. (9)

Another area where globalization has influenced relations between the diaspora and its homeland is the involvement of the diasporic community in homeland politics. Diasporic politics, according to Laguerre, is a 'transborder protopolitical system, because its existence depends on its successful encroachment on both the hostland and homeland political system ... it is based on transnational practice and the transnational stretch of state institutions' (3). Members of diasporas participate in the homeland politics, according to Kapur, in a variety of ways: 'in some cases, they have the right to vote, either as dual citizens or as citizens residing abroad ... more importantly, they influence the voting preferences of kin in the country of origin, an influence that is amplified if they send financial remittances. In other cases, they return and run as candidates themselves. Where direct participation is ruled out, diasporas may attempt to influence politics in the country of origin through financial contributions to political parties and candidates' (31).

The other side of globalization which has received very little academic attention is the diaspora's involvement in homeland conflicts by supporting extremist religious, ethnic, secular, or other movements. Diasporic participation (real and virtual) in the homeland is often the result of emotional attachments with the places of origin or birth though the members live far away from it – this according to Benedict Anderson is called 'long-distance nationalism' (42), a nationalism that no longer depends as it once did on territorial location in a home country. The case of ethnic conflicts in Kashmir, the fight for a separate Sikh state 'Khalistan' in Punjab or the Hindutva movement – a movement advocating Hindu nationalism – are some of the important instances where the Indian diaspora has been involved vigorously by channelling huge amounts of funds to achieve the goals of these nationalist movements.

The other aspect of the Indian diaspora's role, which cannot be ignored, is its philanthropic contribution for national emergencies and disaster relief in India like the Kargil War (1999), the super-cyclone in Odisha (1999), and earthquakes in Gujarat (2001). For instance, in 2002, the American India Foundation raised $7.5 million from PIOs in the US. Of the $7.5 million, $1 million went to the victims of the 11 September attacks, with the remainder going toward relief efforts for the Gujarat earthquake (Anand). In addition to the efforts by the Indian diaspora itself, the US Congress even approved, as a result of Indian diaspora lobbying, considerable financial aid packages to India following the 2001 Gujarat earthquake, the 2004 tsunami disaster, and the earthquake in the Kashmir region in October 2005 (Gottschlich 166). More recently, Indian Americans showed their moral support for Indians in the homeland by participating in a 240-mile walk and one-day fast organized by a group of NRIs to express solidarity for Anna Hazare's fight against corruption in India ('Indians in US Rally').

Another field in which globalization has had a significant effect is the strengthening of international relations between diaspora and homeland as a result of the success of Indians in the politics of the host society. The experiences of racism, discrimination, and marginalization of Indian diasporics in the past had put into question their identity and survival as a minority in majoritarian societies. However, the recent forces of globalization and transnationalization have transformed the ideological and political clout of Indians in the diaspora. From old diaspora in countries such as Mauritius, Fiji, Singapore, Trinidad and Tobago, Guyana, and Surinam to that of new diaspora in countries such as the UK, the US, and Canada (Lal et al.), Indians have become successful in mobilizing the host society's public support of India and in entering directly into the politics of these countries, occupying high positions at both the national and state levels. Such developments have had considerable positive impacts on the international relations between India and the Indian diaspora.

Conclusion

Diasporas may transcend geopolitical boundaries, change their functions over time or even disappear as a result of globalization and transnational migration but the homeland persists through such transformations. Sections of the Indian diaspora, for instance, in areas such as East Africa, the Caribbean, and Fiji have produced new 'twice displaced diasporas' in the UK, Canada, the Netherlands, and Australia but their emotional attachment to the original homeland in India remains unchanged and in the wake of globalization it has further strengthened the transnational networks facilitated through the homeland government (Bhachu; Voigt-Graf). GOI initiatives such as the OCI policy, PIO Card, and liberalization of travel visas have all facilitated the transnational linkages and networks between India and the Indian diaspora (Bhat and Narayan). Both India and its diaspora have benefitted greatly from their strong and improving relationship.

Globalization offers both opportunities and challenges, hitherto never anticipated, for diasporas and their homelands. Challenges to diasporas include organizing themselves to take socio-economic and political advantage of borderless markets, information highways, global institutions, and other conditions of globalization. The same challenges and opportunities confront the homeland. Meanwhile, ethnic, political, and religious conflicts in the homeland can destabilize the diaspora's international relations with the homeland, diminishing opportunities for mutual gain. For this reason, homeland governments must focus on domestic stability simultaneously while courting the diaspora abroad. As I have argued in this chapter, diasporas are not only important for the homeland but reciprocally the homeland is important for diasporas: they are interconnected and interdependent. Globalization has facilitated new levels of interconnection and interdependence between the diaspora and its homeland to the mutual benefit of each.

Notes

1. Appadurai identifies five factors that contribute to the global cultural flows: 'ethnoscapes', 'technoscapes', 'finanscapes', 'mediascapes', and 'ideoscapes'. These describe, respectively, the movements of peoples, technologies, capital, entertainment, and ideology.
2. For instance, it is observed that many of the 'temporary migrants' in the US over the years integrated into US society by becoming 'permanent residents'. There are a number of factors that play an important role in facilitating the process whereby these temporary migrants become permanent residents (see Sahoo et al.).
3. What I mean by 'most modern' here is that the 'Indian diaspora' is considered as resulting from the large-scale emigration since the 19th century as compared to the classical diasporas such as Jews, Armenians, and Greeks who had a much longer migration history; for a detailed discussion of the classical and modern diasporas, see Reis.
4. The main motives of traders and merchants during this period were to become successful in their businesses; however, different circumstances led to the permanent settlement of some of these trading communities in faraway places such as Southeast Asia, East and South Africa (see Markovits).
5. This period is called the first phase of globalization of international migration caused by the growth of European maritime powers which led to the discoveries of the 'new world'.

6. The indenture labour system 'took a variety of forms ... but generally was a contractual arrangement with penal sanctions whereby workers agreed to passage to and employment in a foreign country under specified terms, usually for five to ten years' (Goss and Lindquist 389).
7. Cohen offered five types of diasporas based on their historical migration experiences: the 'victim diaspora', 'labour diaspora', 'imperial diaspora', 'trade diaspora', and 'cultural diaspora'.
8. Esman talked about three classes of diaspora based on their functions they perform in the host society: they are: settler, labour, and entrepreneurial diasporas.
9. The Committee was formed under the Chairmanship of Dr L.M. Singhvi, Member of Parliament and former High Commissioner of India to the UK.
10. It should be noted that the OCI does not confer full citizenship of India, as the Constitution of India does not allow dual citizenship, i.e. holding Indian citizenship and citizenship of a foreign country simultaneously.

References

Anand, Priya. 'Hindu Diaspora and Religious Philanthropy in the United States'. Contesting Citizenship and Civil Society in a Divided World. Sixth International Society for Third Sector Research. Toronto. 11–14 July 2004. Paper.

Anderson, Benedict. 'Western Nationalism and Eastern Nationalism: Is There a Difference that Matters?' *New Left Review* 9 (2001): 31–42.

Appadurai, Arjun. *Modernity at Large: Cultural Dimensions of Globalization*. Minneapolis: University of Minnesota Press, 1996.

Basch, Linda, Nina Glick Schiller, and Cristina Szanton Blanc. *Nations Unbound: Transnational Projects and Deterritorialized Nation-State*. New York: Gordon & Breach, 1994.

Bhachu, Parminder. *Twice Migrants: East African Sikh Settlers in Britain*. London: Tavistock, 1985.

Bhagwati, Jagdish. 'India: The Role of the Diaspora'. PBD Conference. New Delhi. 8 January 2010. Inaugural Address.

Bhat, Chandrashekhar and Ajaya Kumar Sahoo. 'Diaspora to Transnational Networks: The Case of Indians in Canada'. *Fractured Identity: The Indian Diaspora in Canada*. (eds) Sushma J. Varma and Radhika Seshan. Jaipur: Rawat Publications, 2003. 141–167.

Bhat, Chandrashekhar and K. Laxmi Narayan. 'Indian Diaspora, Globalization and Transnational Networks: The South African Context'. *Journal of Social Science* 25 (2010): 13–23.

Brown, Judith. *Global South Asians: Introducing the Modern Diaspora.* Cambridge: Cambridge University Press, 2007.

Brubaker, Rogers. 'The 'Diaspora' Diaspora'. *Ethnic and Racial Studies* 28.1 (2005): 1–19.

Bruneau, Michel. 'Diasporas, Transnational Spaces and Communities'. *Diaspora and Transnationalism: Concepts, Theories and Methods.* (eds) Rainer Bauböck and Thomas Faist. Amsterdam: Amsterdam University Press, 2010. 35–50.

Castles, Stephen and Mark J. Miller. *The Age of Migration.* London: Macmillan, 1993.

Chacko, Elizabeth. 'From Brain Drain to Brain Gain: Reverse Migration to Bangalore and Hyderabad, India's Globalizing High Tech Cities'. *Geo Journal* 68.5 (2007): 131–140.

Clarke, Colin, Ceri Peach, and Steven Vertovec, eds. *South Asians Overseas: Migration and Ethnicity.* Cambridge: Cambridge University Press, 1990.

Cohen, Robin. *Global Diaspora: An Introduction.* London: UCL Press, 1999.

Esman, Milton. *Diasporas in the Contemporary World.* Cambridge: Polity Press, 2009.

Faist, Thomas. 'Diaspora and Transnationalism: What Kind of Dance Partners?' *Diaspora and Transnationalism: Concepts, Theories and Methods.* (eds) Rainer Bauböck and Thomas Faist. Amsterdam: Amsterdam University Press, 2010. 9–34.

———. 'Transnationalization in International Migration: Implications for the Study of Citizenship and Culture'. *Ethnic and Racial Studies* 23.2 (2000): 189–222.

Goss, Jon and Bruce Lindquist. 'Placing Movers: An Overview of the Asian-Pacific Migration System.' *The Contemporary Pacific* 12.2 (2000): 385–414.

Gottschlich, Pierre. 'The Indian Diaspora in the United States of America: An Emerging Political Force?' *Tracing an Indian Diaspora: Contexts, Memories, Representations.* (eds) Parvati Raghuram, Ajaya Sahoo, Brij Maharaj and Dave Sangha. New Delhi: Sage Publications, 2008. 156–170.

Government of India. Ministry of External Affairs (MEA). *Report of the High Level Committee on Indian Diaspora.* New Delhi: Indian Council of World Affairs, 2001.

———. Ministry of Home Affairs. *Overseas Citizenship of India.* 2005. Web 15 May 2011. <http://www.mha.nic.in/pdfs/intro.pdf>.

Harvey, William. 'British and Indian Scientists in Boston Considering Returning to Their Home Countries'. *Population, Space and Place* 15.6 (2009): 493–508.

Hyndman, Jennifer. *Managing Displacement: Refugees and the Politics of Humanitarianism*. Minneapolis: University of Minnesota Press, 2000.
'Indians in US Rally in Support of Hazare's Crusade'. *News One*. 9 April 2011. Web 5 May 2011. <http://www.inewsone.com/2011/04/09/indians-in-us-rally-in-support-of-hazares-crusade/42266>.
Jain, Ravindra K. 'Indian Diaspora, Globalization and Multiculturalism: A Cultural Analysis'. *Contribution to Indian Sociology* 32 (1998): 337–360.
Jayaram, N. 'Social Construction of the Other Indian: Encounters between Indian Nationals and Diasporic Indians'. *Journal of Social and Economic Development* 1.1 (1998): 46–63.
Kapur, Devesh. *Diaspora, Development, and Democracy: The Domestic Impact of International Migration from India*. New Delhi: Oxford University Press, 2010.
Kaur, Raminder. '"Ancient Cosmopolitanism" and the South Asian Diaspora'. *South Asian Diaspora* 3.2 (2011): 197–213.
Khadria, Binod. *The Migration of Knowledge Workers: Second-Generation Effects of India's Brain Drain*. New Delhi: Sage Publications, 1999.
Kivisto, Peter. 'Theorizing Transnational Immigration: A Critical Review of Current Efforts.' *Ethnic and Racial Studies* 24.4 (2001): 549–577.
Knowles, Caroline. *Race and Social Analysis*. London: Sage Publications, 2003.
Laguerre, Michel. *Diaspora, Politics, and Globalization*. Basingstoke: Palgrave, 2006.
Lal, Brig V., Peter Reeves, and Rajesh Rai, (eds). *The Encyclopedia of the Indian Diaspora*. Singapore: Editions Didier Millet, 2006.
Lal, Vinay. *The Other Indians: A Political and Cultural History of South Asians in America*. Noida: Harper Collins, 2008.
Lechner, Frank. 2005. 'Globalization'. *Encyclopedia of Social Theory*. (ed.) George Ritzer. Vol. 1. London: Sage Publications, 2005.
Levi, Scott. *The Indian Diaspora in Central Asia and Its Trade, 1550–1900*. Leiden: Brill Publications, 2002.
Levitt, Peggy and Nina G. Schiller. 'Conceptualizing Simultaneity: A Transnational Social Field Perspective on Society'. *International Migration Review* 38.3 (2004): 1002–1039.
Mani, Bakirathi and Latha Varadarajan. '"The Largest Gathering of the Global Indian Family": Neoliberalism, Nationalism, and Diaspora at Pravasi Bharatiya Divas'. *Diaspora* 14 (2005): 45–73.
Markovits, Claude. 'Indian Merchant Networks Outside India in the Nineteenth and Twentieth Centuries: A Preliminary Survey'. *Modern Asian Studies* 33.4 (1999): 883–911.
Mishra, Vijay. *Literature of the Indian Diaspora: Theorizing the Diasporic Imaginary*. London: Routledge, 2007.

Pires-Hester, Laura. 'The Emergence of Bilateral Diaspora Ethnicity among Cape Verdean-Americans'. *The African Diaspora: African Origins and New World Identities*. (eds) Isidore Okpewho, Carole Davies and Ali Mazrui. Bloomington: Indiana University Press, 1999. 485–503.

Portes, Alejandro, Luis Guarnizo, and Patricia Landolt. 'The Study of Transnationalism: Pitfalls and Promise of an Emergent Research Field'. *Ethnic and Racial Studies* 22 (1999): 217–237.

Raghuram, Parvati and Ajaya Sahoo. 'Thinking "Indian Diaspora" for Our Times'. *Tracing an Indian Diaspora: Contexts, Memories, Representations*. (eds) Parvati Raghuram, Ajaya Sahoo, Brij Maharaj, and Dave Sangha. New Delhi: Sage Publications, 2008. 1–20.

Ray, K.A. 'Roots of Ambivalence: Indenture, Identity and the Indian "Freedom Struggle"'. *Ethnicity, Identity, Migration: The South Asian Context*. (eds) Milton Israel and Narendra Wagle. Toronto: University of Toronto, Centre for South Asian Studies, 1993. 269–290.

Reis, Michele. 'Theorizing Diaspora: Perspectives on "Classical" and "Contemporary" Diaspora'. *International Migration* 42.2 (2004): 41–56.

Safran, William, Ajaya Sahoo, and Brij Lal, (eds). *Transnational Migrations: The Indian Diaspora*. London: Routledge, 2009.

——. 'Diasporas in Modern Societies: Myths of Homeland and Return'. *Diaspora* 1.1 (1991): 83–99.

——. 'The Jewish Diaspora in a Comparative and Theoretical Perspective'. *Israel Studies* 10.1 (2005): 36–60.

Sahoo, Ajaya, Dave Sangha, and Melissa Kelly. 'From "Temporary Migrants" to "Permanent Residents": Indian H-1B Visa Holders in the United States'. *Asian Ethnicity* 11 (2010): 293–309.

Sen, Amartya. *The Argumentative Indian: Writings of Indian Culture, History and Identity*. London: Penguin, 2005.

Sheffer, Gabriel. 'The Emergence of New Ethno-national Diasporas'. *Sociology of Diaspora: A Reader*. (eds) Ajaya Sahoo and Brij Maharaj. Jaipur: Rawat Publications, 2007. 43–62.

Tinker, Hugh. *A New System of Slavery: The Export of Indian Labor Overseas*. London: Oxford University Press, 1974.

Tölölyan, Khachig. 'The Nation-state and Its Others: In Lieu of a Preface'. *Diaspora* 1.1 (1991): 3–7.

Vertovec, Steven. 'Transnationalism and Identity'. *Journal of Ethnic and Migration Studies* 27.4 (2001): 573–582.

——. 'Three Meanings of "Diaspora" Exemplified among South Asian Religions'. *Diaspora* 6.3 (1997): 277–299.

Voigt-Graf, Carmen. 'The Construction of Transnational Spaces by Indian Migrants in Australia'. *Journal of Ethnic and Migration Studies* 31.2 (2005): 365–384.

PART 2

Contemporary Indian Diaspora in Fiction

Chapter 5

Globalization, Diaspora, and the Dynamics of Genre

'Imaginative Realism' in M.G. Vassanji's *The Assassin's Song*

KRISHNA SEN

Globalization and the Dilemma of Diaspora

The paradigms of diaspora theory and diasporic writing have altered considerably since the onset of globalization and its corollaries, transnationalism and transculturalism. In 'Transculturality: The Puzzling Form of Cultures Today' (1999), Wolfgang Welsch observed that despite the persistence of 'regional-cultural rhetoric', globalization had engendered transcultural networks that imbricate even those who stay at home, since 'cultures today are in general characterized by hybridization' – '*The new forms of entanglement* are a consequence of migratory processes, as well as of worldwide material and immaterial communications systems and economic interdependencies and dependencies' (198–199, emphasis added). Through modern electronic communications systems (television, internet satellite phones) and economic interfaces produced by multinational capital, cultural hybridity, once the hallmark of the diasporic condition, now pervades the world in rural as well as urban sectors. Nevertheless, by the simple fact of being in one place and belonging to another, the diasporan still has to negotiate the dialectics of home and away.

Globalization has, however, given a fresh turn to this negotiation. When the critical idiom of diaspora as a new interdisciplinary field was initiated in 1991 by Khachig Tölölyan with the launch of *Diaspora: A Journal of Transnational Studies*, the dominant trope to delineate diaspora was the archetypal exile of the Jews from Israel, and its concomitant nostalgia for the originary homeland. The elegiac note was forcefully struck in William Safran's influential essay in the very first issue ('Diasporas in Modern Society: Myths of Homeland and Return'): it was carried forward in the plangent tones of Rushdie's 'imaginary homelands, Indias of the mind' (10) and the knell-like tolling of Bhabha's 'Gatherings of exiles and *émigrés* and refugees; gathering on the edge of 'foreign' cultures ... . Also the gathering of the people in the diaspora ...' ('DissemiNation' 199–200). In *The Location of Culture* (1994) Bhabha famously identified the diasporic displacement between two cultures as 'interstitial', as an 'elliptical in-between' and an anxiety-ridden 'third space' (2, 85, 143).

Yet the contours of the discourse were already changing in the early 1990s. Two strands are visible – the exilic and the entrepreneurial. While one group mourns its lost past, another glories in its cultural bifocality. For many contemporary diasporans, the old pain of enforced assimilation into the melting pot has given way to joyous adaptation – after taking American citizenship Bharati Mukherjee proclaims, 'I am one of you now!' (18); Rey Chow exults, 'Home is here, in my migrancy' (142); and Gish Jen declares, 'We newish Americans leapfrog from world to world, reinventing ourselves *en route*' (16). Schiller et al. (1992) dub the new breed of voluntary migrants globe-hopping for education or economic prospects as the 'transnational migrants' or 'transmigrants' (1) – denizens of Appadurai's 'global ethnoscapes' (48). For Ashcroft, this affluent, mobile and cosmopolitan population, so different from the disenfranchised exiles and *émigrés* of old, constitutes the new phenomenon of the 'transnation' (1 ff.).

This is not to say that all current diasporans are transmigrants. There is a whole underclass of what Sen terms the 'subaltern migrants' or 'submigrants' (241) – indeed, class and subalternity are rapidly inflecting diaspora theory today. For indigent people like those in Monica Ali's *Brick Lane* or illegal immigrants like Biju, the cook's son in Kiran Desai's *The Inheritance of Loss*, diaspora is still exile and home a poignant dream. But for the privileged transmigrant home is just a Skype call or plane ride away, and can also be accessed in other forms due to liberalized policies. Several countries now permit dual citizenship. Even India, which does not, now has its high-priced OCI (Overseas Citizen of India) card that offers the foreign citizen of Indian origin every facility except franchise, Government positions and ownership of agricultural land. Prosperous 'Overseas Indians' are among the largest consumers of Indian real estate, commodities, equities and art objects. Some diasporans are even partially domiciled. Retired expatriates spend winters at home with family and friends, only to fly away to temperate climes when the mercury rises. And for the younger generation, the opportunity for 'reverse diaspora' in professions like information technology and finance combines homeland ambience with hostland passports. So apparently, the tropology of diaspora has shifted from the linear and temporal axis of irreversible departure from the homeland to the circulatory and spatial axis of straddling both homeland and hostland in (for the fortunate) a borderless world.

Arif Dirlik has felicitously described this reclaiming of cultural roots as 're-ethnicization' (220). Shirley Geok-lin Lim (159) once outlined a triadic trajectory for immigrant identity formation in the hostland – 'pre-ethnic' (dysfunctional sense of exile and loss), 'ethnic' (clinging to homeland practices to resist total assimilation), and 'post-ethnic' (desire to be accepted by the hostland). By this yardstick, the oxymoronic figure of the re-ethnicized diasporan, moving fluidly between homeland and hostland and effortlessly switching languages and lifestyles, could well be termed 'postnational'. Thus, for Gilroy, the modern Black diaspora 'transcend(s) both the structures of the nation state and the constraints of ethnicity and national particularity' (19).

The paradox is that the drive towards re-ethnicization, postnational though it may be, only re-affirms the potency of home. This surely problematizes Derrida's rejection of the 'ontopology' of the 'arch-originary' in *Spectres of Marx*, as also his contention that globalization renders the age-old tug of 'native soil and blood' a mere *'primitive conceptual phantasm ... (an) archaism'* (82, Point 8; emphasis in the original). The problem is that in this era of rapid modernization, temporality subversively infiltrates the triumphant spatiality of the transnation – neither the physical place nor the cultural space of home remains what it was in the fond memory of the diasporan. As Taslima Nasreen says in *Phera*, one can never go back to the home one has left behind. This is the trauma of Tham'ma in Ghosh's *The Shadow Lines*, or of Bangladeshi-Australian novelist Adib Khan's protagonist Masud in *Spiral Road* (2007), in the shock of his return to a stridently fundamentalist Bangladesh after two decades of fantasizing in Melbourne about the home he had left in the heady days of Mujib. Samir Dayal quotes from a 1996 interview in which Homi Bhabha pertinently articulates a provocatively new 'third space' at the juncture of the imaginary homeland and the actual revisited home – 'the strangeness of the familiar ... ourselves-as-others, others-as-ourselves, that borderline ...' (49). In other words, the diasporan's contact zone of emotional destabilization can now be located even within the homeland.

So the transmigrant's homecoming is ambivalent and uncanny in Freud's sense of 'unheimlich' or 'not-at-homeness' (385). This is due, first, to transformations in the homeland; and secondly, to intersecting interpellations from both homeland and hostland – if the hostland lacks homeland culture, the homeland lacks hostland amenities and liberties. The dilemma of the globalized diasporan is thus an ontological, and not just a localized, homelessness – s/he is not at home anywhere, like Ila in *The Shadow Lines*. As Dr Hata, the elderly diasporic protagonist of Korean-American Chang-rae Lee's *A Gesture Life* (1999) says of both Korea and America – 'I will circle round and arrive again. *Come almost home*' (356, emphasis added). This is also the predicament of Black British novelist Caryl Phillips, born in the West Indies and brought up in Leeds. Yearning for an integrated Black identity, Phillips traverses the four Black 'homelands' enumerated by Stuart Hall in 'Cultural Identity and Diaspora' – Africa, the Caribbean, the United States, and Britain: but in each place his journal records his disappointment through a dirge-like refrain – 'I recognise this place ... but I don't belong here. I am of, and not of, this place' (1–3). Nico Israel's serendipitous term for this perplexing condition is 'outlandish' – '*between* exile and diaspora' (ix, emphasis in the original).

The Dynamics of Genre

The artistic representation of 'outlandish' experience poses its own literary and theoretical challenges. Realism has been the preferred narrative mode of the diasporic canon with its scrupulous chronicling of memories of home, the exigencies of cross-cultural living, and the myriad markers of marginalization and estrangement in the hostland. A more sophisticated option is the post-Second World

War Italian aesthetic movement of neo-realism. Neo-realism sought to extend the objectives of 19th-century realism, that of presenting a 'truthful' and 'objective' or 'scientific' image of external reality, by incorporating in its projection of social structures the Modernist practice of layered and psychological narration (without its freight of subtexts and symbolism) and (usually Marxist) social critique. Peter Liebregts analyses the nuanced and individualized modalities of realism and neo-realism deployed in *The Namesake*:

> *The Namesake* can be seen as part of a general trend in English fiction of returning to a more modernist (neo)realism, without the naivety of 19th century realism because of the poststructuralist/postmodernist revolution. Lahiri in her novel very much works in the tradition of literary realism, which offers a wealth of detailed, metonymic descriptions enabling the reader to imaginatively (re)create the settings and characters .... In the same vein, Lahiri creates historical contexts through period details .... The very last scene suggests that Gogol (Ganguli) has finally accepted his heritage when he begins to read ('The Overcoat'), thus offering us both closure (as in a 19th century realist novel) and an indeterminate open ending (to mark the text as a neo-realist one). (232, 245)

Gogol's effort was to create a sense of belonging while in diaspora. Earlier, several stories in *The Interpreter of Maladies* had sensitively delineated the difficulties of this attempt in the neo-realist mode. But globalization and the accessibility of home have reconfigured James Clifford's pithy adage about the gulf between routes and roots and given it totally new dimensions. In this context, Shirley Geok-lin Lim's apposite comment is that new epistemes mandate new articulations – 'fresh narratives of ethnicity recovery to counter the older narratives of loss of ethnic identity' (160). Some alternative rhetoric is required to fuse within a single experiential field the dichotomous worlds of Asian, Middle Eastern and African homelands that valorize tradition and faith with Eurocentric hostlands that privilege Enlightenment norms of progress and rationality. Rushdie's solution was always magical realism, but other authors are experimenting in different ways.

As it so happens, globalization has turned non-Western homelands into prized cultural capital in the Western literary marketplace. The diaspora canon is no exception. It is not that the homeland had not been projected earlier. But to take just the Indian diaspora, in the 1980s the homeland had largely featured in Rushdie and Ghosh for its political turmoil and complicated social and religious controversies – all the turbulence habitual to India that shocks and baffles the external gaze. The post 1980s endeavour is to orchestrate a more intimate and comprehensive engagement with the polyvalence of India in terms of its history, culture, customs, rituals, beliefs, alternative knowledges, aesthetics, myths, and folk lore – but all of this as refracted from the ground of diaspora, mediated as it is by acquired Western epistemologies. It is the difference, say, between the urban/national/international social and political conflicts in Amitav Ghosh's *The Shadow Lines* (1988) and *The Hungry Tide* (2004) with its rich folklore content of the *Bonbibi Johuranama* and its indigenous rural concerns and identities that constitute the backdrop for the contemporary political conflict at Morichjhapi, but also collectively function as an 'education' for the transmigrant Piya.

Contemporary India represents a complex cultural terrain that synthesizes the ancient, the medieval, the modern, and the postmodern as part of everyday life. High-tech manufacturing units are inaugurated with age-old rituals performed by pundits, globe-trotting sophisticates visit astrologers, and the pre-modern intricately permeates the existential reality of an evolving global power that, with China, may soon challenge Western supremacy. Several non-Western historians and social scientists have identified these processes, so puzzling to the West, as expressions of an alternative modernity. In *Provincializing Europe* **Dipesh** Chakrabarty questions Western progressivist historicism **and its** monologic modernity since Bengali/Indian subjectivity is **'inherently** a *multiple subject*, whose history produces significant **points of resis**tance and intractability when approached with a secular analysis that has its origins in the self-understanding of the subject of European modernity' (147, emphasis added); in 'Anderson's Utopia' Partha Chatterjee avers that '(t)he real space of modernity is a heterotopia' (131); and Chinese intellectual Jinhua Dai's translated Foreword to Xiaomei Chen's *Occidentalism* states that post-Mao China is 'difficult to delineate clearly within a single cultural logic such as (Western) modernization' (ix). In the West the Enlightenment ideal of normative Eurocentrism has been challenged by postmodern and post-structuralist approaches that envisage a striated and relativistic universe in place of homogeneous verisimilitude.

'Imaginative Realism'

This epistemological shift has had its impact on aesthetic representation as well, resulting in the foregrounding of forms that allow for heterogeneity and multivalence. Here magical realism with its sharp critique of the incongruities and inadequacies of a political or social situation is not the only option. The genre of romance has experienced a compelling revival, not in the sense of pulp romantic fiction but in terms of its many literary allies and cognates – fascinating episodes from little-known histories, styles of popular culture, fabulation, fantasy, the gothic, allegory, myth, legend, and variants of science fiction. The point is that they are not used in and for themselves but as they contrapuntally intersect with our everyday life. Like magical realism, all these other metarealistic modes have been appropriated by the modern writer for imaging todays' hyperrealities in a process that might be termed 'imaginative realism'.

Imaginative realism has generated an international literary canon in which diaspora plays a crucial role. In addressing Welsch's 'puzzling' transculturality, transmigrant romance has moved well beyond Northrop Frye's characterization of the traditional romance in which 'subtlety and complexity are not much favoured' (195). Emily S. Davis observes in *Rethinking the Romance Genre* (2013) – '... the instability of the romance makes it an especially malleable tool for representing fluid political, sexual and racial identities and coalitions in an era of flexible global capitalism' (2). She goes on to analyse, among others, the 1999 Booker Prize short-listed novel *The Map of Love* by diasporic Egyptian author Ahdaf Soueif with its poly-generic use of love, history and myth along with social analysis and realism to portray postcolonial Egypt and the political conundrum of Palestine. Yogita Goyal says in *Romance, Diaspora and Black Atlantic Literature* (2010) – '... black Atlantic fiction gains its energy from the friction of two competing modes – nationalist realism and diasporic romance' (8): according to her, 'diasporic romance' in this case is that, while Africa is certainly a physical location, the originary African homeland is an identity-shaping mythic construct of the modern Black Atlantic diasporic imaginary (7). Perhaps the strongest voice for recuperating romance from its conventional escapist connotations and positioning its imaginative realism as a powerful tool to evoke complex, contradictory or painful realities is Toni Morrison's in *Playing in the Dark* (1992):

> It has been suggested that romance is an evasion of history .... But I am more persuaded by arguments that find in it the head-on encounter with very real, very pressing historical forces and the contradictions inherent in them, as these come to be experienced by writers. Romance, an exploration of anxiety ... offered platforms for moralizing and fabulation, and for the imaginative entertainment of violence, sublime incredibility, and terror ... . (36)

The only way to convey the unimaginably horrific reality of slavery in *Beloved*, Morrison says in the same essay ('Romancing the Shadow'), was to employ certain facets of the romance mode such as the irrational and the supernatural.

Even allegory, summarily rejected in the West for centuries as an outmoded medieval convention, witnessed three important new studies from three reputed publishers in the same year, 2010. Jeremy Tambling says in *Allegory* – 'Newer approaches, for example those associated with Walter Benjamin and Paul de Man, threaten to unsettle the older senses of allegory altogether' (2); Brenda Machofsky highlights allegory's potential to express the simultaneous multiplicities of our heterogeneous world – 'Allegory always demands that we think otherwise' (7); and *The Cambridge Companion to Allegory* ends its voluminous historical survey with chapters entitled 'Walter Benjamin's Concept of Allegory', 'Hermeneutics, Deconstruction, Allegory', and 'Allegory Happens: Allegory and the Arts Post-1960'. Finally, the 'worlding' or 'world-making' function of myth and folklore in contemporary cultural practice, as distinct from their antiquarian or anthropological study, is found in several recent publications like Donald et al.'s *The New Dictionary of Cultural Literacy* (2002) or Simon Bronner's *Explaining Tradition: Folk Behaviour in Modern Culture* (2011).

The Indian diasporic writer's interaction with the dialogic complexities of the homeland necessitates a flexible cognitive and narrative framework that is nevertheless rooted in the quotidian reality s/he wishes to explore – a morphing, as it were, of the templates of realism and neo-realism. In their blending of bygone Indian contexts and fabulation with contemporary events and hostland literary traditions such as science fiction and the moral novel, Bharati Mukherjee's *The Holder of the World* (1993) and Amitav Ghosh's *The Calcutta Chromosome* (1996) are examples of experimenting with composite fictional forms different from the (neo)realism of their previous work. The composite form itself, in its hybridity and potential instability, signals a multi-ethnic provenance and the interface of two contrasting cultures. In its literary structure *Holder*, for instance, gestures towards bi-cameral cultural translation involving both India and America in place of the univocal cultural translation of the diasporan by the host culture –the major texts underpinning and referencing the action are *Ramayana* and *Shahnama* along with Mary Rowlandson's early American captivity narrative, Hawthorne's *The Scarlet Letter* and Pynchon's *V*. *The Calcutta Chromosome*, subtitled 'A Novel of Fevers, Delusion and Discovery', juxtaposes the local and the global, native tradition and Western science, in the detection ad cure of malaria in India. It provocatively suggests that the apparently magical charms and potions of Mangala Bibi and the empirical discovery of Ronald Ross tend towards the same conclusion – relief from malaria: the difference being that local knowledge is thought to be non-existent only because it is not disseminated in the discursive terminology of the West. The issue of healing local knowledges and their value in the commercial and competitive West surely brings to mind Chitra Banerjee Divakaruni's best-loved novel, *The Mistress of Spices* (2005). It invokes the strategies of romance – love, mystery, magic, and fabulation – to evoke the mystical power of the homeland in the hostland in place of the marginalization and even ridicule of homeland practices in the hostland as experienced by the characters in *The Interpreter of Maladies* and *The Namesake*.

Other recent Indian diasporic mixed-genre novels evoke India through its lesser-known histories that radiate exotic or romantic charm or conjure up aspects of the past that are partially or wholly occluded over time. One thinks of Kunal Basu's *The Opium Clerk* (2001) and especially *The Miniaturist* (2003), Bharati Mukherjee's *The Tree Bride* (2004), Amitav Ghosh's *The Sea of Poppies* (2008) and *The River of Smoke* (2011), or Tabish Khair's *The Thing About Thugs* (2012). Another group of novels recalls romance modalities despite their realistic narratives in plotting utopian returns of diasporans to India – some of the fiction of Tishani Doshi, Shilpi Somaya Gowda, or Priya Basil, for instance. Even an apparently wholly realistic novel like Bharati Mukherjee's *Miss New India* (2011) is romantic when compared to the gritty and even repulsive realism of Adiga's *The White Tiger*. It essentially replicates the process of identity formation in the adventure mode as in *Jasmine* where Jasmine/Jassy/Jane (the name changes signifying stages of self-empowerment) journeys from rural Punjab to America the land of dreams in the quintessential quest motif of romance. Anjali/Angie Bose, too, travels from the boondocks of Bihar to the bright lights of Bangalore, discovering herself while encountering the equivalents of trolls and guardians along the way. As Northrop Frye says – 'The romance is nearest of all literary forms to the wish-fulfilment dream' (186).

The Assassin's Song

M.G. Vassanji's *The Assassin's Song* (2007) is a moving quest, not just for the homeland, but for a unique and fast-disappearing heritage. Vassanji belongs to the Khoja Ismaili Muslim sect of Sufi persuasion and is a multiple diasporan – his Gujarati ancestors moved to Kenya, his own family shifted to Tanzania, and he himself is now a resident of Canada. While every one of his several other novels is set in his African homeland, *The Assassin's Song* is the only one concerning India. To accommodate his widely divergent Middle Eastern religious provenance, Gujarati inheritance, and Canadian present, Vassanji resorts to the polysemous structures of imaginative realism. The narrative flows fluidly between 13th century Gujarat and 20th and 21st century India and Canada, seamlessly interweaving past and present.

Though Vassanji clarifies in the 'Author's Note' (369) that all characters and locations are imaginary, he also vouches for their actual historical links. Two historical strands from separate ancient pasts converge in this Sufi boy's bildungsroman as he transits from Gujarat to Canada through America and then back again to Gujarat. One strand features the revisionary Islamic sect of the Assassins from whom, so the lore goes, the modern word takes its origin. The Assassins were a feared 11th century radical Persian Shi'a sect founded by the Ismaili Nizari Hassan-i Sabbah to oust the Sunni Seljuk Turks from Persia – they conducted daring raids from remote mountain fortresses, till they were overthrown by the

Mongols some time in the late 13th or early 14th century. The Arabic name of the brotherhood, 'Hash'shashin', is said to relate to their use of hashish during their Sufi rituals, but later leaders conducted rampant assassinations that brought about their retributory downfall. In the early phase the brotherhood despatched several evangelists to propagate their faith in far-off lands. The Assassins and Gujarat come together in the other historical strand. Legend has it that one such missionary, pursued by the Seljuks and Mongols and in danger of his life, landed in Gujarat and was warmly welcomed by the Hindu king Vishal Dev Vaghela, who was a real historical figure reigning between 1243–1262 AD. This episode is considered to be the origin of the Khoja Ismaili sect in Gujarat.

Vassanji reconfigures the legend in terms of a fictitious wandering Persian Shi'a mystic from the Assassins sect, Nur Fazal, whose preternatural powers, visionary insights and many magical feats gain him a place in the court of Vishal Dev. He inspires many followers with his one message of love for all fellow beings irrespective of their caste or creed, and is lovingly named Pir Bawa or 'Holy Father'. Later, with the kin's blessings he marries a girl from the royal family and establishes a Sufi *darga* or shrine named Pirbaag or 'the saint's garden' at a (fictitious) remote hamlet named Haripur, a considerable distance from Ahmedabad: its fame spreads far and wide and for centuries on end Hindus, Muslims, and Sikhs worship there in amity. Pirbaag is obviously modelled on such famous Sufi sites as the Balapeer shrine in Baroda.

Nur Fazal's descendants become the hereditary 'Sahebs' of Pirbaag – the keepers of its mysteries or 'bols', the caretakers of its rare and antique manuscripts, and the purveyors of it 'ginans' or hymns. The protagonist Karsan Dargawalla – Karsan being a homonym of 'Krishna' and hence emblematic of Pir Bawa's ecumenical philosophy (281) – grows up through events like the India – China border war of 1965 and the India – Pakistan war over Bangladesh in 1971 that help date the novel to the mid-20th century. The latter war for the first time sows the seeds of Hindu – Muslim tension in idyllic Pirbaag.

Karsan knows from his childhood that he will mandatorily have to assume his father's mantle as the spiritual guide and seer for the throngs of believers who flock to the shrine. As a modern young boy, passionate about cricket and voraciously devouring news of the outside world from the magazines and newspapers gifted by his itinerant truck driver friend, he bitterly resents what he considers to be an indefensible limitation of his freedom of choice. In the tug of war between modern individualism and ancient tradition (represented by his father, the revered present 'Saheb'), Karsan wins what ultimately becomes a temporary victory. As if by the miraculous intercession of his supernatural alter ego Nur Fazal, he wins a scholarship to Harvard, later marries the Indo-American girl of his choice, and becomes a professor of English literature at a college in Canada. The links with his family, and especially his heartbroken father, become more and more tenuous. But after the romantic idyll of Canada, terrible retribution follows his apostasy. Karsan's only child Julian is killed in a motor accident leaving him emotionally crippled, his distraught wife abandons him, and after so many decades of amnesia he miraculously stumbles upon a tiny Ismaili sect in his city that owes allegiance to Pirbaag and reconnects him with his father. But by the time he comes to Pirbaag in late 2002, the horrific massacres following Godhra have already occurred, his parents and many followers have been massacred for being Muslims (despite their Sufism), the shrine has been almost irreparably vandalized, and Karsan's younger brother Mansoor has in retaliation joined an militant Muslim organization to wreak vengeance on Hindus and is being pursued by the Indian police. Willy-nilly, circumstances force Karsan, the reluctant postmodernist, to relocate to Pirbaag as surviving followers appear as if from nowhere, rebuild the shrine as best they can, and beg him to heal their trauma with spiritual guidance as his father would have done. The novel ends with Karsan musing on his strange destiny that even his America-generated rationality could not evade:

> I am the caretaker of Pirbaag .... There are those who touch my feet or my sleeves, ask for blessings. But as I attend to these people, unable to disappoint, to pull my hand or sleeve away, as I listen in sympathy or utter a blessing, a part of me detaches and stands away, observing, asking, are you real? (367)

Karsan, the 21st century incarnation of Nur Fazal, itself a contradiction in terms in the modern era, and the contingent seer of Pirbaag, symbolizes the unique confluence of many eras in present-day India. As Northrop Frye has observed, the social role of romance, which has been identified here as 'imaginative realism', is to demonstrate the underlying unity between opposite poles of the cycle of existence that rationality misinterprets as discrete.

References

Appadurai, Arjun. *Modernity at Large: Cultural Dimensions of Globalisation.* Minneapolis: University of Minnesota Press, 1996.

Ashcroft, Bill. 'Globalization, the Transnation and Utopia'. *Narrating the (Trans) Nation: The Dialectics of Culture and Identity.* (eds) Krishna Sen and Sudeshna Chakravarty. Kolkata: Dasgupta & Company, 2008. 1–23.

Bhabha, Homi K. *The Location of Culture.* London: Routledge, 1994.

Chakrabarty, Dipesh. *Provincializing Europe: Postcolonial Thought and Historical Difference.* Princeton: Princeton University Press, 2000.

Chatterjee, Partha. 'Anderson's Utopia'. *Grounds of Comparison: Around the Work of Benedict Anderson.* Spec. issue of *Diacritics* 29. 4 (Winter 1999): 128–134.

Chen, Xiaomei. *Occidentalism: A Theory of Counter-Discourse in Post-Mao China.* 2nd rev. (ed.) Lanham, MD: Rowan and Littlefield, 2002.

Chow, Rey. *Writing Diaspora: Tactics of Intervention in Contemporary Cultural Studies.* Bloomington and Indianapolis: Indiana University Press, 1993.

Clifford, James. *Routes: Travel and Translation in the Late Twentieth Century.* Cambridge, Mass.: Harvard University Press, 1997.

Copeland, Rita and Peter T. Struck, (eds). *The Cambridge Companion to Allegory.* Cambridge: Cambridge University Press, 2010.

Davis, Emily S. *Rethinking the Romance Genre: Global Intimacies in Contemporary Literature and Visual Culture.* New York: Palgrave Macmillan, 2013.

Dayal, Samir. 'Diaspora and Double Consciousness'. *The Journal of the Midwest Modern Language Association* 29.1 (Spring 1996): 46–62.

Derrida, Jacques. *Specters of Marx, the State of the Debt, the Work of Mourning, and the New International.* 1993. Trans. Peggy Kamuf. With an introduction by Bernd Magnus and Stephen Cullenberg. London: Routledge, 1994.

Dirlik, Arif. 'Literature/Identity: Transnationalism, Narrative and Representation'. *The Review of Education, Pedagogy and Cultural Studies* 24 (2002): 209–234.

Freud, Sigmund. *Sigmund Freud: Art and Literature.* 1919. Trans. James Strachey. Ind. (ed.). New Delhi: Shrijee's Book International, 2003.

Frye, Northrop. *Anatomy of Criticism.* 1957. London: Penguin, 1990.

Gilroy, Paul. *The Black Atlantic.* London: Verso, 1993.

Goyal, Yogita. *Romance, Diaspora and Black Atlantic Literature.* Cambridge: Cambridge University Press, 2010.

Hall, Stuart. 'Cultural Identity and Diaspora'. *Identity, Community, Culture, Difference.* (ed.) J. Rutherford. London: Lawrence and Wishart, 1990. 222–237.

Israel, Nico. *Outlandish: Writing between Exile and Diaspora.* Stanford, CA: Stanford University Press, 2000.

Jen, Gish. 'The Way We Live Now'. *New York Times Magazine.* 7 May 2000: 16.

Lee, Chang-rae. *A Gesture Life.* New York: Riverside Books, 1999.

Liebregts, Peter. 'A Diasporic Straitjacket or an Overcoat of Many Colours? A Reading of Jhumpa Lahiri's *The Namesake*'. *Writing India Anew: Indian English Fiction 2000–2010.* (eds) Krishna Sen and Rituparna Roy. Amsterdam: Amsterdam University Press, 2013. 231–246.

Lim, Shirley Geok-lin. 'Assaying the Gold; or, Contesting the Ground of Asian American Literature'. *New Literary History* 24 (1993): 147–169.

Machofsky, Brenda, (ed.). *Thinking Allegory Otherwise.* Stanford, CA: Stanford University Press, 2010.

Morrison, Toni. 'Romancing the Shadow'. *Playing in the Dark.* New York: Vintage Books, 1992.

Mukherjee, Bharati. 'Immigrant Writing: Give Us Your Maximalists!' *New York Times*, 28 August 1988. 28–29.

Phillips, Caryl. *A New World Order: Selected Essays.* London: Secker and Warburg, 2001.

Rushdie, Salman. *Imaginary Homelands: Essays and Criticism, 1981–1991.* London: Granta Books, 1992.

Safran, William. 'Diasporas in Modern Societies: Myths of Homeland and Return'. *Diaspora* 1.1 (1991): 83–99.

Schiller, N. Glick, L. Basch, and C. Blanc-Szanton, (eds). *Towards a Transnational Perspective on Migration: Race, Class, Ethnicity and Nationalism Reconsidered.* New York: New York Academy of Sciences, 1992.

Sen, Krishna. 'The (Re)Turn of the Native: Diaspora, Transnationalism and the Reinscription of Home'. *Defining and Re-Defining Diaspora: From Theory to Reality.* (eds) Marianne David and Javier Munoz-Basols. Oxford: Interdisciplinary Press, 2011. 227–250.

Tambling, Jeremy. *Allegory.* New Critical Idiom Series. London: Routledge, 2010.

Vassanji, M.G. *The Assassin's Song.* London: Vintage, 2007.

Welsch, Wolfgang. 'Transculturality: The Puzzling Form of Cultures Today'. *Spaces of Culture: City, Nation, World.* (eds) Mike Featherstone and Scott Lash. London: Sage Publications, 1999. 194–213.

Chapter 6

Known Stranger

The 'Asian' in African Writing

T. VIJAY KUMAR

'References to Asians in black African writing, particularly in the writing from South and East Africa, tend to be of an unfavourable kind', wrote Charles Sarvan in an essay titled 'The Asians in African Literature' (160). The 'unfavourable' representation in writing may well be a true reflection of the societal attitude. Writing of his experiences in the region, Paul Theroux observed that, 'In East Africa nearly everyone hates the Asians' (60).

In the first part of my essay, I will try to understand the 'unfavourable' representations of Asians in the context of their socio-political presence in Africa. In the second part, I look at a couple of instances of the diverse cultural negotiations that the Asians themselves have had with the Africa they live in. In the third part of my essay, I offer a reading of one novel as an example of the literary articulation of Asian-African selfhood that has emerged over the last few years from hybrid postcolonials located in the West.

In this essay, I will use 'Indian' and 'Asian' as if they were synonyms simply to foreground the cultural stereotype – 'Asians' generally refers to people from the South Asian subcontinent: from India, Pakistan, Bangladesh, and Sri Lanka. As a *Washington Post* report (15 March 2000) observes, 'After more than a century in Africa, ethnic Indians are still universally known here as "Asians"' (Vick a21). Africa here encompasses the three East African states – Kenya, Uganda, and Tanzania and parts of central Africa – today's Zambia, Zimbabwe, and Malawi.

I

Summarizing the debate over the Asian presence in East Africa, Dana Seidenberg (1983) writes, 'On the one hand, there were those who believed that the Asians were simply economic mercenaries from South Asia who had come to East Africa to grab what they could and leave ... and were immediately dismissed as the "silent observers" or "fence sitters" ... . On the other, there were those, including most Asians, who believed that the Indians had indeed played an important role in anti-colonial politics, a role which had never been sufficiently recognized' (vii).

Although commercial, cultural and political relations existed between the Indian subcontinent and Africa and continued from 'misty antiquity, through colonial period, to the present era' (Ali 143) and although Indian arrival in Africa dates back to centuries before colonization (Gregory) it was during the colonial period that Indians were brought into Africa for serving specific tasks of the colonial regime. At the turn of the century, some 32,000 'coolie' labourers were brought over by the British to build the 657 mile British East African Railroad from Mombasa to Kampala. Of these, nearly 2,500 workers – four workers per mile of track – died while building the railroad that was dubbed the 'lunatic line'. When the railway was completed, thousands of Indians farmed vegetables on the less desirable land – not the land reserved for British settlers. Others went into business. They ventured into newly 'opened' (colonized) areas and occupied the space between the white settlers and the local natives. It was thus the *dukawalla* (literally meaning 'shop keeper', the term used to refer to Indian merchants) and not white settlers, who first moved into new colonial areas, laying the groundwork for the colonialist economy based on cash for food and goods.

The Asian participation in the public life, the civil society of Africa (in economy and politics, trade unions, and journalism) is well documented in studies in the 1960s and 1970s by scholars such as Ghai, Mangat, Gregory, Seidenberg, and others. But since then, however, as Nandini Patel pointed out more recently, the subject of endowing the immigrant Asian identity with the dignity and position that it deserves in East Africa 'has been largely ignored, with a virtual silence on Asian issues since the 1980s, and particularly in the current years following the new wave of democracy in the 1990s' (1).

The repeated hostility to Asians in Africa is one (tragic) acknowledgement of their presence. The expulsion of (80,000) Asians from Uganda in 1972–1973 by Amin; the violence against them in Kenya in 1982 and 1993, for instance, give us some idea of the perception by black Africa of their role. However, neither their perceived contribution to African life, nor their perceived indifference to African causes, finds significant mention in contemporary African writing. Given the divergent perceptions of Asian presence in Africa, it is puzzling that only one perception that of hostility is represented in African writing. The 'Asian' remains even in much of postcolonial African writing, either a shadowy figure, or is represented as the stereotypical, blood-sucking, opportunistic *dukawallah*.

Part of the 'mystery' of the marginal status of the Asian in African literature may be accounted for by the agendas that contemporary African writers have evolved for their work. Ever since Achebe's classic *Things Fall Apart* (1958), African writing has been re-charting the 'tropics of discourse' drawn by the West: all of Achebe's work, for instance, can be seen to be in dialogue with Conrad.

More surprising, perhaps, is the marginal, denigrated Asian in the writings of the East African Ngugi wa Thiong'o. While relatively few, low-profile Asians in Achebe's Nigeria might argue for their marginality in the literature of that country, the same is certainly not true of Ngugi's Kenya. Constituting roughly 2 per cent of the population in 1966, Asians controlled one-fourth of the country's gross domestic product, and 90 per cent of the retail trade in Kenya. Besides, Asian presence in Kenya also took the 'enlightened' form of the founding of and participation in trade unions and journalism. However, the perfunctory acknowledgement of the Asian participation in trade unionism apart, the prevailing image of the Asian in Ngugi's writings is that of the stereotypical *dukawallah*. In an interview to me Ngugi admitted that although 'the prevailing image, it is true, is that of an exploiter', it is 'not the complete picture. The complete picture is much more complicated' (176). In the next section, I briefly look at attempts by Asians to present a more complete picture.

II

'I think there is a sense that the stereotype is not a fair acknowledgement of the community's role. And conversely, I think the rejection of it is an acknowledgement that the (Asian) community is as much Kenyan as any other tribe', said Pheroze Nowrojee chairman of the Asian-African Heritage Trust. 'The times are changing, I think,' he concluded (quoted in Vick A21). Times indeed were changing, and a sign of the changing times was the first-ever Asian-African Heritage Exhibition held in Nairobi in 2000. Titled 'The Asian African Heritage: Identity and History' and dedicated to the memory of the efforts and sacrifices of the Indian rail workers brought to Kenya by the British, the exhibit (at the National Museum of Kenya famed for the archaeological treasures that established East Africa as the cradle of Mankind) showed how Indians came to East Africa and what they have contributed since. Through photographs, documents and artifacts, the path-breaking exhibition depicted two centuries of Asian assimilation into Kenya.

'There has been a remarkable vacuum or lack of understanding in the way African-Asians were represented' (quoted in Evans), remarked Sultan Somjee, a fourth-generation Kenyan and ethnographer at the National Museum of Kenya who curetted the exhibition. Evidently, not much has changed from the time when Shiva Naipaul after visiting East Africa in the 1970s wrote 'The Asian is the eternal "other"'. Naipaul was struck by how 'the Indian in East Africa brought India with him and kept it inviolate' (121). 'Of course Asian Africans are always accused of being a closed society,' Somjee said in the curator's essay. Intensely focused on family and community, the Asian-Africans, according to Somjee, have become over the decades 'a complex minority *seen from the outside* as living a self-centered life' (quoted in Vick A21; emphasis added).

Contrary to how it looks from outside, the 'closed-ness' of Asian-African society, Somjee argued, contained the very components of 'civil society' so crucial to the struggling democracies of the Third World. Unable to rely on either British colonialists or post-independence governments for protection, the subgroups of the Indian community – Sikh, Ismaili, Goan, Hindu – turned self-reliant, building welfare organizations that not just Indians but all Kenyans have come to depend on.

Another cultural text that makes a similar attempt to represent from within the 'closed' community of Asian-Africans is the quarterly magazine *Awaaz*. The magazine began as a newsletter for the Eastern Action Club of Africa, a forum for business people to speak out against racism and unfair business practices after multi-party democracy was established in 1992. Subtitled 'The Authoritative Journal of Kenyan South Asian History', *Awaaz* 'researches, records and disseminates information on the South Asian community in East Africa, and in Kenya in particular, and acts as a catalyst to record the history, and establish linkages with the Indian subcontinent and the South Asian Diaspora in the United States, Canada, and the United Kingdom.'

Awaaz has a multi-racial oversight board but like a good South Asian enterprise it is a family affair. The editor Zahid Rajan is a printer by training and worked in advertising. His editorial partner, and partner in life, is Zarina Patel, writer, artist, and activist. She is also the granddaughter (and biographer) of A.M. Jeevanjee, the entrepreneur in colonial Kenya who founded the *African Standard* newspaper in 1902 (later the *East African Standard*) and the East African Indian National Congress in 1914.

Awaaz is more than a 'desi' magazine. It is a Kenyan nationalist enterprise that attracts intellectuals throughout Africa and Europe. It sponsors an Asian-African cultural event called the 'Samosa' Festival (which is an acronym for South Asian Mosaic of Society and the Arts). It is also a partner with the Kenya Human Rights Commission on a campaign for the recognition of the Mau Mau movement that played a crucial role in Kenya's freedom from colonial rule. *Awaaz* thus takes an active interest in the national life of Kenya and, according to the editor, it is thought to be 'too controversial' and 'too political' by Kenya's business elite, who refuse to support it financially. Rajan is critical of what he sees as the community's lack of engagement with Kenya's many challenges. 'The South Asian diaspora in Kenya is completely nonpolitical,' he says. 'It stays behind its security fences in (the Nairobi suburb of) Parklands' (quoted in Merchant).

III

A writer who takes a similar critical look at the Asian community and their 'attitudes' is the Kenya born Jameela Siddiqi who is among the very few, if not the only, woman writer of South Asian origin writing fiction based in colonial East Africa. But before I come to this 'new' writer, let me first acknowledge the contribution of more senior writers. In general, Asian writing from Africa has taken the form, both in fiction and non-fiction, of possible cultural negotiations with the majority community. There is, on the one hand, the expression of hope – hope of a harmonious coexistence of Asians and Africans. Bahadur Tejani and J.M. Nazareth have written movingly of just such a possibility. On the other hand are the writings of Peter Nazareth and M.G. Vassanji. Peter Nazareth speaks of the individual survival through exile, all attempts at 'communitas' having failed, while Vassanji's chosen subject matter is the *Indian* sub-community: all the 'others' in his fictions – the colonial masters, and black lovers – merely serve to emphasize the continuities with their Indian past: Africa is 'No New Land'.

'There have been numerous books on Uganda', wrote Jameela Siddiqi in a 2002 essay titled 'Uganda: A Personal Viewpoint on the Expulsion, 30 Years Ago'. 'But few', she feels 'attempt to shed any meaningful light on just what this multicultural, multiracial hotpot actually amounted to on a day-to-day basis'. It is precisely this 'life on a day-to-day basis' that Siddiqi's novels attempt to portray.

Born in Kenya and brought up in Uganda, Siddiqi came to Britain as a refugee from Uganda in 1972. She studied English and History at Makerere University Kampala, and at the London School of Economics. She is an award-winning television journalist and broadcaster, and has written on Indian classical music, and translated Urdu and Hindi poetry.

Siddiqi's first novel *The Feast of the Nine Virgins* (2001) interweaves the story of a *dukawallah* with that of a big-budget Bollywood film being made in London, some 25 years after the Expulsion. The narrative has multiple plot lines. The first one is set in East Africa in the fictional land of Pearl and told from the perspective of an 8-year-old child referred to as The Brat by everyone. The 8-year-old's story captures the race, class, religion, gender, and sexual politics in East Africa in the 1960s. The second plot line is set in London in the 1990s where a young Indophile British filmmaker who speaks fluent Urdu is commissioned by a mysterious millionaire to make a film starring a famous Bollywood actress. The complicated relationships amongst an eccentric cast of characters – the producer, the producer's assistant, the diva actress, a groupie, a world famous composer and a well-known Ustad – makes for an almost Bollywoody masala plot that is quite a self-contained story in itself.

The third plot line looks at the script of the film which is based on a historical character from 19th century Lahore, Tameezan Bibi. The fourth plot line which frames the whole novel is the relationship between two friends Ash and Sonia. The reader has to navigate three time periods and spaces – 19th century Lahore, 1960s Pearl/East Africa, and 1990s London. Siddiqi cleverly builds each line without sacrificing suspense and manages to tie them up at the end in an uproarious yet poignant tribute to and spoof of Bollywood. The novel is fast paced and requires some mental agility on the part of the reader to keep the different characters and plot lines sorted out and followed.

The novel experiments with form and structures the narrative like a film script with elements of magic realism and postmodernism thrown in. The short chapters of the novel, for instance, work like very quick cuts between the 'scenes' offering quick, snappy, glimpses of the several threads running all at once. However, as one reviewer (Iyer) pointed out, the plot which is the narrative's strength also makes it vulnerable. But overloading the plot is a familiar, though not a fatal, flaw in many first novels and *Feast* too suffers from it. Despite this weakness, however, Siddiqi manages to create an intricate and engaging story about identity, gender, love, loss, and exile. By affording a glimpse of the 'inner court yard' of the Asian-African life spaces, the novel adds an important new dimension to diaspora studies in general and to the study of Asian diaspora in Africa in particular.

I would like to end this essay by acknowledging the help of Jameela Siddiqi in making her novels available to me. I 'met' Jameela in a blog and when I wrote to her about my research interest and the general non-availability in India of non-North American diasporic writing, she readily sent me not only her two novels but two of Peter Nazareth's as well. In turn, I put her in touch with a distributor in India for her books. Last heard, Jameela's publisher and the Indian distributor were finalizing the terms of collaboration. I mention these details as a way of surpassing the difficulty of accessing books that would add to our understanding of diasporic experience but which due to the larger politics of publication and location are not always available to readers.

References

Ali, Shanti Sadiq. *India and Africa Through Ages*. New Delhi: National Book Trust, 1987.

Awaaz: The Authoritative Journal of Kenyan South Asian History. Web 28 May 2014. <http://www.awaazmagazine.com/>.

Evans, Ruth. 'Kenya's Asian heritage on display'. *BBC News Online*. 24 May 2000. Web 28 May 2014. <http://news.bbc.co.uk/2/hi/africa/762515.stm>.

Ghai, Dharam P. and Yash P. Ghai. 'Asians in East Africa: Problems and Prospects'. *The Journal of Modern African Studies* 3.1 (February 1965): 35–51.

Gregory, Robert G. *India and East Africa: A History of Race Relations within the British Empire 1890–1939*. London: Oxford University Press, 1972.

Iyer, Nalini. Review of *The Feast of the Nine Virgins*. 16 February 2009. Web 28 May 2014. <http://www.sawnet.org/books/reviews.php?The+Feast+of+Nine+Virgins>.

Mangat, Jagjit Singh. *A History of the Asians in East Africa, ca. 1886 to 1945*. London: Oxford University Press, 1969.

Merchant, Preston. 'One Indian's Kenyan Nationalism'. *Sepia Mutiny*. 21 January 2007. Web 28 May 2014. <http://sepiamutiny.com/blog/2007/01/21/one_indians_ken_1/>.

Naipaul, Shiva. *North of South: An African Journey*. London: Andre Deutsch Ltd., 1978.

Nazareth, J.M. *Brown Man, Black Country*. New Delhi: Tidings Publications, 1981.

Nazareth, Peter. *In a Brown Mantle*. Nairobi: East African Literature Bureau, 1972.

———. *The General is Up*. Toronto: TSAR Books, 1991.

Patel, Nandini. *A Quest for Identity: The Asian Minority in Africa*. Fribourg: Institut du Fédéralisme, 2007.

Sarvan, Charles Ponnuthurai. 'The Asians in African Literature'. *Journal of Commonwealth Literature* 11.2 (1976): 160–170.

Seidenberg, Dana April. *Uhuru and the Kenya Indians: The Role of a Minority Community in Kenya Politics 1939–1963*. New Delhi: Vikas-Heritage, 1983.

Siddiqi, Jameela. 'Uganda: A Personal Viewpoint on the Expulsion, 30 Years Ago'. *Information for Social Change*. 15 June 2002. Web 28 May 2014. <http://libr.org/isc/articles/15-Siddiqi-1.html>.

———. *Bombay Gardens*. Raleigh, North Carolina: Lulu.com, 2006.

———. *The Feast of the Nine Virgins*. London: Bogle-L'Ouverture Press, 2001.

Tejani, Bahadur. *The Day After Tomorrow*. Nairobi: East African Literature Bureau, 1971.
Theroux, Paul. 'Hating the Asians'. *Transition* 33 (1967): 60–73.
Vassanji, M.G. *No New Land*. Toronto: McClelland & Stewart, 1991.
——. *The Book of Secrets*. New York: Picador USA, 1994.
——. *The Gunny* Sack. London: Heinemann International, 1989.
——. *The In-between World of Vikram Lall*. Toronto: Doubleday Canada, 2003.
Vick, Karl. 'A New View of Kenya's "Asians"'. *Washington Post*. 15 March 2000. A 21.
Vijay Kumar, T. 'The Writer as Activist: Interview with Ngugi wa Thiong'o'. *South Asian Responses to Ngugi*. (eds) Bernth Lindfors and Bala Kothandaraman. New Jersey: Africa World Press. 2001. 169–176.

CHAPTER 7

Interrogating the 'Other' in Contemporary Indian Diaspora Fiction

ANGSHUMAN KAR

> ... either you are with us, or you are with the terrorists.
> — George W. Bush

> I've been trying to tell him since then to take his beard off – it looks very Muslim and stuff.
> — Priya

The first of these two quotes does not need any introduction. The second one does. It is from an interview of Priya (a 46 year old infectious disease specialist of an American university), taken by Sunil Bhatia,[1] immediately after 9/11. Priya was asked by Sunil to recall 'one moment that made her feel different in the past 20 years of her life in the USA' (Bhatia 28). Priya spoke about an incident in which she felt terribly anxious about the safety of her son (who had long hair and 'a little bit of a beard' that, Priya thought, gave him a 'Muslim' look) when two American young men, one of whom was 'draped in the American flag' and was 'sort of very nationalist in attitude' just stared at Priya and her son at an American railway station (Bhatia 28). Nothing happened either to Priya or to her son that day, but after this incident, Priya, a non-Muslim Indian diasporan in the US, asked her son to get rid of his beard as it gave him a mistaken Muslim identity. To Bush, the 'other' was well defined, but what about Priya? In those 'scared moments' (Bhatia 28) at the railway station, and even beyond that, who was the other to Priya? A terrorist? A white American? Or, a South Asian Muslim? Or all of them? Priya's narrative demands a re-examination of the 'us/other' binary in Indian diaspora, particularly in the post 9/11 era.

In fact, even before 9/11, and beyond the Indian context, the old 'native/diasporan' binary was questioned by critics. Avtar Brah in her 1996 book *Cartographies of Diaspora: Contesting Identities*, for instance, coined the term 'diaspora space' and distinguished it from 'diaspora' by prioritizing flux over fixity in diaspora conditions and by arguing that the concept of diaspora space foregrounds the 'intersectionality of diaspora, border, and dis/location as a point of confluence of economic, political, cultural, and psychic processes ... where multiple subject positions are juxtaposed, contested, proclaimed or disavowed; where the permitted and the prohibited perpetually interrogate; and where the accepted and transgressive imperceptibly mingle even while these syncretic forms may be disclaimed in the name of purity and tradition' (208). While saying this, Brah unquestionably had in her mind the re-structuring of the world and the emergence of a new transnational[2] constellation as the inevitable outcome of globalization and neo-liberalism. The 'us/other' or the 'native/diasporan' binary that was almost inseparable from and synonymous with the 'homeland/host country' binary also required a re-mapping in the 1990s as cheap air travel and internet have reconfigured the older notions of home and belonging. The notion of fluidity that Brah was theorizing in 1994, however, received serious challenges after 9/11, particularly in the context of South Asian (and for that matter, of Indian too) diaspora. Suspicion, incredulity and hate crimes[3] have caused re-grouping and re-structuring of South Asian diaspora communities. Raghuram and Sahoo rightly observe:

> Moreover, the politics of belonging, which occupies centre stage in the troubled territories of nationalism and citizenship, has become even more contested in the post 9/11 landscape. The question of belonging is increasingly being territorialized, securitized and penalized. In the polarized discussions of belonging, diasporics are continuously being asked to display how and in what ways 'you are one of us, not one of them'. Multiple identifications and contested affiliation are to be

muffled, congealed into a publicly expressed singular narrative of belonging. (4–5)

In fact, it has also been noted that after 9/11 'there has been a conflation of South Asians Muslims and Arabs with terrorism and "Islamic Fundamentalism" and regardless of their nationality or religion many South Asians are being categorized as suspicious and having links to terrorists' (Bhatia 30).

But this is only one side of the coin, the other side of which, as has already been indicated by Priya's narrative, tells other stories. Sunil Bhatia's survey shows that in the face of racist suspicion and hate crimes, non-Muslim Indians, on the one hand, align with the other Indian and South Asian diaspora communities, and on the other, try to distance themselves from the Muslim communities in particular. The Sikhs, for instance, are scared of the turban and the beard, which are two important markers of Sikhism but, after 9/11, are mistakenly associated only with the Muslim identity in the First World. In fact, immediately after 9/11, a Sikh man was murdered in Arizona as he was mistaken to be an Arab. This is only one of the many hate crimes that the Sikhs were subjected to in the post 9/11 US. Things went to such an extreme that 'many Sikh religious groups in New York and around the USA waged an expensive public relations campaign to educate the public about how Sikhism is different to Islam' and many Sikh leaders had to point out that 'Sikhism is a peaceful religion and that was founded in opposition to Islam' (Bhatia 25). So the 'us' in Indian diaspora is not a homogenous category and should not be considered to be so; it is rather fractured and multilayered.[4]

It has to be pointed out here that this fissure in the 'us' is neither country nor time specific. It should not be seen as a typical post 9/11 US feature of Indian diaspora. The relationships between different Indian religious groups have undergone changes in the host country in accordance with the changes in these relationships in the homeland. For instance, in the US of the 1960s and 1970s, Hindu, Sikh, Muslim, and Christian Indians used to belong to same pan-Indian associations. But as these associations were mainly dominated by the Hindus who were then the majority in the Indian diaspora in the US, gradually the minority religious groups started leaving these pan-Indian associations to form their own associations. The relationships between the Sikhs and the Hindus and between the Hindus and the Muslims in the US have also been mediated by the Indian government's stance on the Punjab issue and by incidents like the demolition of the Babri masjid.[5] Apart from this religious division, Indian diaspora is also divided from within along the lines of caste and class. Tariq Modood in his essay 'South Asian Assertiveness in Britain' observes that 'very few Asians marry across religious and caste boundaries' (127).[6] Though Modood has used the term 'Asian', there is little doubt that he meant the British Indians in the context of caste, as caste is a typically Indian concept. In fact, like caste, class division in the Indian diaspora communities could hardly be ignored. In the UK, for instance, 'the new regulations limit many rights of lesser skilled workers: rights to entry, to bring in dependants, to stay on or to switch to other immigration categories and therefore eventually limit the right to citizenship while engaging in a rhetoric of endowing these rights on those with the right package of skills' (Raghuram 182).

If we keep in mind the fracture in the Indian diaspora and also its relationships and negotiations – marked not only by the mutual sharing of concerns and anxieties but also by conflicts and tensions – with other Asian diasporas, one is tempted to ask who is the 'other' to an Indian Hindu Brahmin skilled professional diasporan in the US or UK? Is the other the white native only? Or is the other an Indian non-Hindu skilled professional diasporan? Or is the other an Indian Hindu non-Brahmin skilled professional diasporan? Or is the other an Indian Hindu Brahmin unskilled professional diasporan? Or is the other a British Nigerian or a Japanese American? Or are all of them the 'others' to him?

Contemporary Indian diaspora fiction, though often labelled as 'transnational' or 'cosmopolitan', with one or two exceptions, seems to show surprising indifference to the recent changes in the actually lived diaspora experiences and to these other 'others'. Raja Rao's *The Serpent and the Rope*, which Prashant. K. Sinha, considers to be 'the first major novel of the "diaspora"' (196), perhaps was the first novel written by an Indian expatriate writer where Madeleine, the heroine, the native woman of the hostland, was presented as the 'other' to the diasporan hero of the novel, Ramaswamy. *The Serpent and the Rope* was published in 1960. Fifty-four years have elapsed since then but it seems that the white native of the hostland is still the sole 'other' to an Indian diaspora writer. The representation of this 'other' by the

Indian diaspora writers – particularly in the fiction of some contemporary writers like Jhumpa Lahiri, Uma Parameswaran, Sunetra Gupta, Chitra Banerjee Diavkaruni, Anurag Mathur, and the like –, again, usually, avoids serious engagement with issues relating to racism, ethnicity, identity, and multiculturalism and fails to get beyond photographic descriptions of some places of the host countries like markets, streets, and workplaces with occasional peeps into the life of the natives. True that in diaspora certain elements like 'food, clothes, language retention, religion, music, dance, myths, legends, customs of individual community, rites of passage and others' are viewed and used as important identity markers (Sharma et al. xi). And of all these constituent elements of diaspora identity, food seems to have received such an importance as an identity marker that a recent work (2010) of Anita Mannur has been a full-length study of the representation of food in South Asian diasporic fiction, titled *Culinary Fictions*. In her book Mannur has argued that 'For South Asian diasporic cultural texts, the "culinary" most typically occupies a seemingly paradoxical space – at once a site of affirmation and resistance. Affirmation, because food often serves to mark defining moments in marking ethnicity for communities that live through and against the vagaries of diasporized realities, marred by racism and xenophobia. Resistance, insofar as the evocation of a culinary register can deliberately and strategically disrupt the notion that cultural identity is always readily available for consumption and commodification and always already conjoined to culinary practices' (8–9). Notwithstanding Mannur's argument, it could be said that the use of not only food but also of other identity markers in Indian diaspora fiction, on the one hand, exploits the exotica of the homeland and, on the other, conceives the identity of the diasporan against the identity of the native. Diaspora realities, which, as Mannur has rightly pointed out, are often marred by racism and xenophobia, are seldom seriously examined through the lens of food. One is, indeed, tempted to ask whether the representation of the complexities of diaspora realities through food is an attempt of making tensions and differences palatable.

In fact, interactions among different diaspora communities and the transformation of relationships between the host country and the Indian diaspora communities due to changes in the nature of capital, transnational trade, globalization and also in the immigration policies of the host countries in the face of terrorist threats are occasionally represented by the contemporary Indian diaspora writers. Instead, most of them, like their predecessors, still continue to write about the processes of acculturation and difficulties associated with them. These difficulties, however, are skin-deep as these writers seldom attempt to seriously examine the issues relating to ethnic and racial tensions. Issues relating to gender and religion are sporadically addressed but made palatable. When I write this, I know that I am generalizing. Let me confess that I am not forgetting and should not forget the works of writers like Vassanji and Aziz Hassim. If Vassanji's *The Book of Secrets* shows how the mukhi, Jamali of the Shamsi clan, is not only married to an African woman but is also 'committed to Africa' (Jyoti 121), Hassim's debut novel, *The Lotus People*, through a cartographic representation of Durban that uses the Grey Street complex as its centre foregrounds the 'segmentation of the city according to race and the subsequent racial tensions' that 'mirror the political history of apartheid in South Africa' (Singh and Chetty 4). The recent works of Chitra Banerjee Divakaruni (like *One Amazing Thing* and *Queen of Dreams*) also need to be mentioned. These are, however, exceptions. To a coloured Indian diaspora writer, the 'other' still seems to be the white native of the hostland.

The representation of the 'other' in contemporary Indian diaspora fiction brings two questions to our mind. To negotiate with the first, I would like to fall back on Amartya Sen, whom I have been using a lot in my recent works while talking on identity.[7] In his *Identity and Violence: The Illusion of Destiny* (2006), while criticizing a 'solitarist approach'[8] to identity which makes one forget one's plural affiliations, Sen has argued that identity, and to be more specific, communal identity, can never be simply a 'matter of self-realization', it is rather a matter of 'choice' (5). Choice is also not one's own discretion. Choice rather has its own constraints.[9] Even if a person wants to be seen in a specific way, in order to be seen in that way, s/he needs to convince others of his/her preference of others' gaze at him/her, something which is usually beyond his/her control.

Sen writes:

> However, even when we are clear about how we want to see ourselves, we may still have difficulty in being able to persuade others to see us in just that way. A nonwhite person in

apartheid-dominated South Africa could not insist that she be treated just as a human being, irrespective of her racial characteristics. She would typically have been placed in the category that the state and the dominant members of the society reserved for her. Our freedom to assert our personal identities can sometimes be extraordinarily limited in the eyes of others, no matter how we see ourselves. (6)

Following Sen's argument, one can ask if in the US a Sikh American is not even seen as an Indian-American and the white native's solitarist gaze petrifies him/her simply as a South Asian and even mistakes as a Muslim, is it possible for him/her to be aware of his/her multiple identities? Impossible. One must admit. This partly explains the genesis of a work like Kazim Ali's *The Disappearance of Seth*. But what about those writers who neither write about intra- and/or inter-ethnic tensions and conflicts in the lives of the Indian diasporans nor directly about the racial discriminations and oppressions that they are subjected to?

This question brings us to the issue of the production and consumption of contemporary Indian diaspora fiction. In this context, mention could be made of Farrukh Dhondy's early short stories and Kamala Markandaya's novel *The Nowhere Man* (1972). If Dhondy's early short stories depict a racist Britain and the relationship of the Indian immigrants with the African-Caribbean diasporans and the native whites, Markandaya's novel documents how an Indian discovers the racist character of London after living there for almost 30 years. Dhondy's early short stories are seldom read and he is usually known as a playwright for his later works. Markandaya's *The Nowhere Man* received a poor sale: 105 copies in the first five years (Ranasinha 2007). Could it be that the failure of these works in the market is a lesson to the contemporary diaspora writers? Is this why they fictionalize the problems of acculturation without raising serious questions about race and ethnicity? Here we need to stop and listen to what an Indian diaspora novelist-cum-poet-cum-critic Uma Parameswaran says in her book *Writing the Diaspora*. Parameswaran writes: 'If we note that most of our diasporic writers are still occupying that safe space of their original homelands, we need to figure out why this pattern persists. Are they afraid of writing about the place they are standing on? Or is it that they are not really standing here but back there? Or is it because they have realized it is more marketable to stand there and not here? Is it because the world around us dictates the marketability of our writings in the eyes of publishers, establishment, and readers? Do we write what readers want to hear? Or rather, is it that only those who write what the establishment wants readers to hear get published? Is it that writers too are conscious of these pressures and so choose to write in a safe space where they can narrate, satirize, and occasionally celebrate the obsessions of their original homeland?' (323).[10] Such an introspection is rare among the Indian diaspora writers and it raises serious questions about the authenticity of the fiction produced by some of them.

I know that the term 'authenticity' will raise many eyebrows, as in this so-called 'postmodernist' era, the term itself has become a suspect.[11] I shall still use the term to question which and whose diaspora experiences most of the contemporary Indian diaspora writers are representing. We need to know who is speaking for whom. When I write this, I repeat, I am aware of the uneven character of contemporary Indian diaspora fiction and of the fallacy of generalization. But, I would like to argue that this very uneven character of contemporary Indian diaspora fiction calls for not mere analysis but a proper evaluation of this fiction. The 'authentic' has to be differentiated from the 'inauthentic'.

Notes

1. Bhatia's paper, based on interviews taken by him, shows 'how members from the Indian diaspora re-examined their ethnic and racial identity after the events of 9/11' (19) in the south-eastern Connecticut in the US.
2. The relationship between transnationalism and diaspora has also been critically examined. In *Theorizing Diaspora* (2003), by defining transnationalism as 'the flow of people, ideas, goods, and capital across national territories in a way that undermines nationality and nationalism as discrete categories of identification, economic organization, and political constitution', Braziel and Mannur have differentiated diaspora from transnationalism explaining that 'diaspora refers specifically to the movement – forced or voluntary – of people from one or more nation-states to another' (8). 'While diaspora may be regarded as concomitant with transnationalism, or even in some cases consequent of transnationalist forces,' they argue, 'it may not be reduced to such macroeconomic and technological flows' (8).

3. Sunaina Maira in her 'Citizenship and Dissent in Diaspora: Indian Immigrant Youth in the United States After 9/11' writes: 'Some of the most extreme examples are media stories about South Asian Muslim youth linked to allegations of terrorism, for example, the case of a Bangladeshi teenager who was arrested in New York because of an essay she wrote about suicide bombing and Islam and the conviction of a young Pakistani American man in Lodi, California, for presumably attending a terrorist training camp, with no proven evidence' (132).
4. The so-called homogeneity of the native 'other' could also be questioned. For instance, one may ask how pure is the 'British' identity of a native citizen of Great Britain who considers the Indian culinary as the best of the world. This is something that Brah perhaps was trying to indicate by claiming that 'diaspora space is the site where *the native is much a diasporian as the diasporian is the native*' (209, original emphasis).
5. See Aminah T. Mohammad's article 'Relationships between Muslims and Hindus in the United States: Mlecchas versus Kafirs?' Mohammad writes:

> 'in the case of Indians in particular, Hindus, Sikhs, Muslims and Christians used to belong to the same associations at the beginning of their arrival to the United States (1960s and 1970s). But as these organizations were dominated by Hindus (forming the majority), minority groups progressively left these associations to form their own organizations from 1980s onward). Sikhs were mostly motivated by political reasons (since Hindus were supporting the position of the government on the Punjab issue whereas many Sikhs of the diaspora were backing the separatists' claim in India), Muslims and Christians by religious reasons, Hinduism occupying a space seen as too important by minorities in Indian cultural associations (each meeting would begin, for instance, with a *puja*). The impact of the BJP/VHP ... has reinforced this trend, urging non-Hindus to leave these associations'. (293)

6. Modood's essay is based on the findings of The Fourth National Survey of Ethnic Minorities done under the leadership of Modood himself in 1994.
7. One of these two papers has been published in *The Visva-Bharati Quarterly* (Vol. 22, Nos 3 and 4). The other paper will soon come out in the December 2014 issue of *Antipodes*.
8. In his *Identity and Violence: The Illusion of Destiny*, Amartya Sen laments that 'solitarist' approach often determines one's identity:

> 'Indeed, the world is increasingly seen, if only implicitly, as a federation of religions or of civilizations, thereby ignoring all the other

ways in which people see themselves. Underlying this line of thinking is the odd presumption that the people of the world can be uniquely categorized according to some *singular and overarching* system of partitioning' (xii, original emphasis).

But this is not how identity should be conceived. Sen writes:

'A solitarist approach can be a good way of misunderstanding nearly everyone in the world. In our normal lives, we see ourselves as members of a variety of groups – we belong to all of them. The same person can be, without any contradiction, an American citizen, of Caribbean origin, with African ancestry, a Christian, a liberal, a woman, a vegetarian, a long-distance runner, a historian, a school teacher, a novelist, a feminist, a heterosexual, a believer in gay and lesbian rights, a theatre lover, an environmental activist, a tennis fan, a jazz musician, and someone who is deeply committed to the view that there are intelligent beings in outer space with whom it is extremely urgent to talk (preferably in English). Each of these collectivities, to all of which this person simultaneously belongs, gives her a particular identity. None of them can be taken to be the person's only identity or singular membership category. Given our inescapably plural identities, we have to decide on the relative importance of our different associations and affiliations in any particular context' (xii-xiii).

9. Sen argues:

'Many communitarian thinkers tend to argue that a dominant communal identity is only a matter of self-realization, not of choice. It is, however, hard to believe that a person really has no choice in deciding what relative importance to attach to the various groups to which he or she belongs, and that she must just 'discover' her identities, as if it were a purely natural phenomenon (like determining whether it is day or night). In fact, we are all constantly making choices, if only implicitly, about the priorities to be attached to our different affiliations and associations .... The existence of choice does not, of course, indicate that there are no constraints restricting choice. Indeed, choices are always made within the limits of what are seen as feasible. The feasibilities in the case of identities will depend on individual characteristics and circumstances that determine the alternative possibilities open to us' (5).

10. I have used this excerpt from Parameswaran in one of my presentations to raise the same questions about the writings of South Asian diaspora writers in general.
11. Though I consider postmodernism's celebration of pluralism its greatest contribution to academia and society at large, I have many reservations about some of its ideological contours and parameters.

The scope of this essay, however, does not allow me to engage myself with a debate with the postmodernists on these issues.

References

Bhatia, Sunil. '9/11 and the Indian Diaspora: Narratives of Race, Place and Immigrant Identity'. *Transnational Migration: Indian Diaspora.* (eds) William Safran, Ajaya Kumar Sahoo, and Brij V. Lal. London: Routledge, 2009. 19-44.

Bhattacharya, Gauri. 'The Indian Diaspora in New York City: Cultural Identities and Transnational Relations'. *Transnational Migration: Indian Diaspora.* (eds) William Safran, Ajaya Kumar Sahoo, and Brij V. Lal. London: Routledge, 2009. 76-96.

Brah, Avtar. *Cartographies of Diaspora: Contesting Identities.* London: Routledge, 1996.

Braziel, Jana Evans and Anita Mannur, (eds). *Theorizing Diaspora.* Oxford: Blackwell, 2003.

Espiritu, Yen Le. *Asian American Panethnicity: Bridging Institutions and Identities.* Philadelphia: Temple University Press, 1992.

Jyoti, Rashmi. 'A New Poetics of Nation: M.G. Vassanji's *The Book of Secrets* and *America*'. *Contextualizing Nationalism, Transnationalism and Indian Diaspora.* (eds) Kavita A. Sharma, Adesh Pal, and Tapas Chakrabarti. New Delhi: Creative Books, 2005. 119-130.

Maira, Sunaina. 'Citizenship and Dissent in Diaspora: Indian Immigrant Youth in the United States After 9/11'. *Tracing an Indian Diaspora: Contexts, Memories, Representations.* (eds) Parvathi Raghuram et al. New Delhi: Sage Publications, 2008. 131-155.

Mannur, Anita. *Culinary Fictions: Food in South Asian Diasporic Culture.* Philadelphia: Temple University Press, 2010.

Modood, Tariq. 'South Asian Assertiveness in Britain'. *Transnational South Asians: The Making of a Neo-Diaspora.* (eds) Susan Koshy and R. Radhakrishnan. New Delhi: Oxford University Press, 2008. 124-145.

Mohammad, Aminah T. 'Relationships between Muslims and Hindus in the United States: Mlecchas versus Kafirs?' *Community, Empire and Migration: South Asians in Diaspora.* (ed.) Crispin Bates. Hyderabad: Orient Longman, 286-308.

Parameswaran, Uma. *Writing the Diaspora: Essays on Culture and Identity.* Jaipur: Rawat Publications, 2007.

Paranjape, Makarand, (ed.). *In Diaspora: Theories, Histories, Texts.* New Delhi: Indialog, 2001.

Raghuram, Parvati. 'Immigration Dynamics in the Receiving State: Emerging Issues for the Indian Diaspora in the United Kingdom'.

Tracing an Indian Diaspora: Contexts, Memories, Representations. (eds) Parvathi Raghuram et al. New Delhi: Sage Publications, 2008. 171–190.

Raghuram, Parvati and Ajaya Kumar Sahoo. 'Thinking "Indian Diaspora" for Our Times'. *Tracing an Indian Diaspora: Contexts, Memories, Representations.* (eds) Parvathi Raghuram et al. New Delhi: Sage Publications, 2008. 1–20.

Ranasinha, Ruvani. *South Asian Writers in Twentieth-Century Britain: Culture in Translation.* Oxford: Clarendon Press, 2007.

Sen, Amartya. *Identity and Violence: The Illusion of Destiny.* New York: W.W. Norton, 2006.

Sharma, Kavita A., Adesh Pal, and Tapas Chakrabarti. Introduction. *Theorizing and Critiquing Indian Diaspora.* (eds) Kavita A. Sharma, Adesh Pal, and Tapas Chakrabarti. New Delhi: Creative Books, 2004. xi – xviii.

Singh, Jaspal K. and Rajendra Chetty (eds). *Indian Writers: Transnationalism and Diasporas.* New York: Peter Lang, 2010.

Sinha, Prashant K. 'The Indian Diaspora in the West and the Literary Imagination: A Study in the Larger Context of Immigration in America and Europe'. *Theorizing and Critiquing Indian Diaspora.* (eds) Kavita A. Sharma, Adesh Pal and Tapas Chakrabarti. New Delhi: Creative Books, 2004. 192–200.

Chapter 8

Contextualizing *The Lowland*

NILANJANA CHATTERJEE

This paper will examine Jhumpa Lahiri's representation of the three major issues in her second novel, *The Lowland* (2003), namely, issues relating to the Naxalbari movement in Bengal, sexuality, and, the interface between displacement and belonging. The representation of each of these three issues, I shall argue, is heavily mediated by the diasporic subject position of Lahiri. In fact, in arguing so, I shall also try to raise a few questions about Lahiri's representation of all the three issues mentioned above. For instance, I shall try to see how Lahiri looks at the historico-political situations of the Bengal of the late 1960s and early 1970s. I shall examine whether the sexual relations in the novel privatize and thereby decrease the importance of the Naxalbari movement, and I shall also investigate whether the main characters' migration to the USA from Bengal loosens their socio-political tie with the nation and, in due course, weakens their responsiveness to and understanding of the homeland.

Jhumpa Lahiri, the author of *Interpreter of Maladies* (a short story collection published in 1999), *The Namesake* (a novel published in 2003) and *Unaccustomed Earth* (a short story collection published in 2008), is the winner of the 1999 O. Henry Award and 2000 Pulitzer Prize for Fiction. *The Lowland* has also been nominated for the Man Booker Prize and The National Book Award for Fiction. Her previously written fictions, for the most part, deal with the diasporic Bengali communities in the US and their behavioural patterns that foreground the problems of acculturation and a sense of exile in the host land. In fact, Lahiri herself has said,

'The older I get, the more I am aware that I have somehow inherited a sense of exile from my parents, even though I am so much more American than they are' (Interview by Houghton Mifflin Company 177). However, in connection to those diaspora writers who highlight their exilic experience in the host land, Meenakshi Mukherjee has noted:

> I think Aijaz Ahmad's plea for avoiding the word 'exile' to describe the new diaspora, that is those who voluntarily moved to greener pastures for economic or professional gain as different from the coercive dislocation suffered by the indentured labour of an earlier age, is generally accepted now. (*Elusive Terrain* 186)

Although eminent critics like Mukherjee and Ahmad invalidate the exilic experience of the diaspora writers of the new generation in general, Lahiri – like many of her contemporary diaspora writers – expresses her sense of exile in the host land and strives to represent a diasporan's problems regarding his/her journey through acculturation, resultant identity crisis and inter-generational differences in his/her own community. In this context, Lahiri, along with other diaspora writers, occupies a very important place in diaspora since literary works are a major source of knowledge about the diaspora and these writers are the privileged informants. But the question is: whom are these writers representing? While talking about this issue, Natarajan observes, 'the writers are distinct from those they write about. Typically they have led cosmopolitan lives. Often, they have received acclaimed awards, held prestigious academic appointments' (xvi). Since Lahiri and other diaspora writers write from an elite diasporic subject position, their representation of the diasporic experiences in their fictional works may be suspected to be inauthentic. As far as Lahiri is concerned, though her novels deal with the diasporic experiences of the ordinary Bengali immigrants in the US, she herself belongs to the President's Committee on the Arts and Humanities, appointed by the US President Barack Obama himself. So, Lahiri seems to hold an ambivalent position as a writer. Though in her fiction, she seems to play the role of a knower of the diasporic experiences of the ordinary Bengali immigrants, she is perhaps not completely acquainted with the experiences of their lives. The question regarding the authenticity of Lahiri's representation of the Bengali diaspora, therefore, could hardly be ignored.

II

When America revealed its true state-terrorist character during the post-9/11 backlash of hate crimes, many Indian subcontinental diasporic writers raised their voices against the atrocities committed by their hostland. Khaled Hosseini in *A Thousand Splendid Suns* (2007), Shaila Abdullah in *Saffron Dreams* (2009), Mohsin Hamid in *The Reluctant Fundamentalist* (2009), Nafisa Haji in *The Writing on My Forehead* (2009), or, Marina Budhos in *Ask Me No Questions* (2007) criticize the US government's post – 9/11 strategies and immigration laws. However, in her fiction, Lahiri has not touched on these issues yet. This seems to be strange as Bill Ashcroft in his Forword to *Arundhati Roy: Critical Perspectives* observes 'If there was ever a time when writers could take refuge from politics in the world of the imagination, then that time has long past' (7). Interestingly, though Lahiri remains silent about the political strategies of her hostland, she takes up the subject of the Naxalbari Movement of Bengal in *The Lowland*. As a matter of fact, the entire novel rivets round the direct and the indirect effects of the Naxalbari movement upon its chief characters.

The Lowland tells the story of two brothers – Udayan and Subhash – who wish to choose two different lives in two different halves of the world. While Udayan chooses to stay where he grew up, (i.e. Kolkata) and join the Naxalbari movement, Subhash decides to go to the USA and pursue his research work from the University of Rhode Islands. By 1972, the Naxalite movement is banned by the government and Udayan is assassinated by the paramilitary force for carrying on secret organizational work. Hearing this, Subhash comes to Kolkata and eventually meets Gauri, the wife of Udayan who is now expecting. In the course of the events, Subhash marries her. Gauri settles with Subhash at Rhode Islands and gives birth to Bela. The story moves forward with Bela's coming of age, her discovery of the hidden past and her attempts to cope with the complicated present.

A reader, who has read Lahiri's interviews on *The Lowland* and is about to take up the novel, expects a lot from Lahiri about the representation of the Naxalbari movement in the novel. In an interview with Leyshon, for instance, Lahiri asserts:

> I wanted to understand that history completely and digest it before I started to write ... for seven years .... I would read them

(two books borrowed from the library) ... take notes, and I would put them away ... I went to Calcutta. I'd been speaking to people all the way along .... The final key moment was when, suddenly, I was able to write the novel *without feeling as though I needed the crutch of all the research and all of the books* (italics mine), and I felt that the characters were strong enough and their motivations had become more or less solid for me and satisfying for me to just go deeper with them, knowing that this was part of who they were and part of their world. And that was the final phase. The initial phase was a lot of research, but it remained opaque, and then slowly the research, the history, became more clear to me, and the clearer it became, the less I felt that I needed it. ('Unknown Territory')

Lahiri also chooses the realistic narrative mode – the purpose of which is to illustrate the absolute essentiality of likelihood in the depiction of time. She succeeds as long as she is depicting the private life of Subhash, Udayan, Gauri, and Bela as a miniaturized family saga, but her realism seems to fail when she depicts the eventful years of the Naxalite movement and its forceful suppression by the then West Bengal government.

So many questions could indeed be raised against Lahiri's representation of the Naxalbari movement in *The Lowland*. Lahiri puts 'brief, bombastic' (*The Lowland* 24, hereafter *TL*) words in the mouth of the Bengali Maoist revolutionary Kanu Sanyal, 'We will certainly be able to make a new sun and a new moon shine in the sky of our great motherland' (*TL* 33) and ignores the laconic text of the 'Historical Eight Documents'.[1] Lahiri demonstrates the initial uprising of the Naxalbari movement during April 1969, and then gives a blurry image of its evolution:

> Disorganised mobs representing rival communist parties, running helter-skelter through the streets .... Naxalites were operating underground. Members surfaced only to carry out dramatic attacks .... Then the targets turned specific. Unarmed traffic constables at busy intersections. Wealthy businessmen, certain educators. Members of the rival party, the CPI (M). (ibid. 87)

Lahiri even winds up the issue declaring, 'Udayan had given his life to a movement that had been misguided, that had caused only damage, that had already been dismantled' (ibid. 115). What she evades is the fact that the Naxalites were able to leave an ineffaceable imprint on the Bengal psyche with their selfless aim at hitting out at the Indian bourgeoisie's slavish loyalty to their Western mentors. A sensitive critic like Satya Prakash Dash divides the 'eventful years of the Naxalite movements', ranging from 1969 to 1972, into 'five distinct phases' (Dash 25). The first phase was the Naxalbari revolt itself. The second phase began when the revolt collapsed but the movement continued till April 1969, when the CPI (ML) was formed. In the third phase, the Naxalites participated in several rural uprisings. The fourth phase began in April 1970 after the movement moved to the urban areas and Calcutta became the centre of activities. The fifth phase, beginning in July 1972, marked the end of the movement. Lahiri, however, seems to be completely unaware of this phase-wise development of the Naxalbari movement. From Lahiri's representation of the movement it seems that she has an ideological incapacity to affectively grasp the politics and ideology of the movement. Lahiri also fails to substantiate the actual causes behind the failure of the movement. Despite her so-called 'lot of research', Lahiri fails to see the 'volunteer squads of hoodlums' (ibid.) under Siddhartha Shankar Ray's leadership to fight the Naxalites. While talking about the reasons of the failure of the movement, Sumanta Banerjee, again, has pointed out that the 'petty bourgeois background of the leaders' also exerted a baneful influence on the course of the movement (quoted in Dash 25). The 'excessive identification with China', Banerjee further argues, also robbed the Naxalites of a nationalistic image (*TL* 26). These arguments, however, do not figure in Lahiri's novel.

Lahiri's misreading of the Naxalbari movement becomes clear when she makes all her characters, including Udayan, draw the same conclusion about the Naxalbari revolution. Subhash thinks, '... after all these years it remained uncertain, the extent of what he (Udayan) had done' (ibid. 267). Gauri considers Udayan's militant activities criminal in nature. Bela does not want to know anything about this movement or about her father, Udayan. Dipankar, an NRI scholar, 'studied the movement's self-defeating tactics, its lack of coordination, its unrealistic ideology. He'd understood, without ever having been a part of things ...' (ibid. 280). At the end of the novel even Udayan repents and accepts the futility of his revolutionary idealism. Immediately before his death, the third person narrator comments, 'But in this case it (the Naxalbari movement) had fixed nothing, helped no one. In this case there was to be no revolution. He (Udayan) knew this now' (ibid. 334). Interestingly, the only solution to the political crisis that Bengal faced in the 1960s and 1970s that Lahiri seems to present is to migrate to the West in pursuit of a better life.

Lahiri's portrayal of sexuality also appears to be transgressive in nature, but a careful examination of the same shows its conventionality. For instance, the inter-racial relationship between Subhash and Holly (Subhash's American girlfriend) is nothing unconventional, as far as diasporic writings are concerned. The inter-racial homosexual relationship, between Gauri and her research scholar, Lorne, is not an uncommon issue either. Subhash's drastic decision to marry his brother's widow is also a common theme in Indian Literature and therefore nothing unconventional. Nevertheless, Lahiri's use of these sexual relations would have been creatively acceptable had these depictions been helpful to the characters to gain, what Aijaz Ahmad would have called, 'artistic courage, realism, authentic experience, transgression of oppressive social fetters and so on' (Ahmad 35). However, in *The Lowland*, except Udayan-Gauri relationship, not a single sexual encounter leads to any kind of crucial social or political revelation or understanding in any one's life. They seem to merely serve the purpose of private erotic pleasures.

It has to be admitted that unlike other sexual relationships, Udayan-Gauri bond is shown to be the fulcrum of the novel. Udayan-Gauri's sexual experiences during the two years of their married life haunt Gauri even in her late fifties when she dreams, 'He undrapes her sari ...' (*TL* 230). But, even this otherwise powerful short-lived relationship does not leave any deep impact on Gauri's life. In fact, the sexual compatibility between Udayan and Gauri fails to inspire each other, either politically or culturally. Neither can Udayan channelize Gauri's patriotic zeal towards her motherland, nor can Gauri, with all her knowledge and understanding of the militant nature of the Naxalite movement, suggest Udayan some better path to serve the nation. The more Lahiri makes Gauri dream of her sexual experiences with Udayan, the more she projects the loss of Udayan not as a public loss of an individual who selflessly dreamed of an egalitarian society, but as a private loss of Gauri. In fact, immediately after the death of Udayan, Lahiri shifts the readers' focus from the politics of Bengal to the funeral ceremony of Udayan. The readers are also told that Gauri for 10 days after Udayan's death, 'did not wash her clothes or wear slippers or comb her hair. She shut the door and the shutters to preserve whatever invisible particles of him floated in the air' (ibid. 108). Thus, after Udayan's death, by prioritizing the private loss of Gauri over the public loss of a potential leader Lahiri veils the actual political crisis of the period.

Questions could also be raised about Lahiri's representation of the Bengali diaspora experiences in *The Lowland*. After reaching Rhode Islands Subhash realizes, 'he had been waiting all his life to find Rhode Islands. That it was here, in this minute but majestic corner of the world, that he could breathe' (ibid. 65). He starts sending a portion of his stipend 'to help pay for the work on the house' and writes that 'he was eager to see them (his parents)' (ibid. 63). But then, day after day, cut off from them, he starts ignoring them. Along with his psychological estrangement from his parents, Subhash's political attachment towards Bengal also begins to die. When Richard (an American friend) asks Subhash about the solutions for caste system and poverty in India and the government's stance on these issues, Subhash coldly replies to his American friend Richard that, 'it (India) was an ancient place that was also young, still struggling to know itself' (ibid. 41) and then washes off his hands by saying, 'You should be talking to my brother' (ibid. 41). Subhash's lack of awareness of the socio-economic conditions of India leads him to invent a vague understanding of Indian politics. By the end of the novel, we find an assimilated Subhash, who is completely cut off from his dead parents, his Tollugunge-house and his motherland. He marries an American lady, Elise, 'exchanging their vows on the grounds of a small white church' (ibid. 330) and never returns to India.

Gauri, like Subhash, also establishes herself in the US in search of a better living. Compared to Udayan, she is insensitive to the socio-political needs of her homeland, India. Gauri even believes that California is 'her only home' (ibid. 235). During her initial days of immigration to Rhode Island, she wants to 'look like the other women' she notices 'on the campus' (ibid. 134) and at the end of the novel she arrives in India in 'her American clothing and shoes' (ibid. 319). As far as Bela (the second generation immigrant) is concerned, her single visit to Bengal in her early days leaves her with a lackadaisical attitude towards India and makes her look at a

Contextualizing The Lowland • **109**

curious neighbour of her grandparent's house as someone who has a pair of 'unkind' eyes and 'stained teeth uneven' (ibid. 195). Bela's attitude towards a Bengali stranger establishes the fact that she has not only inherited an indifference towards India from Gauri and Subhash but also feels awkward in India. Lahiri's projection of the Bengali rituals should also be examined critically. This is, for instance, how Lahiri describes Subhash's father's funeral ceremony: 'Before the ceremony a barber came to the house and shaved her (Bela) father's head and face in the courtyard, turning his face strange and small. Bela was told to put out her hands, and without warning, the nails of her fingers, then her toes, were pared off with a blade' (ibid. 194). The funeral ceremony here is described from Bela's point of view. Expressions like 'strange' and 'without warning' underline the rude shock that Bela receives from the unfamiliar funeral ceremony of her grandfather. In fact, neither does Bela know her grandfather nor is she acquainted with the Bengali funeral ceremony held in honour of him. That is why the representation of a Bengali funeral ceremony from Bela's perspective gives it an exotic value.

Considering all this, the authenticity and sincerity of Subhash's longing for West Bengal – something that the novel foregrounds sometimes – could be questioned. The authenticity of Subhash's depression – the readers are told that Subhash feels that in Rhode Islands 'some part of him' is 'missing' (ibid. 40) or, for 'a year and a half' he has not seen his family and not 'sat down with them, at the end of the day, to share a meal' (ibid. 63) – is in question as he does not take any initiative to return to his family in Kolkata or to solve their problems. Subhash's take on the Bengali practice of arranged marriage cannot escape criticism as well. In the 21st century Bengal, arranged marriages are 'out-of-bounds' (ibid. 262) though Subhash thinks that, 'If he'd raised her (Bela) in Calcutta it would have been reasonable for him to bring up the subject of her marriage. Here it was considered meddlesome, out-of-bounds. He had raised her in a place free from such stigmas' (ibid. 262). This is unquestionably a distortion of what the Bengalis think of marriage in the present. Lahiri also exoticizes the otherwise busy evenings of Kolkata by showing how in Rhode Islands Subhash recollects the evenings of Kolkata where, 'conch shells were blown … to ward off evil' (ibid. 38). There is little doubt that by exoticizing Bengal and the Bengali rituals, Lahiri is able to deviate the readers' attention from the actual socio-cultural conditions of Bengal and thereby build a fixed and dated image of Kolkata.

III

In an interview taken after the publication of *The Namesake*, Lahiri has pointed out that a writer enjoys more freedom in writing a novel than a short story: 'there's something more forgiving about novel. It's roomier, messier, more tolerant than a short story. The action isn't under a microscope in quite the same way' (Interview by Houghton Miflin Company 179). With this authorial license, Lahiri seems to have written *The Lowland* which represents certain politico-historical, sexual, and cultural images of Bengal and the Bengali immigrants in Rhode Islands. What concerns me about this kind of representation is its repressive potential: representation of this kind often ends in becoming mis-representation. Lahiri's representation of the political, historical, and cultural histories of Bengal in *The Lowland* results in the supply of the erroneous knowledge about Bengal in general to the Western readers. Though Lahiri claims to have made an extensive research on the Naxalbari movement, her research seems to get restricted to two books only. Bookish research has also not enabled Lahiri to understand the commitment of the Naxalites to the cause for which they were fighting: they had no other priorities in their lives than to put their lives at stake for eradicating poverty and feudal oppressions in Bengal. Lahiri's failure to understand the spirit of the movement is reflected in her simplistic evaluation of it by each of the major characters, including Udayan. Udayan-Gauri relationship even privatizes the significance of the Naxalbari movement and reduces Udayan's death to a personal loss of Gauri. Subhash and Gauri, again, could be seen as escapists who migrate to the US and in course of time get assimilated into the American culture. They lead a life, 'without the burden of what had happened (in Bengal)' and where 'it would all cease to matter' (*TL* 119). Lahiri also exoticizes the Bengali culture and projects it as something fixed and dated. In representing Bengal, Lahiri could have written, as Singh remarks in the context of the Indian diaspora writers in general, with a 'real enough commitment' (8) and a mind-set free from any kind of socio-political bias. Interestingly Lahiri who is so critical of the lack of direction in the Naxalbari movement seems to be almost silent about the US atrocities against the third world countries. She could have been more vociferous about it, instead of making some fleeting references to Iraq War (*TL* 246) or the My Lai incident (ibid. 41).[2]

In the context of Lahiri's (mis)representation of Bengal in *The Lowland*, it would not be wrong to refer to Alex Tickel's observations on the emergence of an 'intermediary genre' of fiction, a category to which, probably, Lahiri's fiction belongs. Referring to Timothy Brennen's observation in *At Home in the World: Cosmopolitanism Now* (1997), Tickel goes on to provide a 'formulaic definition' of this kind of 'intermediary genre', (i.e. hybrid and culturally-cosmopolitan fiction) which comprises, amongst other things, 'an irreverence towards national politics and literatures of national liberation, forms of transculturalism and dialogic abundance, and an often magic-realist combination of epic scope and personal, impressionistic memory' (61). In Lahiri's *The Lowland* also the main characters show 'an irreverence' to the Naxalbari movement and the history of a nation is captured through a 'personal, impressionistic memory'. True that impressionistic memory is now considered to be very much a part of history, but we need to seriously re-think about the historicity of memory that is inauthentic.

Notes

1. The 'Historic Eight Documents' are a set of eight monographs authored by the Indian Maoist revolutionary Charu Majumdar that outline the ideological principles on which the Naxalite militant communist movement in India was based.
2. The My Lai incident is the mass murder of 347 and 504 unarmed civilians in South Vietnam, during the Vietnam War, on 16 March 1968. It was committed by the US Army soldiers from the Company C of the 1st Battalion, 20th Infantry Regiment, 11th Brigade of the 23rd (American) Infantry Division. Victims included men, women, children, and infants. Some of the women were gang-raped and their bodies mutilated.

References

Abdullah, Shaila. *Saffron Dreams*. Pontiac Trail, USA: Modern History Press, 2009. Google Books. Web 15 June 2014.

Ahmad, Aijaz. 'Reading Arundhati Roy "Politically"'. *Arundhati Roy: Critical Perspectives.* (ed.) Murari Prasad. New Delhi: Pencraft International, 2011. 32-43.

Ashcroft, Bill. 'Forword'. *Arundhati Roy: Critical Perspectives.* (ed.) Murari Prasad. Delhi: Pencraft International, 2011. 7.

Budhos, Marina. *Ask Me No Questions.* New York: Simon and Schuster, 2007.

Dash, Satya Prakash. 'Formative Years'. *Naxal Movement and State Power: With Special Reference of Orissa.* New Delhi: Sarup & Sons, 2006. 1-32.

Haji, Nafisa. *The Writing on My Forehead.* London: Random House, 2009.

Hamid, Mohsin. *The Reluctant Fundamentalist.* Canada: Doubleday Canada, 2009.

Hosseini, Khaled. *A Thousand Splendid Suns.* New York: Riverhead Books, 2007.

Huggan, Graham. *The Postcolonial Exotic: Marketing the Margins.* London: Routledge, 2001.

Lahiri, Jhumpa. *Interpreter of Maladies.* Boston: Houghton Mifflin, 1999.

——. Interview. *Jhumpa Lahiri: Critical Perspectives.* (ed.) Nigamananda Das. New Delhi: Pencraft International, 2000. 176-181.

——. Interview by Arun Aguiar. *Jhumpa Lahiri: Critical Perspectives.* (ed.) Nigamananda Das. New Delhi: Pencraft International, 2000. 171-175.

——. *The Namesake.* New York: Random House, 2008.

——. *Unaccustomed Earth.* New York: Random House, 2008.

——. *The Lowland.* New York: Random House, 2013.

——. 'Unknown Territory: An Interview With Jhumpa Lahiri.' By Cressida Leyshon. 2013. Web. 23 June 2014. <www.newyorker.com/online/blogs/books/2013/10/the-lowland-novel-jhumpa-lahiri-interview.html>.

Mukherjee, Meenakshi. *Elusive Terrain: Culture and Literary Memory.* New Delhi: Oxford University Press, 2008.

Natarajan, Nalini. 'Introduction: Reading Diaspora'. *Writers of the Indian Diaspora: A Bio-Bibliographical Critical Sourcebook.* (ed.) Emmanuel S. Nelson. Jaipur: Rawat Publications, 2010. xiii – xix.

Singh, Manjit Inder. *The Critical Space.* New Delhi: National Publishing House, 2005.

Tickel, Alex. 'The God of Small Things: Arundhati Roy's Postcolonial Cosmopolitanism'. *Arundhati Roy: Critical Perspectives.* (ed.) Murarari Prasad. New Delhi: Pencraft International, 2011. 59-76.

CHAPTER 9

Remapping the Fiction of Indian Diaspora

Zadie Smith's *White Teeth* and the Conundrums of Multiculturalism

ASHOK K. MOHAPATRA

Having to discuss Zadie Smith's novel *White Teeth* (2000) in an anthology of critical essays on the fiction and cultural representations of Indian diaspora begs many questions. First and foremost, why Smith, when she is a British writer born of Jamaican mother and white British father? Secondly, why a novel which, like Hanif Kureishi's *The Buddha of Suburbia* (1990), Monica Ali's *Brick Lane* (2003) or Andrea Levy's *Small Island* (2004), is more about the issues of multiculturalism in England, about the second-generation migrants and about what Stuart Hall calls the 'New Ethnicities' (1988). Moreover, where in *White Teeth* is India represented as a cultural memory of home or as a set of inherited imperatives interfering with those of the host society in the First World? In this novel the family genealogies that crowd the North London cultural space are traced back home to Jamaica and Bangladesh, not India. Where is the community of the diaspora in the novel to provide foothold to the newly arrived immigrant or communitarianism from which diasporic identity usually derives as in the diasporic fiction? Where in Smith's novel is the recurring trope of failed marriage which we find, let's say, in Bharati Mukherjee's *Wife* (1975), Sunetra Gupta's *Memories of Rain* (1992), Jhumpa Lahiri's *The Namesake* (2003), Adarshir Vakil's *One Day* (2003), or Amit Chaudhury's *New World*

(2000), to cite a few examples? Where, indeed, are the elements of pain, trauma and angst of alienation that characterize the experience of the migrants as they relocate themselves, and where is the endless search for home – a common theme in the genre of diasporic fiction? Isn't *White Teeth* an odd ball?

By way of countering the above questions my essay seeks to justify the inclusion of a study of *White Teeth* in this anthology on diasporic fiction with a view to rethinking the basic underlying premise: the ideological responsibility of a 'genuine' cultural representation of the diasporic subjects – be they the fictional characters or the author. The issue of the genuineness of representation opens up other theoretical issues like origins, roots, home, biography of the immigrants and that of the author, an immigrant herself or himself. My purpose is not so much to discuss *White Teeth* per se as to use it contrapuntally to bring out the limits of diasporic fiction by thinking through the conundrums of multiculturalism. By doing so I wish to have the conceptual terrain of diasporic literature to be remapped in order that texts that disturb the paradigm of defining literature of the immigrants in terms of the places of their provenance – literature of 'Indian' diaspora as the case is in relation to the present anthology – can be studied alongside those that are pliable and predictable. *White Teeth* which is read as a fiction of multiculturalist diaspora initiates an altogether new discourse of dynamic and performative hybridity interrogating the logic of the static liminality of second-generation immigrants being still marked Indian, African, Pakistani, Caribbean, Sri Lankan, Bangladeshi, and so on.

It is common knowledge that in the wake of post-empire and globalization immigrants have followed routes that meet and intersect at the First World metropoles. They have also struck roots in the new soil, undergoing cultural hybridization. After all this is what diasporization is all about, for, as Monica Fludernik aptly says, emigrating to another country 'no longer allows one to make a clean break with the past; on the contrary, one's ethnic affiliation with all its attendant responsibilities re-emerges – *a ghost* that has followed the emigrant and catches up with him after arrival' (Introduction xxii; my italics for emphasis). The ghost metaphor is quite pertinent, in that it evokes a shadowy presence without signifying a location; it has vague lineaments shot through with fantasy. This is what Fludernik seems to be leading up to, having made a remark earlier that originary claims of the ethnic identities are specious, since ethnic groups 'foreground their specificities and to create abstract identities that have little bearing on actual origin' (Introduction xx). Diasporic fiction deals with the modes of ethnic posturing immigrants make in the host society as part of their politics of difference against the putatively homogeneous and 'pure' cultural and racial entities. But the question we need to address is whether the host society is any longer culturally monolithic and racially pure. How 'British' are the white Britons, or do the WASP in North America have really Anglo-Saxon lineage? *White Teeth* raises this question, as do *The Buddha of Suburbia* or *Brick Lane*, interrogating the ontology of Englishness as a race and culture in the post-war era. To my mind, if the English are not 'English' enough, and claims of purity or origins lose moral authority, then the issues of purity and provenance relating to any culture or race or nation become irrelevant in *White Teeth*. This book initiates a new genre of fiction that goes against the very grain of genealogies being tied to nation-states or racial purity, which seems to be the underlying assumption of diasporic fiction.

Understandably, a minority literature in the diasporic contexts stakes its claims of an *authentic* representation of the specificities of ethnicity, and the author, more often than not, takes it upon her/himself this onerous responsibility of being the representative of a community; s/he writes about the problems of assimilation to the mainstream culture, and so on. We know of the fiction by India-born diasporic authors like Rohinton Mistry's *Such a Long Journey* (1991), Jael Silliman's *The Man with Many Hats* (2013), Kwai-Yun Li's *The Palm Leaf Fan* (2006), or *The Last Dragon Dance* (2008), which make an extraordinarily realistic portrayal of the setting, ambience, customs, cultural values as well as moral dilemmas, and social, political, and existential problems affecting specific communities such as the Parsis of Mumbai, Jews and Chinese of Kolkata respectively. But this is not the rule. In some other cases, the ethnicity of the diasporic writer is not pure or homogeneous. S/he may be of mixed breed, and for that reason cannot represent her/himself as the synecdoche of a whole community. As a consequence, the protocols of representation in the case of the writer of mixed-breed will be different from that of the so called pure breed. Therefore, the mimetic realism of the kind of fiction classified as minority literature, which involves biographic antecedents of the author in the formation of the subjectivities of the narrators and protagonists, does not lend itself to a universal paradigm, since the representational nature and canonical status of fictional texts can be variously fashioned, depending on the history and location of subjects, philosophical beliefs, cultural ideologies, and above all the pattern of their affiliations to the national culture. In this context, it will not be appropriate for us to treat Zadie Smith's *White Teeth* as a representative of minority literature, since it is already part of the canon of the post-war British fiction that has evolved from a narrowly homogeneous and provincial mould to assume an inclusive, diverse and a vibrant cosmopolitan character. In the words of Samantha Reive, this novel presents 'a non-constrained cosmopolitanism' and locates 'the cosmopolitan in the local experience of negotiating parallel cultural communities which are not represented as requiring assimilation or integration, but rather hope to coexist in a space of meaningful transcultural interaction'.[1]

The representational ethics of fiction in which the biographic antecedents of the author have been worked into the content will be different and certainly no more valid than the ethics of the fiction where such links have been dismantled. Rather, as Dave Gunning argues, the former type of fiction is based on a reductive notion of the multiculturalism of homogeneous communities where the implied author tries to divert attention towards her/himself from the imputed authorial persona, but the latter follows a post-Barthesian[2] ethical line where

> (...) several black and Asian writers in Britain, including (Monica) Ali and others, have attempted deliberately to fracture those links between the persona and biography of the author and the content and form of the text that may restrict ethical, storytelling potential. More interestingly still, this process has also often been marked by a reflection upon the idea of decentering the (ethnic/racial) self in order to relate to the other and offer an ethical perspective. (788)

Understandably, Zadie Smith's priorities are not biographical representation of the narrator and characters. Biographical traces are certainly there in the mixed parentage of the character of Irie Jones, whose mother Clara is Jamaican and father Archie Jones is English, like Smith's. The Willesden Green neighbourhood in North

England, where the novel is largely set, was where Smith spent her childhood. And yet, in an interview with Random House, she categorically said, 'none of my family appears in *White Teeth* in any obvious way'.[3] Further, the omniscient narrator of the novel stands ironically aloof from Irie and Archie. Although Smith is interested in portraying scenes of community life in its variety and richness, she said to Kathleen O'Grady in another interview not long after the publication of the novel, 'I didn't want the community in *White Teeth* to be representative of immigrants in England, that's not my job really, I'm not a politician, and I wouldn't claim such an optimistic vision of other people's experience, but I have a good time. I love living here (London)' (107). On the other hand, Smith revels in the life as it unfolds in a multicultural space, without being theoretically optimistic about the future of multiculturalism in Britain. In the same interview with O'Grady, she also said appreciatively of her experience of meeting children from diverse cultural backgrounds as a school teacher:

> You have schools in England which are sixty per cent Asian or schools which are eighty per cent black, but this school is just absolutely remarkable. Like any school, a kind of microcosm of a larger community and you see how well it works and you see the children walking towards the gate and there's a red head and a Chinese kid, a black kid, an Asian kid and it doesn't even seem to concern them. And it really lifts your spirits. It is amazing. And you just want to drag certain people to the school and say 'Look at this, look at how well it can work. Look at how these people are doing'. (106)

This response of Smith typifies the easy and somewhat ludic attitude of many of the writers said as belonging to what Stuart Hall calls the 'second movement' with regard to the representation of black and other ethnic subjects. This movement was in terms of a shift from 'a struggle over the relations of representation to a politics of representation' (442).[4] This politics of representation that problematizes representation itself, demolishing the stereotyping of cultural images and dismantling their commonly believed mimetic links with transcendental forms of reality.

It seems to me that Zadie Smith's genealogical antecedents as much as those of the characters in her novel lose the authority of referential and mimetic truth value once they are laid out in the empty space of textual inscription.[5] Further, we would do well to recall Foucault's argument in 'What is an Author?' (1969) that the author of a text is more than the actual writer, as is the author's name more than a proper name, and it is predicated upon 'author function', which is discursive in nature in so far as it consists in 'the mode of existence, circulation, and functioning of certain discourses within a society' (108). For example, born Sadie Smith, she renamed herself Zadie Smith at the age of 14 just to sound more exotic, and the new name featured in all her novels. This re-naming – an act of self-exoticization, meant to promote herself as an author of multicultural fiction – underscores an authorial identity discursively constructed and delinked from the originary, autobiographic self. She exoticizes herself in a multicultural space as a dynamic figure performing ambivalence of identity – partly exotic 'Zadie' and partly British 'Smith' – and thus unsettles the binarist opposition of 'insider' versus 'outsider'. I shall come back to the binarist issue of insider versus outsider, but via the different implications of the trope of naming and re-naming that we find in the diasporic fiction and that of Zadie Smith. For this purpose, I will refer to Jhumpa Lahiri's *The Namesake*, a well-known novel of Indian diaspora genre.

In *The Namesake*, Ashoke and Ashima hastily christen their son, the protagonist of the novel, 'Gogol' after the Russian author, Ashoke's favourite, to fulfil administrative formalities of the hospital when they cannot consult the parents for a proper name readily. This rather freakish name sticks uneasily to the child, marking out a space and subjectivity incongruent with that of the kindergarten, the site of socialization and acceptance into mainstream culture through peer-group affiliation. The school authorities do not accept this name, for it is odd. Nor does the alternative name 'Nikhil' help him develop affinities with American culture. He hates the name Gogol, because it does not mean anything in Indian, nor indeed does the other name Nikhil mitigate the sense of alienation enough. Un-naming himself, he chooses the later name 'Nikhil' when he goes to Yale, to be re-named 'Nick' in order to be Americanized, although evidently this Americanization and cultural affinity with the host culture is anything but illusory. In her doctoral thesis 'Mapping Subjectivities: The Cultural Poetics of Mobility and Identity in South Asian Diasporic Literature', Aparajita De discusses the inescapable conundrum of interstitiality or liminality of the hyphenated diasporic self of Gogol thus:

Gogol unnames his different name and (re)represents himself as Nikhil – showing his agency over his name, exercising the agency through the unnaming, and empowering himself as Nikhil through acts of social assertions. This process is, however, fraught with conflicts and complexities within Gogol. Gogol's transition to his new name triggers new complications and tensions ... . Lahiri shows how Gogol mediates between the realities of his lived experiences – both as Gogol and as Nikhil – after reconciling with the realities of his heteroglossic and heterogeneous identity. Interestingly, Gogol's performance of identity as signified through his name reaffirms essentialized notions of cultural identities. Gogol is still the interstitial, marginalized, hyphenated character in the Asian American diaspora just as his alternate identity, Nikhil. His act of unnaming puts him into the same paradigm of determining one's ethnic identity through their names, while unwittingly trapping him into the conundrum of 'Can you really escape a fixed ethnic identity conferred through naming?'. (48-49)

All the relationships he develops with various women that have been defined in terms of the axes of cultural differences only pronounce his exclusion from them. At the end of the novel, he discovers the significance of the name in terms of a parental heritage, particularly after the death of his father, which he should hang on to even as he has re-located himself in the interstices of American culture. This is a gesture of reconciliation with one's origins and with the fate of having to live a liminal existence.

In *White Teeth*, however, the exoticism of Zadie Smith does not stymie her in ethnic stranglehold. This is because it is not premised upon the notion of origins as a guarantor of one's identity; nor are the origins conceptualized in terms of linear time to be looked back at nostalgically and re-imagined in the present. Rather exoticism signifies her liberation from a regime of homogeneity and normativity through a playful difference and heterogeneity within a multicultural spectrum of races and ethnicities where whiteness is no longer a British template, and it has no longer any cultural authority and racial purity coded in it. Re-naming herself is indicative of autonomy, agency and energy for Smith, and also for her characters, who, however, de-ethnicize themselves. James Procter astutely ascribes to Smith's act of re-naming herself the term 'strategic exoticism', which he borrows from Graham Huggan, and comments that 'it is a process whereby texts negotiate their incorporation into the cultural mainstream by commenting on, critiquing or satirizing the very exoticist discourses they are bound up in' (113). This will be illustrated through the analysis that follows.

In *White Teeth*, Magid calls himself Mark Smith in his peer group, much to the chagrin of parents Samad Iqbal and Alsana Iqbal, the Bangladeshi immigrants of North London. Samad shouts at him: 'I give you a glorious name like Magid Mahfooz Murshed Mubtasim Iqbal ... and you want to be called Mark Smith!'

The narrator's comment in this context is pertinent:

> But this was just a symptom of a far deeper malaise. Magid really wanted to be *in some other family*. He wanted to own cats and not cockroaches, he wanted his mother make the music of cello, not the sound of sewing machine; he wanted to have a trellis of flowers growing up on the side of the house instead of the ever growing pile of other people's rubbish; he wanted a piano in the hall way ... he wanted his father to be a doctor, not a one-handed waiter, and this month Magid had converted all his desires into a wish to join in with the Harvest Festival like Mark would. Like everybody else would. (*White Teeth* 151)

As far as Magid is concerned, changing his name is a radical gesture of breaking out of the mould of ethnic interpellation by the pompously elaborate Islamic name to which his father has subjected him with patriarchal force. It is also a marker of lowly social status characteristic of the South Asian immigrant, which he discards in favour of an English sounding name that evokes a cultured, well-to-do lifestyle of Europeans. The new name also gives him appropriate cultural credentials for performing the Harvest Festival, a local ritual of charity to the poor in which British school children participate. It is a performativity through which identities are produced, and name is but a cultural protocol enabling such performativity.[6] Zadie Smith subscribes to the postmodernist notion of social identity as performativity and something extremely fluid and malleable. There is indeed nothing pre-given as fixed and essential about the identities of the children, Irie and the twin brothers Magid and Millat, who troop out to give fruit and eatables to the white old man Mr Hamilton, a war veteran, end up insulting him for his racist remarks against Blacks and South Asians as Pakis. Here the attempt on the children's part to construct through performance a British identity vis-à-vis a pre-given white racist British man for themselves in a multicultural space is thwarted by the racism of this man, which is based on his ignorance of the history of the war. What Smith wants to do in this scene is privilege the performative model of multiculturalist identity of Britishness as desirable over the static, essentialist and originary Britishness that engenders racism even after the end of imperialism. Unlike the usual diaspora fiction, Smith's novel puts to relentless question 'Britishness' and dismantles it. In this context, Irene Pèrez Fernández makes an observation in the essay 'Exploring Hybridity and Multiculturalism' that Margaret Thatcher adopted an ideology of cultural conservatism to contain social instability, and 'through appeal to the notion of common sense she put emphasis on the idea of belonging and the construct of the family', which re-articulated 'the divisive boundary of insider/outsider in British society' (147).

During Thatcher's time the black neighbourhoods were constantly policed, much to the resentment of the blacks, and they indulged in acts of protest and riots at places like Brixton (1979), South Hall (1981), and Broadwater (1985). All this resulted in the arousal of the conscience on the part of the politically, economically, and culturally dominant whites as regards fair-play in cultural representation. Therefore, the officially adopted policy of multiculturalism in the 1970s reflected the revisionary zeal of a sanitized conscience of the ruling classes. Accordingly, in educational curriculum and in the public culture multiculturalism became a hegemonic ideology, making a virtue of representing the Blacks 'as they are' in real life. This kind of reflective principle was fallacious in believing as if the Blacks inhabited real life in static ontological terms as beings-in-themselves, not as culturally constructed by the dominant discourses. Zadie Smith challenged the State's ideology of engineering multiculturalism because she not only found it hegemonic, binarist and divisive, but also thought its democratic ethos as well as ethics of political correctness were dubious.[7] That is why Fernández observes in another essay 'Representing Third Spaces, Fluid Identities and Contested Spaces in Contemporary British Literature' that various characters in *White Teeth* resort to the performativity of identity, which make their identities fluid in their everyday life. In this novel, interrogation of the insider/outsider binaries engenders an ambiguous, and dynamic space of hybrid location that constantly plays the notions of *belonging* and *exclusion* off against each other (144). As a result, the exclusionary principles of hyphenated subjectivities, which we find as a common phenomenon in the fiction of Indian diaspora, do not hold good. The possibilities of the second generation immigrants like Gogol suffering from hyphenated ontology and doomed to alienation and also social exclusion[8] do not emerge.

While theorizing diasporic narrative we need to acknowledge that there are certain novels like *White Teeth* that radically redefine the multicultural space in such a way that all identitarian fixities and rigidities are subverted, and new dynamics of the uncertainties, contingencies of forms are called into play. These result in the dismantling of all stereotypical notions and uncritical assumptions about identities. Performatives contextually define what identities are rather than roots and home – the two heavily absolutist factors in the conventional diasporan literature. In *White Teeth*, for instance, Archibald Jones, the person who is British by birth is effete and washed out, compared to his Bangladeshi friend, who prides himself on his English education, sound military training, heroic genealogy, and commission to fight on World War II in the European soil. Indeed, compared to the English man, the colonized Indian is represented as more English. If imperial Britain is conventionally regarded and represented as masculine, Archie is antithetical to it. Taryn Beukema perceptively comments:

> Archie Jones ... is a born and bred Englishman, and is the antithetical representation of 'masculinity' as defined by England's colonial empire. Ironically, it is Archie – not Samad – who exhibits characteristics of the not-quite-not-white Englishman. Archie is the epitome of rootlessness and indecision. Unable to live up to the ideals of reason and rationality at the heart of English masculinity (every decision he makes is based on the flip of a coin), Archie represents a 'failed' masculine identity. Indeed, because of this 'failure,' he is a success within Smith's project of challenging the concept of imperial English masculinity. (4)

As for the Chalfens, who embody reason and culture and want to improve the minds as well as morals of the delinquent non-white children like Bangladeshi Millat and Magid, and Anglo-Jamaican Irie, allegorize the policy of the welfare State of the late 1970s that

Britain was. Their educational and therapeutic ministrations have been treated in a mocking manner by Smith, steeped as these are in British racism and snobbery. Irie looks up to the Chalfens as the very best example of white English people and wants their Englishness, their purity and the Chalfenism for her self-edification. But the supreme irony is that it 'did not occur to her that the Chalfens were after a fashion, immigrants too (third generation, by way of Germany, Poland, née Chalfenovsky, or that they might be as needy of her as she was of them. To Irie, the Chalfens were more English than the English' (*White Teeth 328*). For his part Magid, who was sent to Bangladesh by father Samad to be kept far away from the corrupting influence of Britishness, comes back home to England, speaking Queen's English with RP and being a pucca Englishman, more British than a naturally born Briton. What Smith underlines is an ideological basis of performativity underlying what is perceived and understood as British in an epistemological and representational space.

Henri Lefebvre (1974) has already theorized space in terms of its predication upon the key concepts like nature, production, and social purpose. While space can be conceived of in epistemological and philosophical terms as a scientific concept, it has its ideological coordinates in society and culture insofar as it dialectically relates the neo-Cartesian and neo-Kantian subject to the object of knowledge within the framework of a praxis consisting in production of knowledge and meaning embedded in ideology. Thus the logical and epistemological conditions to conceptualize space get mediated socially into representations. The new protocols of the representation of space as evidenced by *White Teeth* are grounded in Zadie Smith's praxis that challenges the notion of purism of Britishness and divests multiculturalism of the hegemonic and racist elements in British culture. The stranglehold of ethnicity with which ontology of diaspora is usually bound up does not hold good in Smith's case; nor does, as we have seen, biography becomes a component of representation of the subjectivities of the narrator or characters in *White Teeth*. Therefore, a novel like this seems to question the very paradigm of studying the fiction of diaspora in terms of ethnicity, roots or a home left behind – like India as is the present anthology is all about.

We may now consider the idea of home which is implied by the insider/outsider binary. In diasporic literature, this binary has been deeply entrenched by the trope of home and its extension, the nation, in terms of inclusion and exclusion. In this context, Rosemary Marangoly George aptly says that 'homes are not about inclusions and wide open arms as much as they are about places carved out of closed doors, closed borders and screening apparatuses' (18). It is a constructed or imagined space of rootedness, belongingness, contentment and even containment. Denial of access to home produces a sense of alienation, and deprivation of it can lead to nostalgia and feelings of exile. In the postcolonial diasporic context, the emigrant to an alien land, because of voluntary or forced exile, carries a homing desire to relocate her/himself in a new imaginary home even as the home left behind haunts the person concerned as a ghost. The peculiar condition of being neither here nor there within the framework of the inside/outside binaries engenders identitarian liminality, which is to be constantly negotiated through re-imaginings of home and multiplicity of affiliations. A typical condition of such liminality has been best exemplified by M.G. Vassanji's *The In-Between World of Vikram Lall* (2003) in which Vic, the protagonist of Indian origin, suddenly confronts the predicament of being unacceptable and a foreigner in post-independence Kenya. Even after having lived there for three generations Indians like him could not be accepted in Africa, as they were perceived by the indigenous blacks as collaborators of the British colonizers. Having been drawn into the quagmire of corruption as a middleman Vic flees Nairobi, fearing arrest, but comes back to be reunited with his family and lives there as an outsider.

Vijay Mishra (2007) has already explored liminality as inherent to the postcolonial diasporic conditions. As the postwar Indians migrate to the West, their race to occupy 'the space of the hyphen – Indo-Americans, Indian-Americans, Hindu-Americans, Muslim-Britons – signals the desire to enter into some kind of generic taxonomy and yet at the same time retain, through the hyphen, the problematic situating of the self as simultaneously belonging here and there' (185). Whether it is the 'old diaspora', or the 'new', they all are forced to undergo some kind of hyphenation, racialization, exclusion, and subalternization. Mishra has studied the works of Jhumpa Lahiri and Vassanji under the category of new diaspora, and yet, as we have already seen, these two authors explore liminality as a major problem of the second generation immigrants. This indicates that the hyphenated, liminal migrants are subjected to the tyranny of absolutist, nation-state paradigm of race and culture in many western countries that still claim a highly liberal and tolerant ethos of multiculturalism.

In a more recent book *Transformations of the Liminal Self: Configurations of Home and Identity for Muslim Characters in British Postcolonial Fiction* (2011), Alaa Alghamdi studies afresh the issues of home, identity, and liminality in the works of Salman Rushdie, Hanif Kuereishi, Monica Ali, Zadie Smith, and Fadia Faqir, which show the dynamics of the liminal, postcolonial subjects (re)producing themselves, transforming and transcending the values and also imperatives of the old and new cultures. But liminality, as Alghamdi shows, is not necessarily a psychic handicap and existential predicament in these novels; nor are the effects of hybridity necessarily negative. It may be positive and liberating, and *White Teeth* presents itself as a case in point. We might consider the liminality of Samad as a case instantiating the consequence of the epistemic violence of colonization coupled with the violence of World War II that he has suffered. He expresses his predicament to Archie: 'What am I going to do after the war is already over – what am I going to do? Go back to Bengal? Or to Delhi? Who would have such an Englishman there? To England? Who would have such an Indian?' (*White Teeth* 112). But then it is his postcolonial fate to be in England, not to passively suffer the ignominy of working as a waiter in a restaurant and to be taunted by Alsana, his Bangladeshi wife. He spins a yarn about his great grandfather Mangal Pandey, the great leader of mutineers who challenged the British in the Sepoy Mutiny of 1857.

Hardly has any commentator of the novel paid attention to the all-too-obvious gaps and anomalies in Samad Iqbal's genealogical claims of being a descendant of Mangal Pandey, given the fact that Pandey was chaste Hindu, a Hindi speaking Brahmin at that, while he is a zealous practitioner of Islam and Bengali. Curious as it might appear, the narrator offers no clue as to how and at what time a cross-over in Samad's patrilineage from Hinduism to Islam or from Hindi to Bengali mother tongue take place. Given the fact that the mutiny was a combined insurgence of Hindus and Muslims against the British over the use of a type of cartridge that offended both faiths serves to emphasize the religious divide of the subcontinent in the colonial period. It appears weird that Samad would peg his heroic lineage and identitarian claims upon so uncertain a figure like Mangal Pandey, without any documentary evidence to that effect, except for a dubious portrait that he possesses of the legendary hero. Colonial history has dismissed him as a deserter, and the only Indian Hindu historian, who presents Pandey as a hero, remains unread. The narrator's silence is perhaps calculated to demonstrate this blatant omission on historians' part in order to emphasize that absence of roots or origins of someone does not affect the person's identitarian claims, since identity is all about posturing and performativity. One is not sure if Samad is Bangladeshi or Indian, and in any case it does not matter.

In contrast with complete absence of genealogical line of Samad, there is a putative genealogical tree with regard to the antecedents of Clara, Irie's mother. It goes far back to the abysm of time steeped in 'rumor, folk-tale and myth'. What it reveals is complicated branches of unsure paternity, adoption, ignorance of names, and other features of identification of forebears up to a clearly identifiable moment of miscegenation, remarked by the narrator in a tongue-in-cheek way thus: 'Great-grandmother Ambrosia Bowden (1890ish–1950ish) and Captain Charlie 'Whitey' Durham (1880ish-Lord knows)' (*White Teeth* 338). Subsequently, in 1907, the Grandmother Hortense marries Darcus Bowden, from which time the family line assumes historical specificity. But the narrator unearths the shoddy family history of sexual exploitation and proselytization of the Caribbean females in the name of 'English education' to undermine the colonial history of the Anglicization of the natives. In contrast to these cases, the Chalfen family history has been seemingly well documented:

> And the Chalfens actually knew who they were in 1675. Archie Jones could give no longer record of his family than his father's own haphazard appearance on the planet in the backroom of a Bromley public house circa 1895 or 1896 or quite possibly 1897 …. (*White Teeth* 338)

But the positivistic claims of history as staked by the scientist family has been ironically undermined by the narrator's description of Marcus's study where a map of Chalfen family tree shows 'a headshot of Mendel pleased with himself', 'a big poster of Einstein in his American icon image', 'Crick and Watson looking tired but elated in front of their model of deoxyribonucleic acid'

(*White Teeth* 336). Needless to say, all these iconic scientists have been appropriated by the self-serving myths the Chalfen have built around themselves. All the three cases of the Iqbals, the Bowdens, and the Chalfens prove that their genealogical truth claims are entirely invalid, and roots as well as rootedness are untenable concepts. Therefore, various identities are shown largely as performatives played out in ideological spaces with respective epistemological protocols for representation and truth claims that cannot be justified by the conventional notions of rootedness which diasporic literary discourse emphasizes.

As for the idea of home which is generally invested with shared memories, myths, and heritage, it has been configured in a different way in *White Teeth*. In consequence, the angst and tension arising out of liminality have been mitigated significantly. In this novel home is a multicultural space that is continuously produced and negotiated. It is not something to be reduced to fixed rootedness and heritage that people in exilic state usually long for in diasporic fiction. It is not an idyllic place to be nostalgically gazed at and re-imagined in the present. The search for one's authentic self in one's roots, which is a common theme in diasporic fiction, is thought of in a different way. For instance, to Irie England is home and a living reality that is very much embedded in the experience of the present:

> No fictions, no myths, no lies, no tangled webs – this is how Irie imagined her homeland. Because homeland is one of the magical fantasy words like *unicorn* and *soul* and *infinity* that have now passed into language. And the particular magic of homeland, its particular spell over Irie, was that it sounded like a beginning. The beginningest of the beginning. Like the first morning of Eden and the day after apocalypse. (402)

What her imaginary is constituted of is not a web of fictions, myths and lies which Mishra defines as 'diasporic imaginary' – in the 'mirror stage' terms of Lacan – as an idealized, illusory collective self-image that leads to the formation of 'any ethnic enclave in the nation-state that defines itself ... as a group that lives in displacement' (14). On the contrary, Irie's imaginary gestures towards a pure time like the *beginningest of the beginning*, beyond the quotidian temporality stretching from Genesis to Apocalypse. The narrator alerts us to the fact that the affective power of home and all its magical adjuncts are constructed through language. One might consider that this kind of imagining of home on the part of Irie and the author Zadie Smith is tantamount to rejection of the experiment of cultural eugenics of the Chalfens, which can be allegorically understood as the benevolently racist policy of assimilation by the State in the early 1980s. Nor is it congruent with that type of multiculturalism, where one becomes a victim of the history of miscegenation as Irie has herself become. Her body, the site of cultural performance, makes her unacceptable to the British standards of preference of straight hair and white skin colour. The mirror image trope is pertinent here: 'There was England, a gigantic mirror, and there was Irie, without reflection. A stranger in a strange land' (266). Of necessity, she has to seek for a self-image, an identity, to validate herself in her homeland in terms of the relationships of love. She does this in two ways. First, she has to win Millat, the Bangladeshi boy she loves, from her rival Nikki Tyler, the white girl. She changes her coiffure to be more like the dark lady in Shakespeare's sonnet taught in her school, and conform to cultural and racial standards of Britishness, which centered on Shakespeare, the cultural icon of Britishness. But the hair she gets plaited to her own Afro-Caribbean hair is that of an Indian girl. In this way the Britishness aspired for within Irie's libidinal economy is negotiated via Indian racial feature. Secondly, since hybridity is the ontological condition of Irie's natural citizenship in multicultural Britain, she wants to carry it to logical end by sleeping with Millat and also Magid in quick succession, so as not to know whose child she will give birth to. Although the motive may be purely libidinal shot through with feelings of anger, the act has tremendous radical implications in terms of perpetuating miscegenation further through the prospective British baby. This way, whether it is Millat, the father of the child is a functionary of KEVIN (Keeper of Eternal and Victorious Islamic Nation), a radical Muslim outfit that is retrograde, or Magid, the apprentice of Chalfen, the genetics expert and futurist, the patrilineage of the child will remain unknown. This is how Irie subverts the notion of the originary and produces a space of uncertain patrilineage where contradictory temporalities, conflicting ideological imperatives, antithetical practices produce their respective affiliative structures of home, jostling against each other, and liberating peoples not only from their bondage to their pasts, but also from their presents held ransom to nostalgias, and from the futures programmed towards utopias. Irie tells her mother vehemently about such a space that exists in contemporary England where people live in perfect freedom from ideological imperatives of temporalities to which their first-generation predecessors were bound:

> Really these people exist. I am telling you. The biggest trauma of their lives are things like recarpeting. Bill-paying. Gate-fixing. They don't mind what their kids do in life as long as they're reasonably, you know, healthy ... . And they will tell you. No mosque, maybe a little church. Hardly any sin. Plenty of forgiveness. No attics. No shit in attics. No skeletons in the cupboards. No great-grandfathers ... . (515)

And yet the past cannot be forgotten, nor transcended in a multicultural scenario. Katina Rogers in her essay 'Affirming Complexity: *White Teeth* and Cosmopolitanism' says that the novel makes a nuanced critique of cosmopolitanism as it is hemmed between 'past-tense, future-perfect', the phrase that gets repeated in the novel, highlighting the polarities that are most common: 'characters either focus on the crises of the past and become too rooted in history and localism, like Samad Iqbal, or idealize a perfect future or cosmopolitan outlook that ignores the history, like the Chalfens, Poppy Burt-Jones, and the Glenard Oak headmaster. Either perspective is faulty because it is only half the picture. By presenting both standpoints with a heavy dose of irony, Smith implicitly suggests that rather than a simple binary, a more complex, nuanced understanding is necessary' (4).

History seems inescapable for the characters in the novel, and it impinges on all, evoking various responses ranging from heroic pride to anxiety and bewilderment. It is in the root canals of teeth, the central metaphor of identities as these are traced to their respective pasts. Even as rootedness is to be overcome by performativity, its influence cannot be denied. That is why the chapters of the novel that are organized around the characters like Archie, Samad, Irie and Magid, Millat and Marcus cover their past as well as the present and show a complex relationship between these temporalities which is not linear. The narrative of the novel prods one, as it were, to, therefore, understand that gaps, discontinuities, intervening contingencies between the past and the present complicate any conception of linearity. There is no linear link between the present and the future either, for the shape of the future is uncertain. The narrator sums up these uncertainties in terms of Zeno's paradox that movement that is stillness; progress that can be stagnation; multiplicity can be unity and so on. Speaking of Millat and Magid, the narrator presents the two conflicting aspects of the issues thus:

> They seem to make no progress. The cynical might say they don't even move at all ... the two brothers trapped in the temporal instant. Two bothers who pervert all attempts to put dates to this story, to track these guy, to offer times and days, because there isn't, wasn't and never will be any duration .... They are running at a standstill. Zeno's paradox. (465–466)

> (...) the brothers will race towards the future only to find they more and more eloquently express their past, that place where they have just been. Because this is the other thing about immigrants ... they cannot escape history anymore than you can lose your shadow. (466)

So, there will be durational time as a lived reality in the Bergsonian sense, contingent upon the sense of past and future. Nevertheless, reality must be conceived of as a continuum of all moments shuffled together into a seamless durational time of *here* and *now*. It cannot be – and must not be as the narrator suggests – split into moments of time such as the past, present, and future with their meta-history of either the Bowdenian dream of Apocalypse, that was predicated upon Genesis and Fall, or Chalfenian utopia of the end of History. The fragmented sense of time produces enslavement to rootedness and past, nostalgia, discontent, utopianism, and a crippling liminality. History is to be therefore retold, remembered, produced, and staged in the everyday life playfully by the first-generation of immigrants in the eatery O'Connell's Irish pool Hall:

> Simply because you could be without family in O'Connell's, without possessions or status, without past glories or future hope – you could walk through the door with nothing and be exactly the same as everybody else in here. It could be 1989 outside, or 1999, or 2009, and you could still be sitting at the counter with your V-neck you wore to your wedding in 1975, 1945, 1935.

Nothing changes here, things are only retold, remembered. That's why old men love it. (244)

As for the young people, their location is the everyday world where they live history:

It's only late in the day that you walk into a playground and find Isaac Leung by the fish pond, Danny Rahman in the football cage, Quang O' Rourkee bouncing a basketball and Irie Jones humming a tune. Children with first and last names on a direct collision course. Names that secrete within them mass exodus, cramped boats and planes, cold arrivals, medical checks. It is only this late in the day, and possibly only in Willesden, that you find best friends Sita and Sharon, constantly mistaken for each other because Sita is white (her mother liked the name) and Sharon is Pakistani (her mother thought it best – less trouble). Yet, despite all the mixing up, despite the fact that we finally slipped into each other's lives with a reasonable comfort (like a man returning to his lover's bed after a mid-night walk), despite all this, it is still hard to admit that there is no more English than the India, not more Indian than the English. (326–327)

Names carry their own freights of immigrant history and memories and keep jostling about and slipping into one another in family and public domains, and identities tagged with names keep playing about to produce multiplicity, heterogeneity, hybridity, uncertainty, fluidity, and confusion despite the persistent divide between the English and the Indians. In other words, while the colonial memories and racial imperatives of imperialism still continue to inscribe the binaries in terms of the English versus the Indians, still these are negotiated through the production of a contestable space in which as malleable categories identities are 'presented in constant processes of re/vision, re/definition and change' (Fernández 'Representing Third Spaces' 149). As a result, the liminality of being on which the diasporic literature is based is mitigated to a large extent. In addition, Bhabha's concept of hybridity which many commentators on diasporic literature use to discuss theorize in-between liminal space does not prove adequately helpful to account for the kind of hybridity Zadie Smith deals with in her novel. Her kind of hybridity is definitely not about the ambivalent cultural interstice or third-space from where the colonial authority can be destabilized by the enunciation of colonial subject. I would also agree with Laura Moss that it is a quotidian, everyday hybridity of characters that Zadie Smith shows in (or is?) a locus where the imperial authority of the British, and their racial homogeneity has already been replaced by multiplicity of cultures, histories, and ethnicities. 'Cultural and racial hybridities are becoming increasingly ordinary. The significance of this ordinariness lies in the pivotal notion of a tolerance or acceptance of diversity in opposition to the potential fear or prejudice that comes out of a desire for purity' (Moss 12).

To conclude, *White Teeth* does not illustrate and reinforce the conventional themes of diasporic literature. Foregrounding multi-culturalism in its hermeneutic scheme it questions the usual postcolonial paradigm of the conflict between the unitary, homogeneous racial category of whiteness and Englishness or WASP Americanness on the one hand and black or brown raciality and liminality of the diasporic subject on the other. Here the multicultural space, unlike the diasporic one, is fluid and fecund to produce and reproduce the protean and malleable identities that are not stuck up in a static situation of in-betweenness. Even if history haunts the immigrants as a shadow, they play upon its constructedness and gaps through their performativity. Hence the simplistic notions of rootedness, origins, and place of provenance – like Indian or African or South Asian – inflecting diasporic themes become problematic in *White Teeth*.

Indeed, as has been shown, Britishness is a problematic identitarian category in terms of the nation-state in this novel, therefore it does not matter which places the non-British people come from. In other words, in absence of the nation-state as a term of reference for immigrants' identities, ethnic enclaves of immigrants do not simply obtain with respect to the places of their origins. It matters little even if Zadie Smith is not 'Indian'. She is no more Jamaican than Hanif Kuereshi is Pakistani or Monica Ali is Bangladeshi; they all are British writers. One might cite Bharati Mukherjee as an interesting example of being an Indian in terms of the place of her origin. She writes about immigrant experience, but she would acknowledge herself as an immigrant living only *in a continent of immigrants* and not accept the hyphenated Indian-American identitarian tag. In an interview she said categorically that she is an American writer of Indian origin, and that she writes 'in the tradition of immigrant experience rather than nostalgia and expatriation' and therefore her affiliation 'with readers should be on the basis of what they want to read', not in terms of her ethnicity or race (quoted in Cowatt 71–72).

As for the question of India in the novel, it is a deterritorialized home with cultural memories represented through Mangal Pandey trope, and also terms like Paki or Bengali that are used for the identification of Samad with a deictic reference to an Indian origin reinforce the idea of the deterritorialization of India. So, in a way India is very much present in the novel without geographic dimensions. This novel belonging to the class of multiculturalist diaspora is very important in so far as it urges us to remap the conventional genre of the fiction of diaspora and rethink its thematic issues and modes of representation.

Notes

1. See Samantha Reive's 'Constrained Communities: Zadie Smith's *White Teeth*.' Web 10 May 2014. <http://www.inter-disciplinary.net/at-the-interface/wpcontent/ uploads/2013/05/rievedia>.
2. The post-Barthesians are the Konstanz School critics like Wolfgang Iser and Hans Earnest Jauss, and the American Reader-Response critics, namely, Stanley Fish and Jonathan Culler. In various ways they emphasize the role of an active reader and seem to inherit from Roland Barthes the ethics of reading the 'writerly' texts as collaborators, and not as passive readers. The reader ought to be inventive and break the consumerist model of reading and accepting uncritically what is purveyed by the writer, by dismantling the apparent naturalness of the content, and showing the text's constructedness even as it looks self-evident. The post-Barthesians refute the simple, self-evident links between biography of the author and implied author and the mimetic correspondence between what exists outside the literary text and literary content. See Zahi Zalloua's 'An Ethics of the Unruly'. Introduction. *Reading Unruly Interpretation and Its Ethical Demands.* Lincoln: University of Nebraska Press, 2014.
3. See A Conversation with Zadie Smith. Interview. *Bold Type.* Web 22 May 2014. <https://www.randomhouse.com/boldtype/0700/smith/interview.html>.
4. In 'New Ethnicities' Stuart Hall explains that while the struggle over the representation was largely about the biacks and other non-whites trying to counter their negative stereotypes in cultural representations with positive images of themselves, the whole exercise was predicated upon an essentialist concept of identity as

well as a mimetic theory of presentation that 'a reality that exists outside the means by which things can be represented' (443). But once the politics of representation was formulated, the means of representation was conceived of as the discursive 'machineries and regimes of representation' within power structures that constructed images and figures and invested meaning in them. As a result representation was understood afresh as *constitutive* rather than having a 'reflexive, after-the-event role', and the ideologically inflected scenarios of representation pertaining to subjectivity and identity politics had a 'formative, not merely expressive place in the constitution of social and political life'. Hence 'black' was not a 'trans-cultural or transcendental category, but politically and culturally constructed' (443). See Stuart Hall, 'New Ethnicities'. 1988. *Stuart Hall: Critical Dialogues in Cultural Studies.* (eds) D. Morley and K. Chen. London: Routledge, 1996. 441–449.

5. I am indebted to W.J.T. Mitchell's post-structuralist theorization of the representational space created in literary text through its own negation. Mitchell derives this idea from Derrida, who in *Of Grammatology* says that 'a speech supposedly alive' can pronounce its own death as it lends itself 'to spacing in its own writing' (1974: 39). See W.J.T. Mitchell's 'Space, Ideology, and Literary Representation'. *Poetics Today* 10.1 (Spring 1989): 91–102.

6. I have extended Judith Butler's theory of gender and performativity in *Gender Trouble* to identity in general. Her theory, largely postmodernist, is premised on the refutation of the foundationalist notions of originality and essence, denial of the Cartesian dichotomy of surface-depth as well as body-soul, and above all absence of any subject lying outside the discursive means of representation, i.e. language. Hence, gender is a 'corporeal style', 'a regulated process of repetition or a performative' (139–140) that can break through the regimented gender as 'performance', which is, on the other hand, constitutive of a pre-existing subject ('Gender as Performance' 33). Identity can in general be conceived of in postmodernist terms, and Zadie Smith does so in many ways.

7. In *The Guardian*, dated Friday 21 May 2010, Stephen Bates reported that in an interview with BBC Radio 4's Today programme, the author of *White Teeth*, Zadie Smith had remarked that she did not understand the idea of either policy: 'Multiculturalism as a policy or an ideology is something I have never understood ... . We don't walk around our neighbourhood thinking how's this experiment going? This is not how people live. It's just a fact, a fact of life, and once people are able to move freely in the world, by plane or by boat, it's an inevitability. Instead of arguing about it as an ideological concept, you might as well deal with it as a reality. Human problems persist and most of them are

problems of class or money.' Web 27 May 2014. <http://www.theguardian.com/books/2010/may/21/zadie-smith-big-society-multiculturalism>.
8. See the ontological and epistemological problems of Indian diaspora in the racist colonial England and the United States in Ashok K. Mohapatra's *Social Exclusion in Postcolonial Fiction: A Reading of Kiran Desai's The Inheritance of Loss*, Occasional papers on Literatures and Cultures (Monograph 1), Department of English, Sambalpur University, 2011.

References

Alghamdi, Alaa. *Transformations of the Liminal Self: Configurations of Home and Identity for Muslim Characters in British Postcolonial Fiction*. Bloomington: iUniverse, Inc., 2011.
Beukema, Taryn. 'Men Negotiating Identity in Zadie Smith's *White Teeth*'. *Postcolonial Text* 4.3 (2008): 1–15. Web 17 May 2014.
Butler, Judith. 'Gender as Performance: An Interview with Judith Butler'. By Peter Osbornne and Lynn Segal. *Radical Philosophy: A Journal of Socialist and Feminist Philosophy* 67 (Summer 1994): 32–39.
——. *Gender Trouble: Feminism and the Subversion of Identity*. 1990. New York: Routledge, 1999.
Cowatt, David. *Trailing Clouds: Immigrant Fiction in Contemporary America*. Ithaca: Cornell University Press, 2006.
De, Aparajita. 'Mapping Subjectivities: The Cultural Poetics of Mobility and Identity in South Asian Diasporic Literature'. Diss. West Virginia University, 2009. Web 17 May 2014.
Fernández, Irene Pérez. 'Exploring Hybridity and Multiculturalism: Intra and Interfamily Relations in Zadie Smith's *White Teeth*'. *Odisea* (2009): 143–154.
——. 'Representing Third Spaces, Fluid Identities and Contested Spaces in Contemporary British Literature'. *Atlantis* 31.2 (December 2009): 143–160.
Fludernik, Monica. Introduction. *Diaspora and Multiculturalism: Common Traditions and New Developments.* (ed.) **Monica** Fludernik. Amsterdam: Rodopi, 2003. 1–38.
Foucault, Michel. 'What is an Author?' *The Michel **Foucault** Reader: An Introduction to Foucault's Thought.* (ed.) Paul Rabinow. London: Penguin Books, 1991. 101–120.
George, Rosemary Marangoly. *The Politics of Home: Postcolonial Relocations and Twentieth-century Fiction*. Cambridge: Cambridge University Press, 1996.

Gunning, Dave. 'Ethnicity, Authenticity, and Empathy in the Realist Novel and its Alternatives'. *Contemporary Literature* 53.4 (Winter 2012): 779-813.

Hall, Stuart. 1988. 'New Ethnicities'. *Stuart Hall: Critical Dialogues in Cultural Studies.* (eds) D. Morley and K. Chen. London: Routledge, 1996.

Lefebvre, Henri. *The Production of Space.* 1974. Trans. Donald Nicholson-Smith. Malden MA: Blackwell Publishing, 2007.

Mishra, Vijay. *The Literature of the Indian Diaspora: Theorizing the Diasporic Imaginary.* London: Routledge, 2007.

Moss, Laura. 'The Politics of Everyday Hybridity: Zadie Smith's *White Teeth*'. *Wasafiri* 18.39 (2003): 11-17.

Procter, James. 'New Ethnicities'. *The Novel and the Burden of Representation: A Concise Companion to Contemporary British Fiction.* (ed.) James F. English. Maiden, MA: Blackwell Publishing, 2006. 101-120.

Rogers, Katina. 'Affirming Complexity: *White Teeth* and Cosmopolitanism'. 1-12. Web 12 May 2014. <http://digitool.library.colostate.edu///exlibris/dtl/d3_1/apache_media/L2V4bGlicmlzL2R0bC9kM18xL2FwYWNoZV9tZWRpYS8xNzU3NDE=pdf>.

Smith, Zadie. *White Teeth.* 2000. London: Hamish Hamilton; Penguin Books, 2001.

———. '*White Teeth*: A Conversation with the Author'. By Kathleen O'Grady. *Atlantis* 27.1 (Fall/Winter 2002): 105-111.

Part 3

Contemporary Indian Diaspora in Films

CHAPTER 10

Indian Diasporic Films
Tone, Tenor, and Accents

HIMADRI LAHIRI

South Asian diasporic films[1] – Indian cinematic productions being an important constituent – are gradually emerging as a major area of studies. The onset of globalization in the 1990s coincided with an unprecedented growth of digital technology and made cinematic forms of cultural representations highly visible. This visibility created a global interest not only in the Bollywood products but also in the diasporic films which are 'located in the interstices of Hollywood and Bollywood' in terms of 'mode of production' (Desai, *Beyond Bollywood* 37). Films now cross geographical borders more smoothly than ever before, creating a large global market of production and consumption. The introduction of Film Studies and Cultural Studies Departments and inclusion of films as legitimate texts in the syllabi of literature studies departments created professional groups of film viewers and critics. Such viewers now take the diasporic films seriously and consider them as yet another form of representation of the lived experience of the South Asians produced from within a 'multicultural' ground reality in the diaspora.[2] The diasporic film still maintains a close relationship with novels and novelists. This is evident from the fact that many of the cinematic productions are based on novels. One can obviously cite the examples of *My Beautiful Laundrette* (1986), *The Namesake* (2006), *1947 Earth* (1998), *Midnight's Children* (2012), and so on.[3]

An interesting aspect of the South Asian diasporic films is indeed the close liaison between the novelists and the filmmakers. The novelists have contributed to the films in various ways. Some authors have written scripts for the films (Hanif Kureishi, Salman Rushdie). This gives them the scope of going back belatedly to the earlier experience of story writing in the framework of the novelistic genre and to 'rewrite' them in the context of the new medium. In the process they create turns and twists in the old materials and negotiate the new terrain. Some have appeared in the films in short character roles (Jhumpa Lahiri in *The Namesake*, Bapsi Sidhwa in *1947 Earth*, Kunal Basu in the Bengali film *The Japanese Wife*). This perhaps offers them scope to participate in the lives they created. The directors too want to see their stories grow in the company of those who originally conceived them. And some others have maintained close touch with the directors during the production of the films, creating a collaborative platform. The authors, on the whole, must have realized the cinematic potentials of their works or are interested in the cinema as a parallel art where they want to experiment with the life materials they negotiate on a regular basis. The films therefore become a very functional site of artistic cooperation, a dynamic field where multiple aspects of the already represented diasporic experiences need to be compressed and honed within a shorter time frame of visuality.

Cinema is also a capital intensive medium and its success as a commercial venture depends on distribution networks, liaison between different stakeholders, financial sponsors and interest of the theatre hall owners in the films. Prior to 1980s/1990s, all these aspects limited the scope of the distribution of Indian/South Asian diasporic films over wider sections of audience. Jigna Desai argues that in the 1980s and 1990s 'South Asian diasporic filmmakers in Britain (and elsewhere) gained access to the means of greater circulation and production' (*Beyond Bollywood* 42). She further observes that 'the political economy of minority cultural production did not enable the entrance of minority discourses into national public spheres (in the seventies) as it did in the eighties and nineties' (42). The policy of multiculturalism in the West allowed the ethnic minorities to engage themselves in creative and financial ventures. There were provisions of state funding of multicultural ventures. Srinivas Krishna's film *Masala* (1992), for instance, received state funding as part of Canadian government's policy of helping multicultural artists. Although there might be politics in the financial encouragement of multicultural projects, it nevertheless gave a boost to the new diasporic cinema. The filmmakers 'employed them (discourses of multiculturalism) to gain wider access to production and distribution, which meant negotiating the preestablished media networks of dominant white society' (Desai, *Beyond Bollywood* 42–43). Taking advantage of 'the extended distribution networks', ethnic, diasporic, and exilic films now reached 'wide audiences and soon became significant to the process of imagining diasporic communities and identities' (43). She mentions Hanif Kureishi's *My Beautiful Laundrette* (1986) and *Sammy and Rosie Get Laid* (1988) as 'two of the first diasporic films to gain access to distribution and reach international audiences' (43).

From the historical point of view it may be easier to trace and map the history of the Indian or South Asian diasporic film but from definitional perspective diasporic films certainly pose probing questions regarding its nature. A Bollywood based director often depicts the lives of people settled abroad with settings divided in two countries. The major cast may be Indian with the presence of a few (white or black) non-Indians to suggest its otherness. The language itself may be Hindi (*Dilwale Dulhania Le Jayenge*). Will that be enough to call such a film diasporic? A diasporic director may come back to India and make an India based film (*Monsoon Wedding* or *Midnight's Children*). Will that be a diasporic film? What then makes a film diasporic – identity of the director or those of the characters or of the cast? Is the story of the work the most important factor? What role does the setting or geographical location play in creating a sense of diaspora? Corey K. Creekmur, in his review of Jigna Desai's *Beyond Bollywood*, adds another criterion, that of state funding in the diaspora which basically attests to a diasporic location in a multicultural context. He asks, 'Are they "foreign" despite North American funding? Does an "Indian" director living in Canada make national or international films? Is *Monsoon Wedding* a Bollywood film? Is it even an Indian film?' (49).

In his book *An Accented Cinema: Exilic and Diasporic Filmmaking* (2001) Hamid Naficy seems to have dealt with the question in an indirect way. His project in the book, he observes, 'is precisely to put the locatedness and historicity of the authors back into authorship' (34). Concerned in a predominant way with the filmmakers in the exile – Iranian and other exilic filmmakers hog the limelight in his book – Naficy is rightly concerned with the condition of hardship and struggle in which their films are made. In such cases, directors look back, in an authorial way, to both the 'internal exile' and the 'external exile' (in the book he accepts exile in the latter sense) that lead to a claustrophobic environment for the characters who live the stories. Forced to live in alien countries, the directors recreate a diasporic consciousness in the films through plots, exilic characters far removed from their home that are not 'homely'. Naficy's conviction on the issue therefore hinges greatly on the concept of the director as the author who breathes and articulates diaspora. He asserts,

> Any discussion of authorship in exile needs to take into consideration not only the individuality, originality and personality of unique individuals as expressive film authors but also, and more important, their (dis)location as interstitial subjects within social formations and cinematic practices. (34)

While explaining the second feature of the 'accented mode' of the diasporic/exilic films, Naficy explains that the filmmaker, by performing multiple functions, 'is able to shape a film's vision and aesthetics and become truly its author' (49). Diasporic consciousness of the director helps shaping the film's 'vision and aesthetics'. He then makes an important comment, 'Authorship, therefore, is not only in the economic and aesthetic but also in the total control of the film' (49). It is through this 'total control of the film' that the diasporic consciousness of the filmmaker, I believe, percolates and circulates in every vein of the work. It is for this reason that Satyajit Ray's films (which are not diasporic films) are overwhelmingly the works of Satyajit Ray the 'author'. Naficy then draws our attention to the legal aspect of authorship and observes that 'authorship' is defined differently in different countries:

> Laws and regulations define authorship differently in each country, and this may also influence the filmmaker's decision to serve multiple functions. The 1957 intellectual property law in France, for example, confers authorship on the film's director and not to the producing, funding, or institutional agency. In other countries where authorship is not so clearly ascribed to the director, performing multiple functions helps to settle the question. (49)

Naficy thus links authorship intimately to the director's performance of multiple functions in the making of the film. The definition of the diasporic film depends largely on the director's 'author' functions. I accept his emphasis on the director's authorial role in creating a diasporic consciousness that determines the nature of a diasporic film. I believe that it is because of this consciousness that a film (e.g. *1947 Earth*) that does not apparently have anything to do with the diaspora may have diasporic dimensions. It is more so if a character in diaspora returns home temporarily (Jhumpa Lahiri's short story 'Interpreter of Maladies') and 'gazes' around, creating a diasporic perspective. Even in a film like *Monsoon Wedding* which has its location in Delhi, the worldview of the director is overwhelmingly diasporic. One immediately perceives a sense of distance and detachment with which the 'authorial' gaze operates in the film. The components of a diasporic author's/director's oeuvre evoke a diasporic consciousness. In the overall fluidity[4] of such a work, lies the diasporic consciousness deeply seated at the centre, coming directly from the perspective of the 'author' of the film.

In this article I shall try to probe into the nature of the diasporic consciousness that informs the representations of some Indian diasporic filmmakers. Taking Hamid Naficy's term 'accented film' at the core of my arguments, I shall try to see how it applies to films like *Monsoon Wedding* (2001) and *Masala* (1991). Naficy takes the term from the field of linguistics and applies it to diasporic and exilic films to emphasize their unique inflections which differentiate them from the mainstream studio-based film industry. I also want to investigate how diasporic consciousness takes different forms in different locales and in different socio-cultural formations. The tone, tenor, and intonation of these accented films affect the contours of the works in different ways.

Monsoon Wedding, written by Sabrina Dhawan and directed by Mira Nair, is generically a comedy. 'Combining elements of Hollywood and Bollywood, the film is the seventh top-grossing foreign film in the United States and cost just over a million dollar to make' (ibid. 49-50). 'Set in the contemporary moment, the film is nostalgic in its employment of the genre of the wedding film to propel a heterosexual narrative of family, community, and belonging' (Desai, *Beyond Bollywood* 204). It presents a picture of the metropolitan India through the event of a wedding which brings together members of an extended family dispersed in different parts of the world. In the process it foregrounds the cohesion and ruptures in the family networks, particularly from the point of view of sexual and gender relations. Wedding in India is not an occasion for just two individuals. It is a family, even a community, event attested by the participation of its members and solemnized by social and religious rites and rituals. This gives an unmistakable ethnic touch to the film. To the non-Indian viewers the ethnic underpinning of the film is not lost. Many Western reviewers of the film, for instance, are baffled by the elaborate wedding preparations that the Indian wedding entails in the film. The dance sequences, background music, particularly women's overtly erotic marriage songs, the rites and rituals that accompany the wedding all give ethnic colour and substance to the film. As Jenny Sharpe comments, 'The crossover success of Mira Nair's *Monsoon Wedding* (2001), whose characters speak English, Hindi, and Punjabi, lies in the skill with which the film acquaints a Western audience with the sights and sounds of new global India' (58). Nair's selection of the theme is unique, but its 'accented' nature is accrued through her diasporic consciousness. The gaze is diasporic as the camera moves and captures the moments and situations related to the familial relationship and cultural practices that a transnational subject nostalgically returns to and records for future reflections. Such films also act as sources of learning *deshachars* (cultural rites of the *desh* or home country) in the *pardesh* (other or foreign country) for the members of the younger generation who had to learn these cultural practices vicariously to a large extent.[5] As a wedding film *Monsoon Wedding* reimagines the old cultural practices in a changed globalized context. It also links the diasporic community with those in India in a globalized network of kinship relationship. As Desai argues, wedding films like the present one 'function to suture and soothe in complex manners in relation to processes of globalization'. They, she observes, consolidates 'transnationally dispersed kinship networks' and maintain 'cultural practices and traditions' (216). Such films serve as 'mechanisms of reassurance for women and their families who experience hope and anxiety in relation to the vulnerability of transnational brides due to separation and isolation' (*Beyond Bollywood* 216).

It is quite apparent that although the film largely caters to the Western audience it works from within the conventions of Bollywood films. The Western audiences indeed have become consumers of Bollywood films. Sharpe points out,

The indebtedness of *Monsoon Wedding* to this genre of Bollywood film is unmistakable in its integration of song-and-dance sequences into the storyline, its indulgence in the rich culture of Punjabi weddings, and its tribute to the extended family. In addition, through the shared knowledge its characters have of songs from popular Hindi films, Nair's film dramatizes how a commercialized, hybridized, and low cultural form such as Bombay cinema operates as the site of a collective Indian identity throughout the diaspora. (61)

But *Monsoon Wedding* also departs from the Bollywood traditions in that, despite the presence of entertainment elements like music and dance sequences and emphasis on family networks, it tries to control the melodramatic elements and offers feminist turns in the plot by offering agency to female characters whose attempts at shaping their own future is quite visible. That their agency still operates under the broad protective umbrella of patriarchy is nevertheless obvious. But that aspect I will not discuss here.

Lalit Verma (Naseeruddin Shah) and his family occupy the centre stage in the film. Lalit is busy supervising the preparations of the marriage ceremony of his daughter Aditi (Vasundhara Das). The bridegroom Hemant Rai (Parvin Dabas) is an engineer based in the United States. Relatives from different parts of India and the world arrive in Delhi to attend the marriage ceremony. The assembly of relatives in the film suggests how Indian middle class families have gone global. The economy of family relationship is apparent, for example, in the proposal of Uncle Tej Puri (Rajat Kapoor), who is located in the diaspora, to financially support Ria Verma's (Shefali Shah) dream of pursuing Creative Writing Programme in America. Ria who lost her father in her early childhood was brought up in Lalit's family. As the preparations progress and family members begin to pour in, the politics of relationships begins to surface. While the young members of the extended family find their romance blossoming as they find their partners, we become aware of Aditi's affair with a married man, the host of a Delhi.com reality show. 'Aditi is not an innocent Punjabi girl whose honor is potentially under attack; rather, she is a savvy Delhi woman who reads *Cosmopolitan* magazine and is having an affair with a married man' (Sharpe 70). She goes to meet him in his studio and even gets intimate with him. Her positive response to the erotic sounds mimicked by a female actor in the reality show displays how, as a modern girl, she does not have inhibition regarding the public exhibition of sexually explicit sights and sounds. All this indicates the changes that have taken place in India. Nair in this scene blasts the stereotype of Indian sexual prudishness. Just before her wedding day she does not hesitate to go out in a nocturnal adventure with her boyfriend. She escapes a police raid and later decides to disclose her affair to her would-be husband because, as she says, a new life cannot begin on a lie. Initially angry and frustrated, Hemant ultimately decides to forgive her. He too had an affair with a girl. Aditi's cousin Ria also divulges the secret during the wedding preparation that as a young girl she was molested by Uncle Tej. This results in the ouster of Tej from the wedding scenario. This brings back a sense of peace and justice among the participants.

The responsibility of managing the lavish wedding ceremony is invested in P. K. Dubey (Vijay Raaj) who, picking up the current business terminology, calls himself an event manager. The introduction of Dubey and his fiancée Alice brings the class dimension in the film. He is a representative of the globalized India. Armed with visiting cards and modern gadgets like pager, wristwatch calculator and cell phones which have now become accessible even to the lower middle class people, he does what a traditional 'decorator' does – building temporary bamboo structures for marriage site and decorating the venue with flowers.[6] He invests in share markets and discusses market fluctuations with his mother. His mother, however, bewails her son's indifference to marriage and cites the example of his cousin who with less income manages a family and is even blessed with children. This is an abiding concern of the Indian mothers which is evident even in upper class families. While blessing Aditi on the eve of her marriage, an elder female member of the groom's family raises the same issue. Dubey now falls in love with Alice (Tilottama Shome), the Verma family maid who hails from Bihar and belongs to a different religious community (Christians) and lower social strata, and after some initial hiccups marries her. Nair thus also focuses on the changes taking place in India in the fields of class, caste, and religion. Dubey-Alice marriage across religion, class, and caste lines adds new dimensions to the film. When the groom for Aditi arrives in the midst of 'cathartic' rains, marriages of both the couples merge and all of them dance together. These weddings taking place at the same site seems to indicate

Nair's emotional investment in a new post-feudal, metropolitan India. 'If the marriage between a woman from Delhi's wealthy cosmopolitan class and the son of a Houston NRI is complicated by prior relationships and family obligations, the relationship between Dubey and Alice is extraordinarily uncomplicated. The latter belongs to the film's Utopian desires for an egalitarian nation' (Sharpe 74). 'The film's final shot, however, shows Lalit reaching out for Alice's hand as he invites her to join the wedding guests dancing exuberantly to a Bally Sangoo fusion of bhangra and disco music' (Sharpe 74). The Verma household in the film is thus the performative site of the changing cultural practices and socio-cultural values, a space that exhibits the ongoing trends of cultural hybridity.

Situated in the interstices of two cultures, Nair knows how India of her ancestry has been changing fast. It is not an India of the age-old traditions or of the mythic past. Nor does it present the India that lives in the villages.[7] It does not inhabit what Naficy calls an 'open form' – vast open spaces like hills, fields and rivers, or spectacular natural objects in natural settings like the flora and fauna of the country. Elaborating on the term, Naficy observes:

> Spatially, the open form is represented in a mise-en-scène that favors external locations and open settings and landscapes, bright natural lighting, and mobile and wandering diegetic characters. In terms of filming, openness is suggested by long shots, mobile framing, and long takes that situate the characters within their open settings, preserving their spatiotemporal integrity. (Naficy 153)

Except on a few occasions (like the golf course where Lalit goes to play golf or the park where Aditi and her lover go on an amorous nocturnal visit), there is clearly no open space visible in the film, neither is there any scope for long shots or long takes. One notable long shot in the film is the scene where a dejected P.K. Dubey looks from his own flat at the cityscape over the mosques and minarets, and houses. The space is marked by narrow lanes, congested streets, overflowing crowds of vendors and pedestrians, cycles, rickshaws, and cabs. This is a Delhi that is old and constricted. It resists change. There are in fact montages of street scenes: a street urchin enjoying monsoon rains, school children walking through rains, vendors of fruits and other wares, moving rickshaws and cycles, and cars. The city comes alive through such visuals 'shot in the cinema vérité style of documentary filmmaking' (Sharpe 73).

It does not necessarily mean that the film projects a 'closed cinematic form' which is defined by Naficy as follows:

> The spatial aspects of the closed form in the mise-en-scène consist of interior locations and closed settings, such as prisons and tight living quarters, a dark lighting scheme that creates a mood of constriction and claustrophobia, and characters who are restricted in their movements and perspective by spatial, bodily, or other barriers. (Naficy 153)

Naficy is overwhelmingly concerned with exilic films where such claustrophobic environment is quite natural. But the homeland in *Monsoon Wedding* does not have any such environment. It is, as we have mentioned earlier, basically a metropolitan space of the upper middle class people who have big houses with sprawling gardens. Most of the shots are either in the interior of the house (which contains all the amenities suitable for an upper class house) with sufficient light or in the garden which looks fresh during the monsoon. There is no sense of constriction. On the contrary, there is a sense of family warmth and a strong feeling of bonding and belonging. The handheld Super16 camera moves in the rooms and the gardens and settles on the faces of the characters, bringing out in the process the subtle plays of emotional nuances on their faces.

There is, in a way, a 'return to homeland' motif in *Monsoon Wedding*, and the homeland has been constantly on the focus. But the easy traffic between the homeland and diaspora is the constant reference point to remind us that the homeland itself is not a site of pure and unadulterated tradition and that it has opened up to a globalized world resulting in new consumer habits and hybrid cultural practices of its people. And the family as a unit is no longer what it had been decades ago. In the diasporic consciousness of the director there is certainly a nostalgic longing. This nostalgia is broadly missing in *Masala*, a film written and directed by Srinivas Krishna who also plays the role of Krishna, the main character (an anti-hero), in the film. 'My film,' says Srinivas Krishna in an interview, 'is full of history, really recent history, but there is no nostalgia' (Chua). There are, on the contrary, visible attempts to mimic the nostalgia evident among the immigrant characters. Lord Krishna's appearance, for instance, 'through the VCR parodies Hindu émigrés' nostalgic attempts to recapture their national ties and to reproduce their cultural roots, as well as portray worshipping, through repeated viewings of the video epics' (Desai, *Beyond Bollywood* 109). The recurrence of the figure of Krishna the God throughout the film is an innovative idea. It suggests the importance of the figure in the religious and cultural practices of the devout Hindus but at the same time it points out the growing irrelevance of the divine presence in the diasporic space. The God in fact at one point of time in the film admits this. His appearance in the VCR which can be activated at the consumer's will is highly postmodernist in approach. It suggests the extent of inroads the electronic goods have made in the diasporic Indian households so much so that the possibility of God's direct *darshan* believed in by thousands of common people back in India is dispensed with – the spectacle has now to be channelized through the electronic medium. Divorced from the homeland in a direct way and forced to continue devotional rites in the new space as a natural continuation of religio-cultural habit, the immigrants are in the process of re-inventing and dis/re-orienting themselves.

Masala is a 'wicked comedy'. It contains elements of shock and surprise. Krishna, recently released from jail, is at the centre of all attention. He lost all the members of his family when the Air India flight they were travelling exploded in the mid-air. This has an uncanny resemblance to the 1985 terrorist bombing of Air India Flight 182. It was a flight heading to India. The blast of the flight with his family in it may be taken as a kind of disruption of interaction with the homeland and extended families there. Krishna is now to survive without the support of his immediate family. Although there are motifs of escape from the unhappy situations suggested by the recurrent sights and sounds of airplanes, Krishna and others, like Rita Solanki (Sakina Jaffrey), cannot leave the place and their situations. The 'open form' of the cinematic shots here underscores the necessity for mobility, freedom, and free imagination. *Masala*, as Desai suggests, 'focuses on mobility but does not resolve diaspora into a state of nomadology or interminable travel' (ibid. 118). Krishna is obviously a 'bad guy', disliked by both the multicultural avatars (like the white Minister of Multiculturalism played by Les Porter) and the members of the family and community. The moment he knocks at the door of the hall where the Minister is announcing the setting up of a temple for the Hindu community at the heart of Toronto in a self-congratulating manner, there is a flurry of activities to keep him out of the place. Bibi Solanki (Madhuri Bhatia), his aunt on the mother's side, and her husband Lallu Bhai Solanki (Saeed Jaffrey), a sari dealer, are distinctly unhappy at his appearance. The moment he enters the hall, the white Canadian Minister is shell-shocked. Shot from a mid-close position, his discomfiture becomes clearly evident. Following the minister's eyes, everybody turns back. All eyes settle on him. There are moments of silence in which he surveys the people gathered there and is surveyed by them. The moments of silence seem to be a comment on the inner hollowness of the professed multiculturalism which creates a stereotype of Indians as a model minority community. Krishna is an odd-man-out in such a context. The camera then cuts to the figures of three white racist youths who chase an Indian boy. It proves the hollowness of the official claims of multiculturalism being the norm in Canada. Krishna then begins to live in the Solanki family, develops affection for Rita, daughter of Harry Tikkoo (Saeed Jaffrey again), who wants to take a flying lesson instead of going to the medical school. Harry Tikkoo who works in the postal department gets possession of a rare stamp which he wants to keep in his possession. He is coerced to donate it to the multicultural museum in exchange of a lucrative financial offer. Krishna in the meantime tries to fit in different working positions but fails to do so. He is stabbed to death when he was trying to save the young boy from the clutches of the racist boys. The *ratha yatras* with multicultural participation goes on. Preparations for the opening of the multicultural museum also continue. But there is apparently no effect of the racist murder on the characters (except of course on Rita). The film ends with the grandmother triumphant in the kitchen of the museum (of course it has one) and the Minister of Multiculturalism is seen looking dazed at the spectacle of the ecstatic old woman who finds herself at the helm of the kitchen affairs.

Although Shanti (Zohra Sehgal), the grandmother, as a first generation immigrant, observes at one point of time that she and her people are 'outsiders', she does not really want to return to India; on the contrary, her wish to stay back in the new country is proved by her interest in 'no-money-down' real estate advertisements, her chiding of her son to sell the valuable stamp to pay off the housing debts, her excitement at the new found responsibility to supervise the heritage museum inaugurated by the Minister of Multiculturalism. Interest in buying land and house is the first sign of an immigrant's willingness to settle down in the new country. But Desai adds a new dimension to this – a threat perception – when she observes that 'real estate and private property become the imagined protective refuge from the violence of exclusion and discrimination' (Desai, *Beyond Bollywood* 117). By foregrounding the ground reality in the diasporic space and the new social formations there, the director underscores the development of the fissures in the society.

Naficy feels that when the impossibility of return becomes all too evident, the objects associated with the homeland assume nostalgic values. It is only then that the 'postmodernist semiosis' sets in. He observes,

> Only when the grand return to the homeland is found to be impossible, illusory, or undesirable does the postmodernist semiosis set in. Then the nostalgia for the referent and the pain of separation from it may be transformed into a nostalgia for its synecdoches, fetishes, and signifieds – the frozen sounds and images of the homeland – which are then circulated in exilic media and pop culture (including wall calendars, as in Egoyan's *Calendar*). (27–28)

In the film there are some references to India. Some synecdochic items of decoration and different idols and pictures of Lord Krishna are also very much visible. But they are not associated with diasporic desires of symbolic return. They do not function as fetishes of the homeland. They are rather suggestive of the fact that the culture being practised now in the diasporic space has its origin in the homeland. They suggest that diasporic cultural journey is one of hybridity and experimentations. The nature of postmodernism of which Naficy speaks lies not in such objects of semiotic significance but in the director's attempt to blast the mainstream attempt to foist a centre of power in the Canadian multiculturalism and in its 'masala' style.

Unlike *Monsoon Wedding* which is set in the homeland, *Masala* has multicultural Toronto, as its background. 'Made within the auspices of the Canadian state-supported film industry, *Masala* functions as part of, but also is critical of, this state-sanctioned multiculturalism in its own process of disidentification' (Desai, *Beyond Bollywood* 97). In an interview Krishna comments that multiculturalism 'is not an ideology. It's actually a lived experience' (Chua). He further observes, 'In Canada, the actual political purpose of multiculturalism is clearing more space and it's given the debate power' (Chua). In the film Krishna really participates in the debate on the nature of multiculturalism as practised in Canada and as it affects the Indian immigrants there. He brings out how there is a huge gap between how multiculturism is projected and how it is practised. Rathayatra as a Hindu religious occasion is duly observed and the construction of a temple 'at the heart of the city' is proudly announced by the Minister. The note of self-congratulation that ensues from a sense of power is however clearly evident in his voice. When Harry Tikkoo refuses to part with the rare stamp that is in his possession, the Minister of Multiculturalism is quite angry. Racism is an aspect that destroys the spirit of multiculturalism. The scenes where three white youth men mouth racist slurs against a young Indian boy and a young Indian woman and chase the boy give a lie to the ideals of multiculturalism. The Sikhs are shown as less privileged than the Hindus perhaps because they are stereotyped as terrorists. Such stereotypes are blasted when Canadian Mounties raid their store only to discover toilet papers with the history of the Sikhs written on it. But what is of vital concern is how subtle forms of racism operate in the official policies and practices of multiculturalism. This is evident in the speeches, gestures, and practices of the Minister of Multiculturalism. Desai calls him 'an opportunistic, slick, hypocritical civil servant – a symbol of the ineffectual and elaborate bureaucracy designed to appease Francophone separatists and 'visible minorities through tokenism that does not disturb the racist power structure' (*Beyond Bollywood* 123).

As Lysandra Woods argues, the film targets 'the structures, strictures, and myths of a putatively harmonious multicultural nation … . *Masala*'s critical work is very much about pulling off the blind from "us" and "them" relations, deconstructing the ideals on which the modern state fashions itself' (210). Woods suggests that the official policy is to project the Canadian government's successful implementation of the policy of multiculturalism while keeping the community away from real power. She cites the case of the opening of the multicultural museum. This, she opines, will be 'spin doctored as another instance of a multicultural success' (211). The projection is indeed more on the display of state gestures rather on the empowerment of the minority communities. Quoting Slavoj Zizek, she observes that *Masala*'s perspective is that

> Multiculturalism is a disavowed, inverted, self-referential form of racism, 'racism with a distance' – it represents the Other's identity conceiving the Other as a self-enclosed 'authentic' community towards which he, the multiculturalist, maintains a distance rendered possible by his privileged position. Multiculturalism is a racism that renders its own position devoid of all positive content ... the multicultural respect for the Other's specificity is the very form of asserting one's own superiority. (quoted in Woods 211)

Srinivas Krishna feels that 'masala' is a better term than 'multiculturalism'. In fact, the term has been used at different levels to suggest varieties and variations. Originally a Hindi term from the culinary register, it not only suggests the Indian emphasis on food and spice, it also refers to the mixture of materials, styles, and approaches that the film adopts. Hindi is interspersed here with English as the characters get more ethnic – there are regular code-mixing and code-switching. Heterogeneous characters crowd the space, and in technical terms Bollywood is in dialogue with the Hollywood. The songs (both in English and Hindi) and dance sequences create a Bollywood environment of romance and melodrama. There are a number of fantasy sequences too. Rita has her own dream of flying in the air with Anil (Heri Johal) whom she liked initially. Anil has an open sexual fantasy of uniting with the girl chosen by his parents and in this sequence the film shows nudity, male and female, in an uninhibited style which verges on the pornographic. Lallu Bhai who dreams of constant upward mobility by advancing his business interests also fantasises of being surrounded by semi-clad dancing girls. Lord Krishna, blue skinned, is presented in bright garish colour. He even wears a 'Maple Leafs' jersey. All these are masala elements taken from the Bollywood. Woods observes,

> Maintaining a few Bollywood style musical sequences, *Masala* goes on to toy with the formula: moving the setting from Bombay to Toronto, switching the Westernized daughter-in-law for the Westernized ex-con Krishna .... Refusing to play the popular off the authentic, the film upsets distinctions between the two,

charting the difficulty of situating them as wholly disparate entities: the masala movie is 'authentically' Indian; it is also 'authentically' pop. 'Krishna' is a god; he is also an ex-con. (Woods 207)

What, however distinguishes the style is Srinivas Krishna's firm control over the emotional and melodramatic elements as tools of satire. Woods rightly points out that 'if (Srinivas) Krishna exhibits a radical documentary spirit, his films eschew any aesthetic of the *cinema-vérite*/direct cinema brand, opting instead for a studied artifice' (207). This artifice turns out to be a postmodernist mishmash of varieties of elements and styles. '*Masala* especially throws reality and realism to the wind, offering up a concoction of postmodern pastiche – high camp, musical numbers, outworldly communications, historical incidents and caricature ...' (Woods 207). Most of these elements are used in subversive ways.

The two films I have discussed here demonstrate how the diasporic English films operate at the intersties of the cultural practices of the homeland and the host land. They are a mélange of Hollywood and Bollywood traditions and cinematic practices. The directors and their diasporic visions and consciousness are strongly present in the films. They emerge as real 'auteurs' which is amply proved by the choices and preferences they make in terms of plot, characters, and styles. Stylistically seen, the films are free of the claustrophobic environment that Naficy speaks of in the context of exilic films. The 'open' cinematic form is more or less represented in the mise-en-scène. Although they have to work from within a well-established network of production and distribution, the director's control (and not the control of the big mainstream studios) over the entire process of the filmmaking is unmistakably evident. By owning production companies (e.g. Divani Films by Srinivas Krishna and Mirabai Films by Mira Nair) and by collaborating with the pre-established prominent mainstream media and distribution networks, the directors take considerable control over the production and selling processes of their films. *Monsoon Wedding*, for instance, was produced by Caroline Baron and Mira Nair with a low budget of 1,200,000 US dollars and distributed by USA Films. Premiered at Venice on 30 August 2001, it was released worldwide on 30 November 2001. Produced by his own company Divani Films, Krishna's *Masala* is the first feature film produced by a South Asian in Canada. Distributed by Wellspring US Alliance Atlantis Canada and Icon Entertainment International, it has the participation of Telefilm Canada, the Ontario Film Development Corporation, and the Ontario Arts Council. The Indian diasporic cinema thus is not exactly 'accented cinema' in Naficy's sense of the term. Due to specific socio-historical factors (which we cannot discuss here for lack of space) Indian diasporic films participate in the production processes and cultures, and cinematic practices of the West more easily than those made by diasporic filmmakers from Iran or Palestine. They are in the process of overcoming the hangovers inherent in the very conditions of early diaspora. In the near future, we hope, more and more experimental films, freed of the early diasporic angst, will be made by the emerging Indian directors located in the diaspora.

Notes

1. Indian diasporic films are usually discussed under the nomenclature of South Asian Diasporic films. It is because of this that it is very difficult to discuss Indian diasporic films separately from South Asian diasporic films. Moreover, a large number of actors, actresses, editorial and technical staff and script writers, who have their national origins in different South Asian countries like Pakistan, Bangladesh, and Sri Lanka, are involved in the film projects.
2. In these areas of studies diaspora is used as a very useful tool to examine a number of issues that emerge from a unique lived experience. Jigna Desai argues, '(T)he concept of "diaspora" has become a powerful discourse for producing knowledge about nation, migration, displacement and transnationalism' ('The Scale of Diasporic Cinema' 207). Her observation about the nature and significance of the phenomenon will be useful for our purpose:

   'Sometimes understood empirically as a 'deterritorialized' national community or used synonymously with refugee, exile, guest worker and immigrants, diaspora has also become a critical concept for theorizing and imagining the broader socioeconomic, political, psychic, and cultural modalities of migration and displacement. Popular academic and state discourses employ 'diaspora' as a nomenclature empirically to describe migrant communities, but also to theorize the complex transnational social, affective, cultural and political processes that link those communities to South Asian nation states' ('The Scale of Diasporic Cinema' 207).

3. An important deviation from this trend is the case of *Water* which was first written as a script for Mira Nair's film and then transformed into a novel.

4. The difficulties we face in defining a diasporic work emanates from its fluidity. It spills over to different locations as it has broad and complex associations. Its lack of fixity characterizes it as an ongoing process of becoming. Speaking of diasporic films, Creekmur observes, '(T)hese films, like their creators and typical characters, resist being located' (49). Diasporic films have multiple locations, divided characters, mixed casts with several national affiliations and multilingual textualities. It is because of this that the films move beyond national borders. Diasporic films are essentially, as Eva Rueschmann observes, 'a truly international genre of contemporary cinema ... in a variety of national and transnational contexts ... in a "world on the move"' (quoted in Martin and Yaquinto 22). Martin and Yaquinto assert that 'diasporic cinema is at once global and local, expressive of a distinctive transnational style ... while also reflecting national specificities. In doing so, diasporic cinema deconstructs and challenges hegemonic understandings of national identity as it mediates a re-imagining of the nation (and national cinema) from the point of view of the postcolonial subject' (23).
5. Documents about Indian wedding, as Desai argues, are a site of learning rituals, traditions, and social practices for the later generation of South Asian American viewers. This, she observes, is evident from her own empirical investigations in the field. Moreover, these provide spectacles for the anthropological consumption of others' cultures. She says, 'Cross-cultural consumption of wedding films relies on the rejuvenation of an anthropological desire for knowledge of and intimacy with the other. Weddings have been a site of fascination in anthropology and the ethnographic film' (*Beyond Bollywood* 210).
6. Sharpe rightly points out that since 1991 India went through social and cultural transformation. It initiated a period 'when a new economic policy eliminated the bureaucratic red tape restricting imports and foreign investment. For the first time, the marketplace became flooded with consumer goods that had previously been available only on the black market, and designer labels became commonplace' (Sharpe 58). Dubey's proud exhibition of his gadgets in connection with his business can be accounted for by this phenomenon. Sharpe also observes that 'Indian television went from the two channels of the state TV to more than 60 channels available on cable and satellite in some urban areas ... the new satellite TV channels broadcast sexually explicit music videos and Hollywood soap operas such as *Santa Barbara* and *Baywatch* that engendered Indian imitations. Sexual topics that were previously unmentionable were now being openly discussed, and television brought these discussions into the inner sanctum of the home' (Sharpe 58).

7. The changing trends of representing India in the Bollywood films so far as its rural and urban geographies are concerned have been briefly dealt with by Sharpe. She points out, 'The rural exists in the post-1990s films not as a geographical location so much as a signifier for a simpler way of life prior to globalization'. She cites 'a member of the new generation of directors' who declares: 'The village has been pushed to the farthest periphery of our imagination. Any reference to a rural background today is only a synthetic nod to the roots. The insistence is on gloss' (60). 'The commercially successful films made since the mid-1990s,' she observes, 'in contrast, emphasize wealth, fast cars, youth culture, and cosmopolitan lifestyle' (60).

References

Chua, Lawrence. 'Srinivas Krishna: Artists in Conversation'. *BOMB* 43 (Spring 1993): n.p. Web 25 July 2014. <bombmagazine.org/article/1645/srinivas- krishna>.
Creekmur, Corey K. Rev. of *Beyond Bollywood: The Cultural Politics of South Asian Diasporic Film*. Jigna Desai. *Film Quarterly* 59.1 (Fall 2005): 49–51. JSTOR. Web 20 May 2014.
Desai, Jigna. *Beyond Bollywood: The Cultural Politics of South Asian Diasporic Film*. New York: Routledge, 2004.
———. 'The Scale of Diasporic Cinema: Negotiating National and Transnational Cultural Citizenship'. *Routledge Handbook of Indian Cinemas*. (eds) Moti Gokulsingh and Wimal Dissanayake. Oxford: Routledge, 2013. 206–217. Google Book Search. Web 28 June 2014.
Krishna, Srinivas, dir. *Masala*. Perf. Srinivas Krishna, Saeed Jaffery. Alliance Atlantis Communications (Canada) and Wellspring (US), 1991. Film.
Martin, Michael T. and Marilyn Yaquinto. 'Framing Diaspora in Diasporic Cinema: Concepts and Thematic Concerns'. *Black Camera* 22.1 (Spring/Summer 2007): 22–27. JSTOR. Web 20 May 2014.
Nair, Mira, dir. *Monsoon Wedding*. Perf. Naseeruddin Shah, Vasundhara Das. USA Films, 2001. Film.
Naficy, Hamid. *An Accented Cinema: Exilic and Diasporic Filmmaking*. Princeton: Princeton University Press, 2001.
Sharpe, Jenny. 'Gender, Nation, and Globalization in *Monsoon Wedding* and *Dilwale Dulhania Le Jayenge*'. *Meridians* 6.1 (2005): 58–81. JSTOR. Web 20 May 2014.
Woods, Lysandra. 'Srinivas Krishna and the New Canadian Cinema'. *North of Everything: English-Canadian Cinema since 1980*. (eds) William Beard and Jerry White. Edmonton: University of Alberta Press, 2002. 206–15.

Chapter 11

Evolution, Manifestation, and Future Trends of Indian Diasporic Cinema in Britain

SOMDATTA MANDAL

Over the last few decades, the interest in multicultural studies, ethnicity, pluralism and interdisciplinary areas has already become the thrust area in the United States, as it has in Britain and Canada, and the development is interesting to survey. With the emphasis on the concept of cultural pluralism across the globe, the particularities of individual cultural distinctions owing to race, class, gender, ethnicity, language, and religion are amalgamated into the various hyphenated groups. What interests us is the existence of diasporic Indians in these countries who contribute a great extent to the 'browning' of the population. Since most diasporic Indians are debating not whether to adopt multiculturalism, but rather what kind of multiculturalism to adopt, the issues are now spread across different genres and boundaries to extend under the broad umbrella of cultural studies. The old Kipling lore that the East is East and the West is West is passé and the twain do meet.

Communication is the first step to appreciating the value of the differences in people, cultures, and beliefs. The central issue of this paper will be an attempt to render what is at stake in making 'Indian-ness' an object of scrutiny and how far the diasporic film media as site of knowledge production in Britain is implicated in reproducing racialized accounts of 'Indianness'. It will primarily highlight the myriad voices of the Indian diaspora through films. These range from regular features, to short documentaries made either for art's sake or for finishing graduate school projects, or as a vehicle for expressing social problems like acculturation, hybridity, and identity politics. Many of them also focus on the gay/lesbian/bisexual existence of some of the members of this community who have found a better chance of opening up and expressing themselves than they would be able to do in their 'home' culture. Living in a space between two cultures, most of these independent filmmakers focus upon their Indian tradition and how it collides with Western individuality. Apart from a few established diasporic Indian film directors who have reached a stage when their films are easily distributed, many of the films made by others do not see the light of day in commercial theatres at all. A lot of them have to wait for film festivals and word of mouth for their circulation.

Stuart Hall, in his 'Introduction: Who Needs "Identity"?' states that '(I)dentities are never unified and, in late modern times, increasingly fragmented and fractured; never singular but multiple constructed across different, often intersecting and antagonistic, discourses, practices, and positions. They are subject to a radical historicization, and are constantly in the process of change and transformation ... . Identities are therefore constituted within, not outside representation ...' (4). Precisely because identities are constructed within, not outside, discourse, we need to understand them as produced in specific historical and institutional sites within specific discursive formations and practices, by specific enunciative strategies. Moreover, they emerge within the play of specific modalities of power, and thus are more the product of the marking of difference and exclusion, than they are the sign of identical, naturally-constituted unity – and 'identity' in its traditional meaning (that is, an all-inclusive sameness, seamless, without internal differentiation). Taking the cue from Hall, we can state very categorically that the first essential quality of Indian diasporic cinema is its manifestation of fluid identity.

In many ways, the diaspora epitomizes the notion of a 'minority': small percentage of the population, usually self-identified with traditionally Eastern religions (Hinduism, Islam, Sikhism), and in 'white' nations classified as 'non-white'.

However, a substantial number of Indians who come/settle in these countries are middle-class and well educated. As such, this group does not confront the economic disadvantages faced by most minorities. So, what kind of media representations do we expect to come out of, or reflect this group? Though some of the Indian films are primarily family drama rendered as thoroughly entertaining comedies, all of them are the manifestations of the 'racial problem' that faces the members of an 'ethnic minority' in Britain. Sometimes they are not complete in themselves, what with low budgets, difficulty in obtaining viewership and moving towards the mainstream. On the other hand, it is interesting to note that positive Indian images have also entered the national consciousness through film and television. Along with the task of entertaining an audience of millions, these productions have a huge responsibility as they are defining perceptions of Indians living in Britain. Primarily produced by independent filmmakers, most of these films explore the process of how communities and identities are constructed in the Indian diaspora, where the dynamics of class structure and racial formation contribute in specific ways to the evolving self-definitions of being 'minority', and also the rendering of stereotypical roles. Some of the questions the films examine include acculturation problems, dual existence, how racism and gender norms reconfigure families and how particular intersections between class, sexuality, and race are worked out in a cross-cultural setting. Also, as commentators on modernity and social change, understanding of cinema as a social medium, sometimes there are doubts as to whether these films can keep alive issues on realistic, socially relevant cinema.

The films of the Indian diaspora in Britain can be roughly divided into three categories. In the first group fall the films that are made 'from' the diaspora – films that look back at the 'home' culture with a sense of nostalgia. The form this homesickness takes in diaspora films can vary a great deal. It can manifest itself through a literal longing for the home which has been left, an emphasis upon comparing the new and old homes, and a clinging to the iconographies and beliefs of home which is less about any cultural superiority and more about a community which can be said to still share a common culture. The second category can be films that are made 'of' the diaspora – located within the settler nation and talking about it. Being produced in a multicultural nation, one of the significant factors in these diaspora films is that they are also rooted deeply in the generic and narrative tradition of British cinema. The third category is those films 'about' the diaspora – made by outsiders who talk about it. For convenience of discussion of the multifarious types of films being made, I have classified Indian diasporic cinema roughly into two broad groups, namely feature films and short narratives in the first group and documentaries or non-fiction films and videos in the second. Within each category there are various subgroups, according to the multiplicity of themes and techniques, and according to the ways they approach the issues of acculturation and hybridity.

Considering cinema as a part of the cultural studies scenario today, one is often baffled when Indian diasporic films that are classified under the commercial category as well as those experimental/documentary/short narratives – all deal with the issue of diasporic identity of the immigrants trying either to acclimatize themselves in a new and alien world, or lost like the mythical *'trishanku'* figure, belonging neither here nor there, or focusing upon the inter-generational conflict arising out of this kind of issues related to acculturation. Whether the tone is comical, serious, or critical, the primary role of the director is to focus upon these problems, most of the time within the community in which he or she belongs (though exceptions also prove the rule). Here we have to consider four specific areas:

(a) *Cinematic realism:* With most of the diasporic directors taking recourse to the *cinema-verité* style of documentary filmmaking, more importance is given to thematic explorations than to techniques. In the case of full-length feature films, depicting real life situations either through comic touches or through serious observations becomes the primary motive of the director.

(b) *Identification:* The anthropologist Thomas Hylland Eriksen offers a typology of overarching identities that include ethnic identity, class identity, gender identity, age identity, religious identity, local identity, political identity, linguistic identity, kinship identity, and supra-ethnic national identity. For the

Indian immigrant in the western world, it is difficult to identify which form of identity he is most concerned with as sometimes, categories overlap. Eric Hobsbawm calls the 21st century the age of displacement. In spite of the bouncy humour and chocolate box ending of certain diasporic films, most of the characters in these films are parts of those flotsam and jetsam on an uncertain tide.

(c) *Subjectivity:* Several Indian diasporic feature films and documentaries are made with conviction of the directors themselves and speak about their own personal situations. They highlight the plight of the minority; expose the exile's essential loneliness. But at the same time it has to be kept in mind that most of the directors do not want to stick to the rules, i.e. be labeled as 'diasporic' filmmakers only. They long to venture into mainstream productions as well.

(d) *Spectatorship:* Question naturally arises as to who is the target audience for such films and videos. Over the course of the last 20 years, Indian diasporic cinema has been able to make itself more visible, moving from the festival circuits to more commercial distribution networks. With more crossover films with bigger budgets entering the arena, the scope of viewership has also opened up to include the average western viewer.

Feature Films

The earlier diasporic films in Britain primarily focused upon culture-clashes. But there are many more diaspora films that go beyond the clichés, and tackle issues of race, identity, hypocrisy and racial and sexual politics, delving into individual dilemmas, contradictions, vulnerabilities and triumphs, and often touching a universal chord – such as, *My Beautiful Laundrette, Brothers in Trouble, My Son the Fanatic, East is East, Bhaji on the Beach, Anita and Me.* Some of the most heartbreaking moments in these films have been, for instance, when Om Puri, who befriends a prostitute in *My Son the Fanatic,* loses the respect of his son, who turns to fundamentalist Islam. To Meena, in Metin Huseyin's *Anita and Me,* discovering that her best friend and idol, the white-skinned Anita, has a Paki-bashing boyfriend is a kind of betrayal. These are strong characters that transcend mere diaspora labels and leave their signatures on our hearts.

Here one must remember that the Indian diasporic situation in Britain is different from the American and the Canadian context in the sense that in Britain we find a larger component of Bangladeshi, Pakistani, and Indian directors. The United Kingdom is the one place outside India with an exceptional concentration of 1.3 million Britishers of Indian origin on a small island, engendering a relatively more mutually nurturing relationship between audience and film talent. In Britain, apart from the migration of people from the South Asian area, migration from other ex-colonies has also occurred, which has resulted in the migration of those originating in India but from countries such as East Africa, Guyana, Trinidad, and Mauritius. Moreover there are several generations of Indians residing there who share a colonial heritage and their identities are formed by once, twice, or even thrice migrations. From first generation settlers from India in the 1960s, it is now time for the second generation Indians to define their histories and melting pot cultures. The question naturally arises, how does this definition of identity get carved out in films? Films made by British Indians explore stories from their communities and interface with their mainstream culture. Films have looked back at the chapters of the 1970s and 1980s when settlers tried to fit in against the pressures of racism and intolerance (*My Beautiful Laundrette*, *Brothers in Trouble*). Films have examined changing values in traditional families with self-reflexive humour (*East is East*). Other filmmakers have turned a serious eye at the rapid spread of religious fundamentalism amongst youth in ethnic communities (*My Son the Fanatic*). With more recent films like *Anita and Me*, a young girl's memory of growing up in an English village stands sharply juxtaposed with the relentlessly grim and powerful story of Shakeela Tarannum Mann's *A Quiet Desperation* (2001) which looks at the dark underbelly of the migrant's success story. As Meera Syal, who had entertained viewers with the Channel Four serial *Goodness Gracious Me*, succinctly puts it in an article entitled 'Goodness Gracious Meera!' published in April 2003 issue of the British Council newsletter for Eastern India called *Connecting*:

> Britain is inevitably and will always be from now on a multicultural society and that will always upset a small minority of the indigenous Brits. But it is precisely Britain's multicultural mix that has made the country so vibrant, so challenging and productive. Satire is one of the best ways to win over the Brits because they do have

the best sense of humour in the world and truly appreciate wit and playfulness. As I write, far right groups are winning local elections in the north of England, yet alongside them, *Bombay Dreams* plays to packed houses, Asian millionaires emerge every year ... life continues and we hope to change outdated attitudes by our presence and most of all, our successes. (9)

Thus through these different kinds of interesting films made by Indians to define themselves, we see their sense of belonging to an alien culture. There are films that tackle the difficult issues of racism, sexuality, violence, and politics. From feel-good comedy to razor sharp incisive drama, from personal storytelling to experimentation with form and content, all this finds reflection in both features and shorts. We get to see a fair representation of happy integration stories as well as those that raise complex questions about minority identity and social space. But that is not the entire story. As Gurinder Chadha is reported to have stated in July 2002 issue of *Connecting* after making *Bend it Like Beckham*, times are also changing:

One of the most exciting possibilities for Asian filmmakers is that we aren't only making films for the UK but we're making international films that communities from all over the world identify with. We're presenting a new vision of what Britain looks like today and our audience is global. (10)

A last point to be kept in mind while going through the numerous feature films and documentaries on the Indian diaspora is that not all the films discussed or mentioned are technical masterpieces or brilliant in their production methods. But, they are relevant because of their content matter and with the sincerity with which they are made. Also, while we can celebrate the arrival of diasporic filmmakers offering as they do a much-needed perspective on the complex lives of the Indians in the western world, and for challenging the constrictive boundaries of patriarchy which some of their films offer, we have to be careful not to be seduced by a nostalgic and undifferentiated representation of a dynamic and complex society. However, transgressions within one context can become unproblematized celebrations of difference within another. Cultural productions never occupy an absolute, static space, but when they undergo transnational crossings, we have to be particularly aware of the interplay of longing and nostalgia, nation and diaspora, fundamentalism and liberation, democracy and difference; in the end, these texts have to be interrogated with particular attention to the disjunctures and shifts that take place as culture moves from one site to another within a process of uneven geographical development.

The discourses of the self – sexual, racial, historical, regional, ethnic, cultural, national, and familial – intersect in the lives of the diasporic people and form a net of language that they share with the community. This 'collective memory', like individual memory, is a function, not an entity. They 'remember' events, language, actions, attitudes, and values that are aspects of their membership in groups. Thus they want to preserve them or recover them when they venture into the film medium. The Indian diasporic filmmaker therefore often employs his or her storytelling to redefine history and culture and to legitimize personal and collective memory. As the stories pass from one generation to the next, memory interrupts linear conventional narrative patterns in order to make room for multiple voices and perspectives and allows for a narrative exploration of the past that rejects or circumvents positivistic assumptions about truth and history. It must be mentioned here that I use the term Indian as opposed to the use of distinctive groups within the South Asian diasporas, as the media usually portrays them as a homogeneous entity.

Some of the new Asianization of Britain comes straight from India and Pakistan, much of it from an Indian culture in Britain. It's the idea of India that binds India and Indians in Britain in a togetherness culturally unseparated by passports. Today the British eat Indian, hear Indian, wear Indian, look Indian, read Indian – and nobody notices. George Mikes wrote in the 1960s that an immigrant has two choices: to try to be yourself and be ridiculous, or to try and be like the English and be even more ridiculous. That has changed. England has changed. India and the Indians have made their impact by being themselves and letting the British find out. In some measure, an Indianness has changed them. Nowhere is this phenomenon more discernible than in films.

Narrating Reality: The Bi-cultural Predicament

Like all immigrant communities, the major issue that plagues the mind of the Indian diaspora settled in the western hemisphere is the problem of their bi-cultural status. They can neither adapt themselves fully into the alien culture, nor can they forget their roots. Again, a new group of immigrants has been entering Britain over recent years: older South Asians coming to the west for the purpose of being closer to their American or British settled children. They come to these countries primarily striving to sustain the long-term bonds of intergenerational reciprocity and affection that many view as central to an 'Asian' and 'good' family and old age. But life in the west can never be the same as an envisioned life in India. They take some values, practices, and images from the 'home' country and some from the 'new' one, creating new complex forms of family and a gaping divide between generations and nations. The films resulting out of this kind of situation can be broadly divided into three categories, namely, (a) comedies where the characters and the directors laugh at themselves (b) where the directors assess the predicament much more seriously and try to give a true 'slice of life' presentation, and (c) where the approach is less *avant garde*, but deal with a blend of both the earlier categories, resulting in a new breed called 'crossover' films.

Certain social issues plague many diasporic Indian directors. These range from the question of the expectation that Indian parents have of their offspring – the notion of many Indian parents being that only certain careers are acceptable for their children; the tension of job insecurity in a foreign country; learning to let the children decide things for themselves; the idea that arranged marriages work better; tending to be more protective of their daughters than of their sons; the protest from their children regarding their double standards; parents change their attitude while at home with their children and when in company of other fellow immigrants. Thus in several films we find the recurrence of some of these set themes and ideas. They mirror the predicament of young people who are coming to terms with issues like arranged marriages, steady careers, and premarital sex that were paramount in the minds of their parents when they migrated to Britain in the 1960s and 1970s. At the same time, they are learning to live a life for themselves and on their own terms. Though the filmmakers may be reaching out to a limited audience, their statements are often quite powerful and it is here that their appeal lies.

Laughing at Themselves: Diaspora of Hope

Let us now look at two examples of transnational spaces and the construction of a new imagination for immigrant communities who are forced to migrate. In 1994, a young woman from Britain named Gurinder Chadha directed and released her first feature film, *Bhaji on the Beach*. The director grew up in Southall, a largely Punjabi neighbourhood in West London, after her family was forced to move from Kenya when she was three. The film explores the lives of nine South Asian women, spanning three generations during one day at a seaside resort in Blackpool. The film touches on many aspects of gender identity formation and negotiation for women of Indian descent. Simi, who is a politically committed community worker and who talks about 'the double yoke of racism and sexism', wants the women to just have a good time at the Blackpool seaside resort away from their duties as women.

Question naturally arises, how do Indians who have never been to their 'home' country imagine and feel their 'Indianness' together? Arjun Appadurai explains: 'Part of what the mass media makes possible, because of the condition of collective reading, criticism, and pleasure ... (is) a community of sentiment ... a group that begins to imagine and feel things together' (8). Groups that have never seen each other start to imagine themselves Indians, or Sikhs, or Burmese, or as Indian women. However, even though transnational spaces can become oppressive as can be seen by Pushpa's and Mina's reactions toward Hashida, there are also possibilities for the construction of new mythologies for social action, as can be seen by the resolution of the narrative in *Bhaji on the Beach*. The movie ends with the 'aunties' understanding Hashida's decision to be with her boyfriend, if not completely accepting it. Thus, the film becomes the best example of the 'diaspora of hope'.

Metin Huseyin's *Anita and Me* (2002, 93 minutes) is another movie that insists on the diasporic situation by exploring differences and finding connections. Based on Meera Syal's novel it takes '*a trip back in time to when flares, glam rock and Jackie magazine ruled!*' *Anita and Me* is an amusing look at the 1970s from a different angle. Speaking about the situation in the book as well as in the film, Meera Syal emphasizes upon this tug of cultures in an article entitled 'Goodness Gracious Meera!':

The second generation is certainly coming into its own now, and it is inevitable. We are the kids born and brought up in the UK and have claimed many sections of British culture and achievement as our own, by drawing on dual heritage and creating a dynamic new one which has a unique voice and pulse. There were so many dire predictions of how our 'mongrel race' of kids would turn out and here we are, the huge irony being that it is precisely because of our two cultures that we are creative, challenging the status quo and continually asking questions about identity, belonging and self-expression. Without my strange and sometimes funny upbringing, I know I would not be an actress and writer. I had to ask myself early on, because of being an outsider, the questions that all artists ask themselves; who am I? What do I want to say? What is the bigger picture? (9)

Crying for Themselves: The Diaspora of Despair

As against the series of films discussed above that could be termed as representing a 'diaspora of hope', we also have several diasporic Indian films that deal with issues more seriously and hence can be labelled as 'diaspora of despair'. In most of these films, the directors are careful in depicting Indians and Indianness in the diasporic spaces as part of the continuum of displacement and alienation. They realize that although Indians were taken to many parts of the world as indentured labourers and had to live in abject poverty and face racism, through hard work, finding sustenance and strength in their own cultures (one is reminded of Gayatri Spivak's ideas of strategic essentialism as noted by some postcolonial critics), they have somehow managed to sustain themselves while giving their children a better future.

In the reconfiguration of identity for the diasporic Indian woman in a postcolonial space, the identity of the 'authentic' Indian self is produced sometimes by the Indian community and sometimes by the dominant community as in England, where Indians and Pakistanis and Bangladeshis are all seen as enforcing oppressive 'arranged marriages' due to the Asian patriarchy's backwardness. This reconfiguration occurs because the Indians are situated in a nation state that pride itself on having a homogenous national identity; such nation-states, however also celebrate diversity and multiculturalism. Thus the new space of empowerment, a hybrid space, is where new cultural ideas, forms, and identities are being articulated.

A very frightening sense of reality and acculturation problem occurs in Alex Pillai's *Flight* (1996, 74 minutes). Set in the Bengali community of Accrington and Manchester, it is the story of a 17-year-old girl and her relationship with her father. Based upon a true story that the writer Tanika Gupta came across while acting as a volunteer in a women's refuge home, it tells the story of Sikha, a young Bengali Hindu girl who is the oldest daughter in a very patriarchal family. Sikha is her father's favourite daughter, and he expects her to do what he decided: study at the university to become a doctor. Baba's faith in Sikha is suddenly spoilt, as she is found in a deserted factory together with her Muslim boyfriend Imran. Baba feels that Sikha has betrayed him and has Anil, a relative to the family, to beat her up, then locks her in her room and forbids her to visit school. Sikha's mother cannot argue her husband but takes a brave step when she helps her to escape to a new life of her own. Sikha travels to London and finds shelter in a women's refuge. Little does she suspect that her father's need to contain and frustrate her life is not yet over. Baba wants her daughter back at any cost and asks Anil to trace her. When Sikha wants her freedom, the Bounty Hunter wants her dead. This controversial film casts an unforgiving eye over the subject of mixed race relationships and arranged marriages within the Indian community.

Shakeela Tarannum Mann's debut feature *A Quiet Desperation* (2001) shines a light upon the London based Indian community rarely seen on-screen. Shammi is a wanderer forced to return home to Southall in West London after the death of his brother. His time away has left his friends and family with mixed emotions about his return. Shammi is haunted by the memories of the woman he loved and lost. Thrown into an already volatile situation, he is forced to either face up to his history or to keep running. This tale of one man's journey through a quasi-deserted city and past provides a rare insight into a little known London community.

Udayan Prasad deftly captures the role of religious fundamentalism and identity politics in the South Asian context in Britain in his film *Brothers in Trouble* (1996, 102 minutes) In the mid-1960s, scores of refugees from the Indian subcontinent illegally came to England looking for a better life and found themselves living the very lives they sought to escape. This British drama, chronicles the daily existence of one household of these illegal refugees. Udayan

Prasad's *My Son the Fanatic* (1999, 87 minutes) also deals with issues of inter-generational strife and religious fundamentalism.

Crossover Films: Hollywood, Bollywood, and Beyond

In 1994, Gurinder Chadha's *Bhaji on the Beach* was released in the United Kingdom on five prints on the basis that it was a small, sweet film but with no box office expectations. It sold out for weeks and by public demand returned to multiplexes after playing in art houses. But there was still little recognition by the British film industry of its wider potential. Gurinder was made to feel that it was an 'Asian film' that only Asian audiences would enjoy. In the meantime she had ventured out to America and made a film on the multicultural context of Los Angeles in a film called *What's Cooking?* (2000). Two years later, when *Bend It Like Beckham* was released on more than 450 prints across the UK, it grossed over 2 million pounds at the box office in its first weekend. Made with British finance, there was never any doubt that this was a 'British film' though it featured a British Asian family at its centre. As expressed to Cameron Cook, her reason for directing the film went as follows:

> *Bend It Like Beckham* is my most autobiographical film …. When I wanted to be a filmmaker, he (Dad) knew it would scare away prospective husbands working as pharmacists in Birmingham, but inside he loved the idea of his daughter documenting our community. Fast Forward to the World Cup in 1998. My husband Paul and I go to our local pub and scream and cheer for the England team along with men, women, kids, black, white, Asian – the entire country has gone mad. Our star player David Beckham stands out because he's turned the idea of the traditional macho soccer player on its head. Little boys want to play like him, women (and lots of men!) want to snatch him away from his wife Posh Spice and take him home to their families, everyone agrees he's an amazing player and he looks gorgeous in a sarong. It hits me that I want to take this world and stick a young Indian girl right in the centre of it because it's the last thing anyone would expect of her (or me). I decide then to make a film combining the English passion for football with the Indian passion for marriage.

The film ends with the idea that while all may not be right with the world, globalization will soon bend it just right. As she stated in the July 2002 issue of the British Council newsletter *Connecting*:

In the time between *Bhaji on the Beach* and *Bend It Like Beckham* I haven't changed, and my sensibilities and reasons for making films haven't changed, but the British audience's appetite for films about Britain has. I think in the same way Indian audiences have changed. There is now a tremendous interest in India about how different Indian communities throughout the world live .... (9)

According to the director herself, when she attended screenings of *Bend It Like Beckham* around the United Kingdom, she had the fortune to sit with the audience members of all cultural backgrounds and generations who recognized the characters in the film and the England that is presented as their own. The audience reactions reconfirmed in her that British audiences identify with characters regardless of their cultural background.

With the success of *Bend It Like Beckham,* Gurinder Chadha ventured into another 'crossover film' called *Bride and Prejudice – A Bollywood Musical* (2003). Borrowing the story from Jane Austen's *Pride and Prejudice,* she directed this Bollywood-style retelling of Austen's classic tale of marriage and manners, transplanted to modern-day India, England and America, with lavish musical spectacle. Mixing up both the cultures in terms of the story and the filmmaking, Gurinder tried to attract mainstream audiences from both the worlds stating that the music of the film 'is a mix of *West Side Story, Fiddler on the Roof, Grease* and also Hindi film music'. Incidentally she also had a new musical in mind entitled *Bollywood Untitled* where she got Zoya Akhtar to write the lyrics.

Hybridity Issues Seen from Outside

In the sub-genre of diasporic cinema about the immigrant experience and the meeting of cultures, we also find several offerings made by outsiders – people not of Indian origin or descent. Obviously, the South Asian presence in England must be significant enough for filmmakers who are not from the subcontinent to make films about Indians and Pakistanis abroad. Probably one of the first films to focus on the issue was Peter Smith's *A Private Enterprise* (1974, 78 minutes). It could be the first British Asian Film (or of Large British Asian Representation), which was produced by the British Film Institute. Gathering as it was made during the mass migration of South Asians into Britain, they produced this film for those who found it difficult in adapting to

Britain. So it is a portrayal of an Asian immigrant experience, dealing with issues of integration, against the backdrop of industrial Birmingham. Dilip Hiro wrote the script.

In 1986, British director Ronald Neame made *Foreign Body* (111 minutes) that chronicles the adventures of Ram Das who moved to England after losing his job in India. He winds up pretending to be a doctor after he sees a pretty girl on the street who has been hurt. Then he takes the charade even further when he rents an office and treats many other patients including the Prime Minister. Whether he will win the girl and whether she will ever find out his secret is what the rest of the film is about.

We often see a conflict understood as typical within South Asian Muslim families of the backward Muslim father and his modern advanced younger son or daughter who seeks the freedoms inherent in British liberal society. *East is East* (2000, 98 minutes) by Damien O'Donnell is one such film. Written by Ayub Khan Din originally as a hilarious play script, it is based on his own growing years in Salford in the north of England and the consequences of his father's wish to bring up his children as 'good Muslims'. *East is East* is a delightful slapstick comedy, albeit occasionally overdone. Set in England in 1971, it presents a conservative Muslim immigrant father in England who is in constant conflict with his mixed-race children, seven of them, born to his liberal English wife. Since the story-time is 1971, in the background several news items announce India's dismembering of Pakistan. When the Indian army marches victoriously into Dhaka, Khan commiserates with his cronies, mouthing the Paki Punjabi contempt for the Bengali babu. Though the clichéd culture clash formula is repeated over and over again, praises for Om Puri in the role of George Khan had been pouring in from all quarters, with the actor himself confiding to the *New York Times* interviewer that he considered that role the richest he has had in the English-speaking cinema.

Another interesting film which projects the outsider's point of view is *West is West* (2010) directed by Andy DeEmmony. Written by Ayub Khan-Din, it is a sort of sequel to the earlier movie and the story is set in 1976 in Manchester, north of England. The claustrophobically cohesive and desperately dysfunctional Khan family continues to struggle for survival. Sajid, the youngest Khan, is deep in pubescent crisis under heavy assault both from his father's tyrannical insistence on Pakistani traditions, and from the fierce racist bullies in the schoolyard. Isolated and bored, he resorts to bunking off school and shoplifting useless items to spice up his dull and lonely little life. In a last attempt to make a good son of him, his father decides to pack him off to family in the Punjab. But although resolved to teach Sajid a lesson, the tables are turned on George when he comes face to face with his own transgressions, and realizes that it is he himself who has much to learn.

My Beautiful Laundrette (1986), which was scripted by Hanif Kureishi and directed by Stephen Frears, is set within the Asian community in south London. It is an unusual story, taking a look at an ethnic community concerned with identity and entrepreneurial spirit during the harsh social conditions and the rampant exploitation that is a direct result often of years under Margaret Thatcher. The film breaks racial stereotypes and fearlessly portrays Asians as real, though not always compassionate people. The film certainly did not endear Kureishi to the South Asian community in England. Dubbed as the vanguard of the British New Wave, this of course is exactly the sort of reaction that Kureishi delighted in. One of his aims was to subvert the trend of the 'polite, controlled', English movie, represented by films like *A Passage to India, Brideshead Revisited,* and *Jewel in the Crown.* He definitely created a London that some audiences are shocked to discover resembling their conception of a third world country rather than the genteel land of crumpets and afternoon tea.

Thus it is not surprising that Kureishi opens *Samie and Rosie Get Laid* (1987) directed by Stephen Frears, with scenes of rioting in East London. The story tells of how an elderly black woman is killed by the police while they are trying to arrest her son, and all hell breaks loose. 'The idea for the film started with the image of a man walking down the road carrying a suitcase and the streets were burning', explained Kureishi. The script, however, is a veritable maze of plots and subplots, a characteristic that has become a trademark of his style. 'I don't want my films to be boring! Unlike *My Beautiful Laundrette,* however, *Sammy and Rosie Get Laid* encompasses a wider range of ethnic groups, not just the Pakistani or Indian community'. Pakistani or subcontinent characters predominate because of the author's own Pakistani heritage, 'But this also has to do with the fact that these films are about people who are excluded, people who are marginalized, and people who aren't always in the centre of British films', explained Kureishi. Thus the multiracial mix of characters give the film a vibrancy that is quite unique in British film.

No More Diaspora: Entering the Mainstream and at par with the World

An interesting phenomenon in the evolution of Indian diasporic cinema in Britain is that as time goes on and the idea of transnationalism becomes even more important, we find directors moving away from their binaries of depicting 'us' vs. 'them' or stories seeped in nostalgia of 'homeland'. As with 'crossover' cinema, they move towards entertaining the masses with popular themes and stories that can no longer be labelled as 'diasporic'. Since the early 1990s, the project of modernization that has proceeded hand in hand with processes of globalization and the opening up of the market in India and a more globally mobile middle class, the demarcation of Indian films made in the diaspora on the one hand and Bollywood films with the diaspora as a theme on the other and distinctions begin to blur. As E. Anna Claydon rightly states:

> ... the hybridity of contemporary British cinema is not simply a matter of cross-cultural representation or fulfilling the 'ethnic minority' criteria by which the Arts Council seem to solely define 'diversity' in recent times but that it is, like all art, the complex combination of the small details which belong to many homes and which adapt to create another. That, in a sense, contemporary British cinema is inherently driven by diasporic and intertextual sensibilities which persistently allude to something lost, 'home-like', in the past. (26)

Documentaries or Non-Fiction Films/Videos

Apart from full-length features and short films, there are innumerable documentaries that also focus upon the diasporic Indian's journey from marginalization to assimilation. The range and subject of such documentaries is mind-boggling. In this category both renowned directors as well as amateur Indian artists who are at the forefront of redefining western culture refuse to be typified, and want to make their work out of the experience of displacement. As mentioned earlier Indian diasporic documentaries can be divided under several sub-headings for discussion.

Acculturation, Identity Politics, and Its Challenges

In 'Frontlines and Backyards: The Terms of Change', Stuart Hall talks about the contrary position occupied by the young black British. According to Hall, black identity is organized around its own sense of frontlines and backyards. On the one hand, there was racial deprivation and victimization. On the other, eroticization and stylization of the black body had conferred upon it the status of an object of desire. Public visibility at the frontlines of representation did not ensure much clout in the backrooms of real power (129). The Indian diasporic filmmaker also probably understands the token status he or she enjoys within the industry. They are able to score brownie points only by adopting an exploitative relationship to their own culture, by enthusiastically embracing the role of a culture vulture. They have to use in the interest of the centre the skills that they have inherited and learnt at the margins. This is partly what prompts them to make documentaries of their 'Asianness' – which, while it does constitute a counter-narrative to the exoticism, is also a betrayal at the personal and political level. Even when they are reconstructing images on their own terms, they do not really empower the community in any way. Some again lose their radical edge due to the speed with which they are embraced by the mainstream.

Gurinder Chadha's 13-minutes-film *What Do You Call An Indian Woman Who's Funny?* looks at four Indian women cabaret performers to explore who sets the agenda for comedy. Is it culturally specific or can anyone enjoy a joke regardless of race/ethnicity? With hilarious performance clips, this film questions what type of humour 'makes it' onto television and to mainstream audiences.

Another very significant area of Indian diasporic films is those that explore bonds through music. Amidst the plethora of themes, one common area that has drawn the attention of several filmmakers is bhangra, the folk music of Punjab, which has come to acquire new political and cultural resonance for the South Asian diaspora. As in the United States and Canada, bhangra has also gripped the non-resident Indians in the United Kingdom. This new bhangra is very much an immigrant music, incorporating the music played in decaying English industrial cities and Trinidadian neighbourhoods, and has become a cultural marker for second generation diasporic citizens of the country. If the immigrants hadn't come to the United Kingdom, this music would not have been created. As Sadie O observes in *SF Weekly* in 1995:

> Ever since Gandhi, Britons have been embracing certain aspects of East Indian culture (like Vindaloo and Bhangra) with relish (or possibly chutney). Like Vindaloo, Bhangra has passed through the collective digestive tract of the United Kingdom and emerged profoundly changed. Unlike Vindaloo, bhangra will only keep you up all night in order to dance.

This celebratory music of Punjabi farmers transformed by young Britishers of Asian origin has hit the United Kingdom in an explosive way. Some critics see the westernized bhangra scene in Britain as derivative because it is still dependent on music from the subcontinent. Leaving aside the debate whether bhangra in its hybrid forms enriches or diminishes the popular Indian dance form, I will now focus on a couple of documentaries that use the bhangra to show the acculturation process in Britain. The first documentary is by the well-known director Gurinder Chadha who uses this music as a backdrop in her exploration of various notions of Britishness through the eyes of English, Scottish, Irish, and Welsh Asians in *I'm British But ...*, (1990, 30 minutes) thus uncovering a defiant popular culture. It is a witty and perceptive short film dealing with the South Asians in Britain, which looks at what it means to be British and Asian.

Bhangra Jig directed by Pratibha Parmar (1991, 4 minutes) was originally commissioned by Channel 4 to celebrate Glasgow as the European cultural capital. In this short film Pratibha Parmar continues to explore the Asian-Western encounter with a music video. A Scottish Asian woman, in a leather jacket and a tartan skirt walks through superimposed images of Glaswegian architecture, statues and the inside of a Mosque dome whilst these images are cut with young people dancing to a Bhangra soundtrack. In both images and sound Scotland meets Asia in this absorbing testimony to a multicultural Britain.

These different explorations therefore lead us to a better understanding of how the Bhangra, in a mix of the old and the new, becomes symbolic of universal cultural transformation for new generations and how the British cultural scenario is being constantly remixed into newer forms with every passing day. It also explains how a specifically diasporic cultural politics of nostalgia thus ironically has resulted in a transnational impact. As Ashley Dawson rightly points out, this cultural studies model should not be confused with the dominant sociological approaches of the day, which represents Asian youths as trapped in an 'identity crisis' that robbed them of agency. Instead, the styles developed within subcultures should be seen as part of a symbolic repertoire through which young people attempt to win space, in both a literal and figurative sense, in relation to their double articulation.

Coming to more cultural concerns, in Britain, Sangeeta Datta's documentary *In Search of Durga* (2000) tries to capture the ethos of the Bengali Indian diaspora in UK through their most important religious festival, the Durga puja which is always celebrated with fervour. With a large Bengali community in London, there are eight separate Durga puja festivals in the city. This film is shot in the largest Durga Puja festival in London (Kings Cross) where 1,500 people come together. The older generation celebrates with nostalgia and devotion, the younger kids find fascinating myths and colorful rituals. The second generation has brought with them a wider mix of participants from mainstream white and other communities. Datta tries to analyse how people so far away from home relate to the myth and practice of Durga.

Recreating History and Facts

Third world filmmakers in Britain have increasingly confronted the need to construct alternative histories to those of the dominant culture in order to combat the appropriation and oppression of marginalized cultures. They have created narratives that actively confront the dominant culture's attempt to destroy and/or neutralize these marginalized cultures through the destruction or appropriation of the collective history. In Gurinder Chadha's *Acting Our Age* (1993, 30 minutes) with the filmmaker's assistance, the residents of a home for British South Asian elderly shoot their own video. They interview a wide range of subjects – from people on the street to a member of the Parliament which reveal generational attitudes, cross-cultural values, and everyday problems faced by older, often neglected citizens. Ultimately, with passion and dignity, they prove that it is never too late to take matters into your own hands.

A serious documentary, Pratibha Parmar's *The Colour of Britain* (1994, 50 minutes, Channel 4), shows how alternative ways of seeing Britain, as a place of crossings, of cultures in movement, have emerged out of imaginative and challenging developments in theatre, dance, music, and the visual arts. It is a frank and for sometime considered as a controversial film, where internationally renowned artists (such as sculptor Anish Kapoor, choreographer Shobana Jeyasingh, and theatre director Jatinder Verma) talk about their role as artists who inhabit many different cultural spaces and who refuse to be ghettoized on grounds of their ethnicity. The visions, values and images of their work shock us with their brilliance while at the same time illustrate their different views on questions of identity and representation. Again, *A Brimful of Asia* (1998, 24 minutes) is about the explosion of second generation Asian talent in mainstream British culture and features musicians Talvin Singh, Asian Dub Foundation and Cornershop as well as fashion designers and writers. It offers a fascinating guide to Asian culture successfully illustrating the wealth of intelligence, energy and influence being exhibited by young British Asians.

Another documentary full of passion and grit is Pratibha's *Sari Red* (1988, 11 minutes) made in memory of Kalbinder Kaur Hayre, a young Indian woman killed by three young white men in 1985 in a racist attack in England. It eloquently examines the effect of the ever-present threat of violence upon the lives of Asian women in both private and public spheres. In this moving visual presentation, the title refers to red, the colour of blood spilt and the red of the sari, symbolizing sensuality and intimacy between Asian women. Told with intense personal anger, the film is expressive and full of beautiful and haunting images. It also gives keen insight into the often-unarticulated colonial legacy of a racially arrogant society. There have been so many racist murders in England and sometimes these just become part of the statistics. So, Pratibha wanted to make a video which would rescue this brave young woman from being yet another statistic and evoke her life, her dreams and her potential. In the interview given to Lloyd Wong she mentions that at the Flaherty Documentary Seminars in New York when a white man criticized the film for having no universality for him, she was unperturbed:

> For me, I was unable to respond to that whole notion of how *Sari Red* didn't have a universal resonance by actually feeling much more confident in what I was doing. That was his problem that he could not find an access point into it, and I said so to him. I said I thought that he had to go away and do some work on himself and educate himself because I wasn't going to do it for him. (12)

To mark the 50th anniversary of the Independence of India and Pakistan, Sarbjit Ghattaura made a wonderful documentary called *Music, Politics or Culture?* This 1997 film celebrates the Asian influence on popular culture in Britain. It shows how the 'fusion' of Britain and Asian cultures brings in new vitality and colour to music, fashion, cinema, language, literature, food, art, sport, and comedy. Highlighting the vitality of contemporary relations and the respect and affection – often irreverent – between the people of Britain and the subcontinent, it charts the success of British Asian businessmen and their contribution to the British economy.

Reality Bites: Queer Issues

The term 'queer' is controversial even within the lesbian/gay/bisexual/transgender community, but has been reclaimed as a positive term by the community, encompassing its diversity at large.

Pratibha Parmar, who has made several documentaries on gay and lesbian issues, is aware that identity, which is not a fixed construct for all diasporic people, is even more complicated for queer people. In an interview published in *Fuse* in 1990 she tells Lloyd Wong:

> The question is about the multiplicity of the identities we inhabit as lesbian and gay people of colour, who are involved both politically and culturally with anti-racist movements and then involved in the actual lesbian and gay movement too .... Culture isn't static .... I don't want to go wholesale back to the culture that we 'come from', because I think there are problems too within our own cultures. As lesbians and gays within the South Asian communities we are often contradictorily positioned vis-à-vis our families and our communities but at the same time we have to experience the racism of the predominantly white lesbian and gay movements and so we are marginalized amongst that community. (10)

Pratibha Parmar's life as a South Asian lesbian filmmaker puts her out of the mainstream, but her point of view is everything but hidden in her films. She manipulates the traditional male gaze of films, and uses her characters to shape new gazes. She employs the 'look back' of the others looking back on the viewer to deobjectify her characters and the stereotypes they evoke. *Khush* (1991, 24 minutes) deals with the blissful intricacies of being queer and of colour in the United States and Britain. 'Khush' means ecstatic pleasure in Urdu. For South Asian lesbians and gay men in Britain and India, the term captures the blissful intricacies of being queer and of colour. Inspiring testimonies bridge geographical differences to locate shared experiences of isolation and exoticization but also the unremitting joys and solidarity of being 'khush'.

Parmar's *Double the Trouble Twice the Fun* (1992, 24 minutes) is another interesting documentary on queer experience. 'We're crippled and queer, we've always been here ...' sings the acapella group, The Tokens, with saucy signing, taking queer reclamation into yet another dimension. 'We all need mirrors', begins the narrator of the documentary. 'Some of us are shy of mirrors, some of us have never had them', explains Indian writer Firdaus Kanga, who sets out to find a mirror image and gains 'access to himself'. Pratibha Parmar's direction is dynamic, powerful and witty, dealing with a rich range of disabilities without guilt induction or patronage. The Black poet who asserts he would rather die than have someone else make decisions for him is only one of the strong, self-determined voices in the programme. The film-noirish blue on the floating signer is effective, while the drama sequence featuring Nabil Shaban seducing another disabled man is utterly gripping and tender and begins to confront notions of the body beautiful and the tyrannies of perfection.

There are also certain films that evolve around the question of identity in more personal and specific terms. As children of migrants, the question of identity can be a complicated one. So often, the premise of the question assumes specific ideas about culture, geography, nationalism, sexuality and identity as being a seamless entity that is perfectly packaged without wrinkles or contradictions. Pratibha Parmar's interest in documentaries arose from portraying profile artists who through the languages of photography and the written word articulate their new experiences. Thus, in accordance with her declarations, Parmar made two documentaries focusing upon self-representation that would effectively negotiate the history of exoticism. In *Flesh and Paper* (1990, 24 minutes), Pratibha documents writer Suniti Namjoshi, who revisions South Asian mythology into a contemporary lesbian sexuality. This moving and powerful portrait of a unique and brave woman weaves Namjoshi's life and writings into a sensual tapestry. Shot on location in Devon, England as well as at the Old Palace in India, the film includes interviews with young Indo-British lesbians, expressive readings and choreographed dance segments. Sharing her life with fellow writer and poet Gillian Hanscombe, Namjoshi's passionate correspondence with her love reflects the intimacy and detail of this meditative piece. With great visual beauty and lyricism, *Flesh and Paper*, captures the spirit of Namjoshi's poetry in an evocative, multi-layered way.

Towards Artistic Expressions

The debate between form and content and the balance of both has been an issue that is discussed over and over again relating to documentary films. Though documentaries about the Indian diaspora are primarily issue-based, usually the thematic content becomes more significant. Nevertheless, there are some filmmakers who still try to present their views as artistically as possible. Pratibha Parmar's *Memsahib Rita* (1994, 20 minutes) is an unusual fictional short, studded with fantasy and magical realism and with some surprising answers too. In the film Shanti's face is brown and painfully Indian, even though her mother was a beautiful white woman. The film explores whether Shanti survives in London's East End, with the ugliness of racism around her and the bitter memories of a mother who committed suicide, unable to take the pressures of an interracial marriage. Another 24-minute monologue performed by Nina Wadia that Pratibha directed is entitled *Sita Gita* (2000).

Breaking Stereotypes

As in feature films, there are also several documentaries that are not thematically connected to the Indian diaspora *per se*. It seems that after making a few films on the diaspora, each of these directors feel that the rite of passage has been completed and they are now free to make films on whatever topic that interests them. They seem to be keen to shed off the label of diasporic filmmaker from their backs once and venture into ordinary and mainstream issues. It helps them to do away with labels. Udayan Prasad, for instance, who directed such engrossing films on the plight of the Pakistani immigrants in the midlands of the United Kingdom as *My Son the Fanatic, Brothers in Trouble,* also has to his credit several short films and documentaries on the life of Rembrandt or Samuel Johnson. In an interview given to me in 2001, Prasad specifically mentioned that he does not want to be labelled as an immigrant diasporic director.

Pratibha Parmar has made several documentaries relating to the plight of women, about female genital mutilation in Africa (*Warrior Marks*), about a disabled midwife who has pioneered facilities for pregnant disabled women in Liverpool (*One More Push*), about feminism in popular culture (*The Righteous Babes*), current affairs item about gay parenting (*Fostering and Adoption*), the role of African-American women in the civil rights movement (*A Place of Rage*) and about religious attitudes towards disabled people (*Taboo*).

To conclude we might say that like in the United States and Canada, the nature of Indian diasporic cinema in Britain is also changing rapidly over the years. A common tone that binds most Indian diasporic films is their searing honesty that we would scarcely find in Indian cinema today. In spite of the diverse themes and techniques used in their modes of presentation, the one unifying factor of all these films is that they have been able to do away with the negative images of migrants that are portrayed in the mainstream media. Though many recent diasporic films have settled upon a number of comfortable stereotypes, there are many others that look beyond these images to representations that transcend the homogeneous notions and stereotypes of the Indian diaspora. This point serves as a tool, by its very existence, to recognize the heterogeneity within the Indian diasporas, i.e. the recognition of difference within, as opposed to unified 'imagined communities'. But again, one has to keep it in mind that diasporic identity problems are inextricably bound up with questions of globalization. As E.A. Claydon rightly points out, 'the cinema which Britain has produced has always been more or less of a national cinema, it has been Imperial, post-Imperial and, as postmodernism fragments identification with anything other than an American, again false, national identity, it becomes post-national' (28).

References

Alessandrini, Anthony C. '"My Heart's Indian for All That": Bollywood Film between Home and Diaspora'. *Diaspora* 10.3 (2001): 315–340.

Appadurai, Arjun. *Modernity at Large: Cultural Dimensions of Globalization.* Minneapolis: University of Minnesota Press, 1996.

Chadha, Gurinder. *Bend it Like Beckham – Landmark Theatre.* Web 5 July 2014. <http://www.landmarktheatres.com/mn/benditlikebeckham.html>.

Claydon, E.A. 'British South Asian Cinema and Identity I "Nostalgia in the Post-National: Contemporary British Cinema and the South-Asian Diaspora"'. *SACS* 2.1 (July 2012): 26–38.

Cook, Cameron. 'From the Mind of ... Gurinder Chadha'. Blog. 29 November 2006. Web 5 July 2014. <http://www.foxsearchlight.com/post/660/from-the-mind-of-gurinder-chadha/>.

Hall, Stuart and Paul du Gay. 'Introduction: Who Needs "Identity"?' *Questions of Cultural Identity.* (eds) Hall and du Gay. London: Sage Publications, 1996. 3–17.

Hall, Stuart. 'Ethnicity: Identity and Difference'. *Radical America* 23.4 (1989): 9–20.

———. 'Frontlines and Backyards: The Terms of Change'. 1997. *Black British Culture and Society: A Text Reader.* (ed.) Kwesi Owusu. London and New York: Routledge, 2000. 135–139.

Jungblut, Christiane and Wera Reusch. 'Identities, Passions and Commitments: An Interview with the British Filmmaker Pratibha Parmar'. *Lola Press.* Web 12 July 2013. <http://www.lolapress.org/artenglish/parme12.htm>.

Kureishi, Hanif. *Samie and Rosie Get Laid: The Script and the Diary.* London: Faber, 1988.

O, Sadie. *SF Weekly.* Web 5 July 2014. <http://sadieo.ucsf.edu/music/bhangra.html>.

Ong, Aihwa. *Flexible Citizenship: The Cultural Logics of Transnationality.* Durham: Duke University Press, 1999.

Parmar, Pratibha. 'Hateful Contraries: Media Images of Asian Women'. *Ten* 8.16 (1984): 70–78.

Syal, Meera. 'Goodness Gracious Meera!' *Connecting (British Council News from East India)* (April 2003): 8–9.

Wong, Lloyd. 'Fuck You: This is Our Home! Claiming South Asian Identity in Britain'. *Fuse* (Summer 1990): 10–15.

Chapter 12

Hybridity, Humour, and Resistance

The Case of Meera Syal MBE and the British Asian Diaspora

VIMAL MOHAN JOHN AND AYSHA IQBAL VISWAMOHAN

'Diaspora' has been theorized prominently since the 1990s as a displacement of individuals and communities from the 'homes' through exile and migration and their subsequent anchoring in host communities and countries. Considering the implications of dual national and cultural identities, the term itself has served the purpose of forcing a rethinking of ideas of nationhood, borders, exclusions and challenges to identity. In more recent discourses, as Sabo (2012) points out, there is a shift from the notion of 'diaspora as an alternative paradigm for the nation' and from 'a preoccupation with the construction of diasporic identities as culturally hybrid, to the idea that diaspora entails lived and embodied experiences of diasporic subjects and communities, which are predicated on factors such as class, race, ethnicity, age, gender, and sexuality' (2).

In 'Another Kind of British' (2001), Cary Rajinder Sawhney talked about an emerging spate of British films with Asian themes that developed their own distinctive identity and aesthetics of hybridity, notable among which were their homage to Hindi films in their use of song and dance elements and narrative structure. She pointed out how the emergence of this new class of films reflected not only the creative innovation of their cast and crew, 'who (were) *simultaneously British and Asian*, but also a gradual desegregation of the British society, which (was) slowly forgetting its colonial past (58, emphasis added). Meanwhile, one of the more prominent voices in British-Asian filmmaking circles, Director Gurinder Chadha has noted the change in attitudes between the release of her first film, *Bhaji on the Beach* (1994), and her third, *Bend it Like Beckham* (2002): saying 'People are much more aware of difference, what was once foreign is now familiar' (BFI interview) At the same time, these films arguably subvert prominent Asian archetypes. Chadha's own *Bhaji on the Beach* is a story of a group of Asian women, all striking different from each other. They are women who are tired of working their drab corner shops, women who love flirting with British boys and women who are in love with men outside their class and race – all toppling the idea of the demure, passive Asian woman. Even before Chadha put the trend on the map, Harwant Bains penned *Wild West* (1992) where he showed a bunch of British-Asian boys forming a club of country-and-western lovers.

Whether or not these films adopt an 'anti-ethnic, "feel good fare"' very consciously is a matter of debate. However, as Ahmed Jamal points out, Asian filmmakers were beginning to occupy a position of 'reacting, of feeling strongly about depicting the reality of (their) experiences and resisting what has been imposed on (them)' (quoted in Sawhney 58). In *Indian Popular Cinema: A Narrative of Cultural Change* (1998) Dissanayake and Gokulsingh also further the case of the synergy between British-Asian films and their relationship with (for instance, through homages) the cinematic tradition of their original 'homeland'. Arguably then, British-Asian films since the 1990s exhibit a sense of hybridity that accommodates a spectrum of cultural experiences and as Chadha's own case points out, they describe their work in terms of a broader, more international perspective. This phenomenon is significantly, not just restricted to the filmmaking environment. Case in point is the extremely popular sketch comedy *Good Gracious Me!*, that originally aired on BBC's Radio 4 from 1996–1998 and was later made for television from 1998–2001. The show's primary cast were mostly British-Indian actors including Sanjeev Bhaskar, Nina Wadia, Kulvinder Ghir, and Meera Syal. The show was interestingly subversive in that it explored issues of both confrontation and assimilation of British and Asian cultures, tradition and modernity, and was equally irreverent of stereotypes from both cultures.

In 'Foreign Accents: Notes upon My Return to the Diaspora' (2002) Sharmila Sen asks a series of questions concerning our understandings of the term 'hybrid', starting with identifying and problematizing hybridity and ending with 'Are all hybridities, to put it bluntly, built equal? How useful is it to read Shani Mootoo, Meera Syal, Jhumpa Lahiri, and Anita Desai as all part of the South Asian diaspora?' (8). The paper is an attempt to answer some of these questions with respect to the curious case of Meera Syal MBE. Meeral Syal was also one of the writers of the show (as well as a star in it). The show could very well resonate with Syal's own experiences as a second generation Asian living in Britain. Syal attained prominence as a British comedian, writer, actress, journalist, and singer, among many other roles. Following *Goodness Gracious Me!*, Syal also starred in the hugely popular *The Kumars at No. 42*, which also explored similar themes as *Goodness*.

While Syal was born in Wolverhampton and grew up in a small West Midlands mining village, her parents were Punjab-born immigrants. Her experience of growing up in Essington here (of belonging to the only Asian family in a mostly white village) influenced her profoundly and was something which she would use later as a backdrop to her first novel, *Anita and Me* (1996). After reading English and Drama at Manchester University, she started her career by penning the script for *My Sister Wife*, a television series made for the BBC followed by the script for *Bhaji on the Beach* produced by Channel 4 and directed by Gurinder Chadha (of *Bend it Like Bechkam* fame).

Bhaji is also Chadha's first feature film. Penned by Syal, the film's script ensures the work is a piece of social realism coated in smart, comic presentation. Like her first novel *Anita and Me,* the film explores a narrative in which three generations of middle class, working women navigate the terrains of England. They take a pleasure trip from Birmingham to the working class, seaside retreat of Blackpool. Full of comic subplots and livid confrontations, the film (considered a feminist text), ultimately explores how Asian women experience and navigate the physical and experiential host country. The metaphor of travel has frequently been used to describe the diasporic experience of migration, tourism, pilgrimage and exile (Clifford 6.) Stuart Hall also talks about defining cultural identities through a process of continuous 'positioning' that topples ideas of cultural essence and fixed identities (237) while

Appadurai mentions models for circulating cultures through flows and cascades (*Modernity at Large*) and these are all viable frameworks to approach the text of *Bhaji*.

The characters in the film comprise a couple of 'aunties' wearing sarees; traditional, parochial and moralizing, a stereotypically 'smart' Indian girl, the pride of her community (*but pregnant from her Black boyfriend*), a couple of teen girls loudly playing their boom boxes (reminiscent of Harwant Bains' *Wild West*, referenced earlier) and gossiping about British boys and the organizer of the trip itself, Simi – a passionate feminist, who while deeply connected to the Asian community is highly critical of some of its value systems. As can be observed, the film offers fertile ground for playing out feminist politics as well as politics of race. However, as Leonard Quart observes, '(*Bhaji*) is a feminist film which makes its political points more through seductive humour than through polemics .... Still, the film's prime interest does not lie in illuminating the women's internal states or psyches, but in providing a nuanced perspective on their feelings about ethnicity and gender' (49). Part of the charm in *Bhaji*, attributable in no little measure to Syal's script, is that it refuses to sentimentalize Asian/Indian 'culture'. Chadha doesn't dwell on racist issues. When it is revealed that Hashida has a Black boyfriend and is pregnant, the film captures the racism and parochialism inherent in both communities (Asian and British) simultaneously and brilliantly. Though the revelatory scene happens in a cafe frequented by the working-classes in Blackpool, we see the *proprietress* screaming racist abuse at Pushpa for bringing her own food into the cafe, while she herself rages against Hasida, lamenting that England has cost the (British-Asian) community their children.

In *Bhaji*, both the British and the British-Asian are intolerant and yet funny in equal measure. The film's script refuses to make a distinction between the oppressed and oppressors. This hybrid that permeates the film is helped along by its use of music; a hybrid mix of Bhangra, English and Indian pop songs. 'Bhangra music's ability to fuse cultures (e.g. in *Bhaji on the Beach* Chadha takes Cliff Richard's "Summer Holiday" and rewrites the lyrics in Punjabi, and then has a bhangra band remix the music) is a perfect reinforcement of the film's commitment to the idea that Asians must create a new identity in England. It's not assimilation or, obviously, traditional immigrant culture that Chadha holds out as an answer, but a fluid, open, bilingual identity that represents for her the new England. For Chadha, "difference is celebratory", but not exclusive' (Quart 49).

Speaking of representing diasporic spaces in contemporary British films, Ciecko (1999) argues how Asian identities and Black identities may find points of overlap, 'presenting images and narratives authored by hybrid diasporic subjects working in the "United Kingdom" (68) ultimately arguing how a film like *Bhaji on the Beach* might constitute a "third cinema", grounded in an understanding of the dialectical relationship between social existence and cultural practice' (70).

One of the ways in which *Bhaji* achieves its subversiveness is through its deployment of pop culture references and celebration of a carnivalesque mode. This is especially important considering the resonance 'carnival' has for African and Asian cultures where the carnival as a practice may strongly be linked to street festivals, uprisings and activism simultaneously. As Ciecko points out, 'carnival' with reference to contemporary British cinema 'needs to acknowledge its complicated connection to the carnival as 'event' in Britain-in terms of diasporic Afro-Caribbean (and South Asian) culture' (76). Thus, the wonderfully quirky film that is *Bhaji* takes its audience on a trip where a South Asian women's community take a road trip almost a la mode Ridley Scott's *Thelma and Louise* (1991). Their end is to escape the oppressive household of Birmingham, a landscape of confinement, maleness and general ennui and disenchantment; seeking escape and freedom in the form of pubs, candyfloss, and even strip shows. The film ends with an erosion of the sense of *Indianness* the community felt it originally had, culminating in a comic excursion and intelligent interrogation of British-Asian identities in England, setting the scene for further films that explored the idea (*East is East, Bend it Like Beckham*).

The script for *Bhaji* was followed by Syal's first novel, *Anita and Me* (1996) and was shortlisted for the *Guardian* fiction prize and won the Betty Trask Award. Autobiographical by her own admission,[1] the novel (which was later adapted into a film) relates the story of Meena Kumar, a little British-Asian girl trying to mediate the cultural influences of her white school friends and her traditional Indian roots at home. In the novel, Meena is shown growing up in Tollington, (a fictional mining village resembling

Essington) in the 1970s. However, as opposed to many diasporic writings, Syal's Meera feels ambivalence towards her British identity. As James Procter (2002) points out, '... it reveals an affection for the local village community, rather than the tropes transatlantic travel preferred by writers such as Salman Rushdie and V.S. Naipaul. The nearest Meena gets to London is on her monopoly board ... .' She prefers the warmth of her friendship with Anita, her white school friend and the working class white community of the neighbourhood to the posse of extended relatives from India who gather in her parents' house. She likes fish and chips more than her family's Punjabi cuisine and loves flirting with the local boys.

Anita and Me occupies many of the same terrains as *Bhaji*; a minority community mediating cultures and evaluating the temptations, gains, and losses that the host community offers the Asian diaspora. Meena's own rebellious spirit makes her a non-conformist; to both the cultures that envelope her. She bites a white girl at a party in her father's office who, driven by curiosity, wanted to touch her brown skin. She remains unapologetic. She finds mutual camaraderie in Anita Rutter, who shares her own instincts of independence, cheekiness, anger, and irreverence. Considering the Kumars are the only Asian (let alone Indian) family in the village of Tollington, Anita turns up being the first white person to dine at Meena's house. However, the same Meena who passionately and unapologetically bit her little friend at the party is severely embarrassed by the sight of her parents eating with their hands while in the presence of her white, best friend, 'apparently unaware that all of us had a great view of a lump of half masticated fish finger sitting on her tongue' (Syal, *Anita and Me* 252).

However, as the novel progresses (and as Meena gets older) she is forced to reassess her loyalties. Racism becomes apparent and she starts reconsidering friendships. The paper argues that this ambivalence is symptomatic of Syal's own negotiation of her cultural identity. Though Syal prefers to dissociate herself from an overtly simplistic and easily contained 'Asian' label, her work, and recent activism foregrounds a sense of resistance from within (as subsequent sections will demonstrate). In the end, the novel itself remains an extremely funny and irreverent rendition of a second generation British-Asian person negotiating cultures, forming identities, and offering resistance without fearing assimilation.

Her latest novel, *Life Isn't All Ha Ha Hee Hee* was published in 1999 and was later adapted into a series for BBC Television, (much like *Anita and Me*). And like much of her former work, *Life* relates the story of a group of young British-Asian women (the children of Punjabi immigrants) growing up in Britain. The three childhood friends in the novel form a sort of bridge between their own conservative, immigrant parent and their own children, who will most likely (being second generation British-Asians) never face the need to break out of a mould of conformity warped from distant relatives and arranged marriages. Like *Anita and Me*, *Life* also treads a fine line between sympathetic portrait and merciless satire when representing both British and Asian culture. As James Procter observes, 'While she pokes fun at the conservative ambitions of her characters, Syal also encourages her readers to consider the wider cultural climate in which they are caught'. For instance, while at a restaurant, Chila (one of the protagonists in the novel) has a bit of a conversation with a receptionist at a restaurant who coos to her: 'Loove your outfit by the way. This stuff is really in at the mo. Is it DKNY?' Chila looked down for a moment. 'No, Bimla's Bargains, Forest Gate, I think ...' (212). While on a sardonic level, *Life* might be interpreted as a look at ways in which ethnic cultures are commodified and marketed as accessories in the West, the ways in which the protagonists (including Chila) navigate these terrains of conflict; with utter irreverence and biting wit, makes a more powerful statement.

As in *Anita and Me* (with the picture of little Meena being embarrassed by the sight of her 'uncouth' parents eating with their hands), *Life* also documents a picture of second generation immigrants feeling embarrassed by their parents in a modern day England. However, under Syal's treatment, these experiences (*and* clichés) become the pivot that subverts and debunks aspects of the British-Asian experience. While Syal rarely uses clichés and stereotypes to document this experience, even if she does, she does it to subversive effect. Like all of her work, in *Life* too, Syal laughs *with* and *at* cultures simultaneously. She uses humour intelligently to push the limits of political correctness as well as to politicize existing narratives of British-Asian Culture.

However, perhaps one can infer a subtle change in her mode of presentation and deployment of humour since her *Goodness Gracious* days. The brand of humour that hallmarked her hit radio/television series, *Goodness Gracious Me* (even through its very title, a thinly veiled lampoon at the *British* way) is discarded in favour of a more sophisticated one towards her later career. As Procter reminds us, 'At a time when Britain's bookshops are flooded with the fictions of comic television celebrities, from Ben Elton to Stephen Fry, it is easy to underestimate the significance of Syal's recent work as a novelist. However for all their comic brilliance, *Anita and Me* and *Life Isn't All Ha Ha Hee Hee* are more substantial, serious works than such comparisons allow'.

Syal was conferred the Most Excellent Order of the British Empire (MBE) in 1997 and has consistently figured prominently in Britain's cultural milieu. She won the 'Media Personality of the Year' award at the Commission for Racial Equality's annual 'Race in the Media' awards (2000), as well as the EMMA (BT Ethnic and Multi-cultural Media Award) for Media Personality of the Year in 2001. She was also listed by *The Observer* in 2003 as one of top 50 comic performers in Britain. She is also an eminent journalist and contributes frequently to *The Guardian*.

While Pollock et al. point out that 'refugees, peoples of the diaspora and migrants and exiles represent the spirit of the cosmopolitical community' (6), Wilson considers 'the immigrant as (a) global cosmopolitan ... carrier of some liberal and liberated hybridity' (352). Talking about assimilation, Syal has herself maintained that 'fitting in meant forgetting who I was ... I loved talking in a broad Black Country accent as much as I loved speaking Punjabi' (Jones). In more recent times, Syal has been very vocal in expressing her annoyance at the way in which she and her colleagues in England are labelled together as 'Asian', maintain that 'It's one of those awkward umbrella terms that's increasingly losing relevance ... . We're not just one homogenous lump' (Owen). At the same time, she also recalls instances of racial abuse that she had to endure growing up in a working class British community where her family was the only Asian one. She cites her identity as the 'odd one out' (unlike many of her contemporaries who lived in more Asian-populated areas of England) as something that defined her, going on to point out that this special case granted her 'real independence', free from the mythical 'policing' of the more conservative Asian communities. She is also acutely aware of the shift in the form and mode of racial intolerance that she experienced growing up (from incurring racial slurs and so on to the more subtle ways in which racism operates in present day England).[2]

Self admittedly, this hostility and her perceived self image as an 'outsider' helped her develop as a creative person, enabling her to deflect racism through humour and education. As Owen documents, 'Spurred on by winning the National Student Drama Award for her play *One of Us* – a semi-autobiographical story about an Asian girl who leaves the Midlands to become an actress – she abandoned plans to do a master's degree in drama and psychotherapy'.

Syal has reiterated her hatred of the term frequently; maintaining that '(the term "Asian") is something you end up saying because it's been used as our collective noun for so long' (Jones). As she found professional success, both as performer and writer (and even as a visiting professor of contemporary theatre at St Catherine's College, Oxford) Syal has arguably developed a more interrogative stance that is yet not entirely placed oppositionally to her embrace of a hybrid identity and neither embracing of her bracketed label as an 'Asian'. She has been openly articulate concerning the lack of ethnic diversity in British television, frequenting occasions such as the launch of 'Act For Change' a project designed to address this question. Maintaining that the problem of ethnic under-representation has been around for too long, she infuses her point with her signature humour: 'For a lot of us this is like *Groundhog Day*; we were having these discussions thirty years ago and I can't believe we are still having them' (Dowell). Suggesting that British TV may need to introduce quotas for black and ethnic minority performers, Syal also stresses that radical change may be needed to grant 'more opportunity to non-white performers' (the most radical of which would be a quota system). She points out how this might be construed as tokenism, but might also be the only way out. 'With all the good will in the world attitudes just are not changing. If things are not changing, you have got to lead people that way', Syal asserts.

Syal herself explained at a symposium on women and film production at the National Film Theatre in summer of 1994 that 'writing was to create roles for women of colour' and as a scriptwriter who was also an actor and a woman, made sure that each woman in her often ensemble cast had substantial speaking parts, instead of the all too common 'that'll be 50p please' (quoted in Ciecko 88).

It might admittedly be an oversimplification to assume that Asian exclusion from British media was a consequence of postcolonial racism. Immigrants facing housing challenges ('don't sell your house to them', Owen) linguistic challenges and general racial hostility might have also contributed by segregating themselves, much like the case of present day Southhall in London. Talking about British-Asian filmmaking practices, Sawhney points out – 'With the development of their own successful media cultures, working-class Asian communities often chose not to engage with white-mainstream, English-language media, which discouraged their representation anyway' (60). However, over the past few decades, with the prominent emergence of many second and third generation British-Asians (with a more hybrid sense of identity, as represented by the case of Meera Syal), more open and less oppositional cultural permeability can easily be perceived. The unfashionable, crude Asian aesthetic sensibility has warped into something that is chic and desirable ('Loove your outfit by the way. This stuff is really in at the mo. Is it DKNY?'). This is aided in no little measure by the fact that major Western communities (Hollywood included) see India as one of its key future markets. Likewise as Sawhney pointed out in 2001, 'The British film industry has gradually begun waking up to the "brown pound"' (61).

While Carmen Wickramagamage argues that 'most people envision relocation as a painful choice between assimilation (betrayal) and nativism (loyalty)' (194), it is easy to see how even a broad survey of diasporic writing/writers illustrate this. While diasporic writers like Kiran Desai explores both aspects of the issue, she seems to ultimately question the desirability of assimilation and the need to maintain difference, '(to inhabit) the margins and (avoid) full and unapologetic participation in the New World' (195). While many diasporic writers' (Kiran Desai's, for instance) work may be construed as an attempt to re-politicize South Asian diasporic narratives through refocusing attention on topical themes and narrative form, we argue that Syal's own model of work and writing doesn't aim to de-politicize but remains an acutely aware, irreverent, interrogative *yet* assimilative stance on hybridized identity politics that seeks resistance from within, to both host and homeland cultures. Syal's rendition of British-Asian communities in many of her scripts for television and film can make fascinating texts for study in a cultural studies course. Her statement that – 'the purpose of the melting pot (of hybridity), it seemed, was to boil all our differences away – the differences that make us so interesting and unique' (Jones) sums up the curious case of Meera Syal MBE – writer, actor, journalist, performer, and racial ambassador who refuses to be bracket as 'Asian'.

Notes

1. Confessing the semi-autobiographical nature of her first novel, Syal declared in an interview to the BBC: 'I did grow up in a very small mining village like that … . I think the emotional landscape is very much how I felt growing up, being the only Asian family in such a tiny mining environment' (Best).
2. Talking of shifting racial reception, director Gurinder Chadha has commented on the way British Asian films have been a regular presence on British Top 10 charts since 1998. Comparing the reception of *Bend it Like Beckham* (2002) to her earlier film *Bhaji on the Beach* (1994), Chadha explains how it was 'a totally different experience … people are much more aware of difference. What was once foreign is now familiar; culture has shifted in this country' (quoted in Sawhney 61).

References

Appadurai, Arjun. *Modernity at Large: Cultural Dimensions of Globalization*. Minneapolis: University of Minnesota Press, 1996.
Best, Jason. 'Meera Syal: Anita and Me'. *BBC UK*. Web 22 July 2014. <http://www.bbc.co.uk/films/2002/10/23/meera_syal_anita_and_me_interview.shtml>.
Ciecko, Anne. 'Representing the Spaces of Diaspora in Contemporary British Films by Women Directors'. *Cinema Journal* 38.3 (1999): 67–90.
Clifford, J. *Routes: Travel and Translation in the Late Twentieth Century*. Cambridge, MA: Harvard University Press, 1997.
Dissanakayke, Wimal and K. Moti Gokulsingh. *Indian Popular Cinema: A Narrative of Cultural Change*. Trentham: University of Michigan, 1998.
Dowell, Ben. 'Meera Syal: It Might be Time for Black and Ethnic Minority Quotas in British TV'. *Radio Times*. 30 June 2014. Web 20 July 2014. <http://www.radiotimes.com/news/2014-06-30/meera-syal-it-might-be-time-for-black-and-ethnic-minority-quotas-in-british-tv>.

Hall, Stuart. 'Cultural Identity and Diaspora'. *Theorizing Diaspora*. (eds) J.E. Braziel and A. Mannur. Malden, MA: Blackwell Publishing, 2006. 233–346.

Huggan, Graham. *The Postcolonial Exotic: Marketing the Margins*. London: Routledge, 2001.

Jones, Chris. 'Meera Meera Off the Wall'. *BBC News Profiles Unit*. 14 March 2003. Web 15 July 2014. <http://news.bbc.co.uk/2/hi/in_depth/uk/2000/newsmakers/2847873.stm>.

Owen, Jonathan. 'Meera Syal: "I Didn't Want to Reach 50 and be Full of Regrets"'. 6 May 2012. Web 17 July 2014. <http://www.independent.co.uk/news/people/profiles/meera-syal-i-didnt-want-to-reach-50-and-be-full-of-regrets-7717628.html>.

Pollock, S., H. Bhabha, C. Breckenridge, and D. Chakrabarty. 'Cosmopolitanisms'. *Cosmopolitanism*. (eds) S. Pollock, H. Bhabha, C. Breckenridge, and D. Chakrabarty. Durham, NC: Duke University Press, 2002. 1–15.

Procter, James. 'Meera Syal'. *British Council Literature*. Web 18 July 2014. <http://literature.britishcouncil.org/meera-syal>

Quart, Leonard. 'Bhaji on the Beach by Nadine Marsh-Edwards; Gurinder Chadha; Meera Syal'. *Cinéaste* 20.4 (1994): 48–49.

Sabo, Oana. 'Disjunctures and Diaspora in Kiran Desai's *The Inheritance of Loss*'. *The Journal of Commonwealth Literature.* Web 14 August 2012. <http://jcl.sagepub.com/content/early/2012/05/24/0021989412450697>.

Sawhney, Cary Rajinder. 'Another Kind of British: An Exploration of British Asian Films'. *Cinéaste* 26.4 (2001): 58–61.

——. 'Asian British Cinema: From Margins to Mainstream'. *BFI Screen Online*. 10 November 2011. Web 20 July 2014. <http://www.screenonline.org.uk/film/id/475617/>.

Sen, Sharmila. 'Foreign Accents: Notes upon My Return to the Diaspora'. *The Women's Review of Books* 19.5 (2002): 8–9.

Syal, Meera. *Anita and Me*. 2012. London: Harper Collins, 1996.

——. *Life Isn't All Ha Ha Hee Hee*. London: Random House, 2012.

The Guardian. 'The A-Z of Laughter (part two)'. 7 December 2003. Web 20 July 2014. <http://www.theguardian.com/stage/2003/dec/07/comedy.thebestofbritishcomedy>.

Wickramagamage, Carmen. 'Relocation as Positive Act: The Immigrant Experience in Bharati Mukherjee's Novels'. *Diaspora* 2.2 (1992): 171–200.

Wilson, R. 'A New Cosmopolitanism is in the Air: Some Dialectical Twists and Turns'. *Cosmopolitics: Thinking and Feeling Beyond the Nation*. (eds) P. Cheah and B. Robbins. Minneapolis: University of Minnesota Press, 1998. 351–361.

PART 4

Contemporary Indian Diaspora in Plays and Poems

Chapter 13

Why the Play *The Black Album*?
Hanif Kureishi, the Playwright and the Publishing Industry

ARNAB KUMAR SINHA

Hanif Kureishi, one of the most popular and prolific contemporary British writers, has worked with different genres like novel, play, screenplay (for television and films), and short story. Recently, when I was browsing over the literary corpus of Hanif Kureishi on the internet, I noticed that the attention of the critics and the publishing house Faber and Faber[1] – significantly Faber and Faber is the only publishing house in Britain which has published all the novels, plays, short story collections, and screenplays of Kureishi – is more on the successful novels and screenplays of Kureishi than on his plays.[2] This evidently tempts us to interrogate the silence of the critics as well as of Faber and Faber about the plays of Kureishi. In fact, except one thesis (Tracy K. Parker's – which elaborately discusses the play *Borderline*) no other researcher or critic has made any significant attempt to analyse the plays of Kureishi. Does this suggest that Kureishi the playwright is less successful than Kureishi the novelist or Kureishi the screenplay writer? This question further leads us to interrogate the factors that determine the success of a writer in a particular genre. In fact, apart from the critical attention, Kureishi has also received a number of awards for his novels and screenplays.[3] These awards that Kureishi received in the last two decades for his novels and screenplays have also shadowed the prestigious George Devine Award that he received for his play *Outskirts*. This award was received by Kureishi in 1981 and conspicuously, after this award, he has received no remarkable recognition for his plays. I hope that it has become clear by now that I am trying to point out the implicit politics in the global reception of Kureishi's works. It seems that the publishing industry and the awards politics have, to a large extent, determined the popularity of Kureishi's novels and screenplays, and this popularity, in turn, has drawn the attention of the critics towards his fictions and screenplays. This paper will therefore attempt to interrogate the factors that led to the shadowing of the dramatic career of Kureishi, and, in doing so, will also try to find out the factors that led Kureishi to write a play like *The Black Album* in 2009, a time when Kureishi was already at the peak of his success as a novelist and screenplay-writer.

Kureishi began his career as a playwright with the Royal Shakespeare Company. In fact, the Royal Shakespeare Company not only introduced Kureishi to the world of theatre, but also to the metropolis London. As an original resident of the London suburbs, Kureishi belonged to a place called Bromley, and his attraction for the London city life and culture developed during his university days. In an interview given to Colin MacCabe (titled 'Hanif Kureishi and London' 2003), Kureishi mentions about the big cultural leap experienced by him every time he crossed the river separating the suburb Bromley from the city London, 'When you got on the train and crossed the river, at that moment there was an incredible sense that you were entering another kind of world. Being in the suburbs, we could get to London quite easily on the train – about 15 or 20 minutes – but it was a big jump' (*AA Files* 40). In the same interview he asserts his love for the theatre during those days when he worked for the Royal Shakespeare Company, 'I loved the theatre and I worked in the theatre in the evenings. London for me was culture. I just wanted to be in a place that wasn't like Bromley, where you could talk about plays' (ibid.). In the 1980s and 1990s, Kureishi wrote four plays: *The King and Me* (1980), *Outskirts* (1981), *Borderline* (1981), and *Sleep with Me* (1999), and all these plays except *Outskirts* went unnoticed. The turning point in Kureishi life came when he met Rushdie in the late 1980s. Rushdie advised Kureishi to write novels and become a serious writer. This is what Kureishi reflects on Rushdie's advice in the interview, 'Hanif Kureishi and London':

> But I also remember Rushdie saying this really cutting thing to me. 'We take you seriously as a writer, Hanif', he said, 'but you only write screenplays'. I remember being really hurt by this, and

provoked by it, and I thought, well, I'll write a novel, and then I'll be a proper writer; that somehow that's what being a proper writer was. Perhaps it is, in the sense that what you write then goes to the reader unmediated: there are no actors, directors or anybody else involved. (*AA Files* 43)

That Kureishi became a 'proper writer' is evident from the fact that following the suggestion of Rushdie, he wrote the novel, *The Buddha of Suburbia* in 1990 and it was an instant hit. Kureishi talks about the success of his first novel in terms of the financial gain that he achieved after its publication: 'So, after being stung by this remark of Rushdie's, I wrote *The Buddha*. I had money as well, for the first time; after *Sammy & Rosie* and *My Beautiful Laundrette* I had what they call a two-year window. *Laundrette* had made money in the US' (ibid.). *The Buddha of Suburbia* was, in fact, the turning point in Kureishi's career because after the publication of this novel he enjoyed financial success. His novels were also (either immediately after publication or later) adapted to films. The financial success of the first novel of Kureishi marks his entry into the culture industry where fictions and films are treated as commodities to be finely packaged and marketed to the readers. In this context, I would like to refer to an essay written by Angshuman Kar where he studies the issue of commodification of post-Rushdie Indian novels in English. In this essay, 'Commodification of Post-Rushdie Indian Novels in English: Kunal Basu and the Politics of Decanonization', Kar examines how the contemporary Indian authors by incorporating different versions of 'India' and 'Indianness' are using India as a saleable product in the global market. In the essay, Kar raises a series of pertinent questions, which, I believe, are important for this essay of mine, because through these questions Kar addresses the issues related to production and consumption of a literary text in an era of open market economy. The questions that he asks are as follows:

> ... who determines what sells in the literary market? Is it the writer, who once sure of the market value of a particular brand of writing goes on repeating him/herself? Is it the publisher who, with his/her innovative 'promo' techniques, can create a demand in the market even for a mediocre work .... Or is it the academic who, for professional reasons, writes papers and publishes books on these authors and even instructs a budding researcher to choose any one of these 'talked about' writers for his/her dissertation. (15)

Based on these questions of Kar, if we try to examine the popularity of the novels and the screenplays of Kureishi, the issue of commodification of a particular brand/genre of literary product becomes very clear. A novel is always meant for private reading and, for the readers around the globe, a novel is like an easy consumable commodity. Similarly, screenplays are meant for mass entertainment and in our times when the film industry is generating a lot of revenue, screenplays have become popular as a product to be consumed by the audience worldwide. Unlike a novel or a screenplay, a play is written for such audience who can manage little bit of time to go to a theatre and see a performance. A play therefore is not an easy consumable product as it demands a more dedicated consumer who is ready to invest time, money, and energy. Why would therefore a publisher like Faber and Faber promote the plays in the literary market when the demand for novels and films is very high? Surprisingly, when for the first time, I tried to buy Kureishi's collection of plays, most of the reputed online bookstores like flipkart.com, infibeam.com, and homeshop18.com displayed the unavailability of the plays by mentioning the phrase 'out of stock'. Contrary to the unavailability of the plays, Kureishi's novels and films are easily available in most of these reputed online bookstores. This apart, I was further surprised when I opened the cover page of the play *The Black Album* to find a tag line below the title of the play, 'Hanif Kureishi: Author of *My Beautiful Laundrette* and *The Buddha of Suburbia*' (1). Is this tag line another strategy of advertising the author's success in the field of screenplay writing (*My Beautiful Laundrette* is a very popular screenplay of Kureishi), as well as in the field of novel writing (*The Buddha of Suburbia*, as already shown, is the first and the most popular novel of Kureishi which gave him a lot of money and success)? By using this kind of a tag line for the play *The Black Album*, is the publisher trying to suggest that they should read this play not because of its own merit but because of the fact that it is written by someone who has written those two screenplays and novels? Hanif Kureishi as a writer therefore could not escape from the cobweb of forces operating within the literary market which promotes specific brands of literature. That he depended more on his novels and screenplays for success is understood when one looks at the number of fictions and screenplays produced by him in the last 20 years. As a full time creative writer Kureishi had to write novels and screenplays for earning money and surviving in the literary industry. But then, why did he write a play like *The Black Album* in 2009 when Kureishi had already emerged as a very popular novelist and screenplay writer in the culture industry? The next section of this essay will particularly deal with the play *The Black Album* to show how in this play Kureishi attempts to seriously deal with issues connected to the life of Muslim immigrants in Britain.

In the Faber and Faber edition of the play *The Black Album* there is an introduction written by the author which appears under the title 'Newness in the World'. In the introduction the author has explained the problems faced by him while converting a popular novel *The Black Album* published in 1995 into a play. The play, as Kureishi candidly claims, demanded more focus on the characters and the debates arising from the discussion between the characters, and so there was a greater need to see the issues related to religion, the conflict between liberal and fundamental forces within Islam, and global capitalism intensely. Kureishi explains how he deliberated on these issues while working on the translation of the novel into a play with his director friend, Jatinder Verma:

> It was a debate, ideological confrontation and physical passion that Jatinder and I had in mind when we sat down to work on the translation from prose to play. The novel, which has a thriller-like structure, is a sprawl of many scenes in numerous locations: foul pubs, a further education college, a mosque, clubs, parties, a boarding house, cafes, Deedee's house and street. As it was impossible in the theatre to retain this particular sense of late-eighties London, we had to create longer scenes and concentrate on the important and dangerous arguments between the characters as they interrogated Islam, liberalism, consumer capitalism, as well as the place and meaning of literature and the way in which it might represent criticism of religion. (*The Black Album* 6)

When we read the play the intense concentration of the playwright on the debates between the characters is noticeable. *The Black Album*, as a play, deals with multiple issues connected to the lives of the people belonging to diasporic Muslim community in Britain. Firstly, the play seriously interrogates Islamic fundamentalism especially in the context of the fatwa against Rushdie given by the Iranian government for blasphemy in *The Satanic Verses*. The Rushdie debate in this play foregrounds the conflict of ideas between two contrary forces within Islam: Shahid (who is a liberal

Muslim) argues in favour of Rushdie by asserting the freedom of an individual writer to criticize religion, whereas Riaz (who is a conservative Muslim) is uncompromising and harshly criticizes Rushdie for writing unwelcome things about Prophet Muhammad. Though Shahid and Riaz are poles apart on the Rushdie debate, yet they are both university students, aware of the harsh world of racism. They unite to fight against racism when the Old Man seeks their aid in order to save his family from the tortures of the whites. Shahid and Riaz even decide to take violent measures to put up a fight against racial intimidation. However, except the issue of racism, Shahid and Riaz are different in their outlook towards Islam in general, and Muslim fundamentalism in particular. Riaz gets the support of a few fanatic conservative Islamic friends like Chad, Taheera, and Hat, who along with Riaz convince Shahid to become a fundamentalist giving no scope to the British culture and religion to penetrate into one's own mind. This strategy of non-assimilation is stated by Chad as follows, 'We must not assimilate, that way we lose our souls. Like that blaspheming writer! We are proud and we are obedient. It's not we who must change, but the world' (*The Black Album* 36). Shahid, unlike this group of fundamentalists, is an open-minded, liberal Muslim who believes in the values of change and assimilation. For him, Rushdie is not a blaspheming writer, and at one point in the play he even argues that Rushdie in his texts have only attempted to write about the immigrant Muslims in Britain: 'He (Rushdie) has said time and again he has your view of the world – the migrant's view. He celebrates what you are because out of you come new things' (ibid. 75). The liberal viewpoint of Shahid is the outcome of his association with a white British teacher named, Deedee. As an influential teacher, Deedee inspires Shahid to read postcolonial literature, and during a discussion on the issue of banning of creative texts like Rushdie's *The Satanic Verses*, she vehemently opposes censorship of creative texts: 'There's nothing new in wanting to ban a book. We've been down this road before – with Joyce, Lawrence, Miller, Nabokov. They were all censored in their time. And what did it change? People still read the banned books. Censorship's never been successful. The last time it was tried was during the Inquisition – and that led to the fall of the very Church it was trying to protect. Not what your friends really want, is it?' (ibid. 70). In Deedee's take on censorship, Shahid locates a warning regarding the fate of Islamic fundamentalism, and he understands that too much of conservatism will surely lead to the downfall of Islam. Apart from the critical issues related to Islam, the play also presents an interesting take on postcolonial literature. As already mentioned earlier that Shahid is introduced to the world of postcolonial literature by Deedee and, on one occasion, when Deedee deliberates on this new breed of literature, she very poignantly states that postcolonial literature is all about new stories coming up from different non-white ethnic backgrounds which are interesting and can add to the variety of stories written by English writers. In fact, when Deedee discusses postcolonial literature, she tacitly emphasizes on the role of the publishing houses in England in giving fame and acclaim to postcolonial writers writing from different locations across the globe. Let us first have a glance at Deedee's viewpoint on postcolonial literature, 'It's very original, the way you weave Scheherazade into your story. *The Arabian Nights* in Sevenoaks. No one's written like this about England – you have a voice and a future, Shahid. This is the new literature – when stories from elsewhere slice into conventional England. Rushdie showed there's a gap in modern writing that can only be filled by stories like yours. You could be the real deal. You could be published by Faber and Faber and go to literary parties, accompanied by me' (ibid. 60). This particular viewpoint of a white English teacher is, I believe, the focal point in the play connected to the main line of argument of this paper. Deedee's opinion about postcolonial literature is indicative of the fact that stories written by postcolonial writers are heavily loaded stories connected to the histories and cultures of the non-white communities. These stories, as Deedee implicitly tries to pinpoint, are commodified by the publishing industry in such a manner that they give fame to the postcolonial writers. Shahid is seen by Deedee as somebody who like a postcolonial writer can weave new and interesting stories, and if these stories which Shahid can write make an impact on the literary market by selling thousands of copies then it could be a 'real deal'. Deedee interestingly talks about the reputed publisher Faber and Faber who can change the life of a postcolonial writer like Shahid by ensuring success, popularity, and money. In Deedee's take on new literatures, one can locate the trace of the publishing world's attitude to a literary text that sees a text only as a commodity to be sold in the market. Kureishi in *The Black Album* is also critical to the policies adopted by the Prime Minister

Margaret Thatcher who introduced the concept of free market economy in Britain, and this new economy led to a new era of global capitalism. In the play, Chad equates Thatcherism with 'extremity', 'ingratitude', and 'hard-heartedness', and Deedee says that, 'the under-classes are fighting back against Thatcher's greed' (ibid. 26, 40). In Heather Ann Joyce's thesis there is detailed discussion of Thatcher's policies and how these policies recast the British economic system. Joyce mentions, 'Thatcherism is characterized by a turn towards a free market economy, resulting in an emphasis on individualism and entrepreneurship' (6).

The Black Album is, therefore, an intense drama of debates on contemporary issues, and it carries the old theatrical spirit of Kureishi which had been marginalized during the era of his popularity as a writer of novels and screenplays. In the novel version of *The Black Album*, Kureishi frames 'a thriller-like structure' story with references to 'numerous locations' in London which somehow dilutes the focus on 'ideological confrontation' (*The Black Album* 6). But the play version of *The Black Album*, as Kureishi opines, is a serious study of characters who are continuously debating on multiple issues related to the life of the Muslim immigrants in Britain. The speeches of the characters have therefore been edited several times by Kureishi to give the audience a feel of natural conversation. The following comment of Kureishi highlights the concern of the author regarding the technical aspects related to the writing of the play:

> If we were to create big parts for actors in scenes set in small rooms, we needed to turn prose into fervent talk, having the conversation carry the piece. We had to ensure the actors had sufficient material to see their parts clearly. Each scene had to be shaped. The piece had to work for those who hadn't read the book. It was this we worked on over a number of drafts, and it was the usual business of writing: cutting, condensing, expanding, developing, putting in jokes and trying material in different places until the story moved forward naturally. (ibid. 6)

The play version of *The Black Album* is, therefore, not simply a theatrical adaption of the novel, it is an independent piece of writing meant for the serious audience who are ready to encounter 'difficult debates and violent outcomes' (ibid. 8).

The novel *The Black Album* was published in 1995, and the play version of the novel was published in 2009. If we try to analyse the reasons which made Kureishi write the play 14 years after the publication of the novel, one needs to study the changes in the socio-cultural environment in Britain during the in-between years of writing the two different versions of the same text. Before the publication of the novel *The Black Album*, the Muslim immigrants in Britain were confronting the problems of racial discrimination and those relating to the issue of the fatwa against Salman Rushdie; they were also adjusting to the nation's transformation from a monocultural society to a multicultural one. Kureishi has dealt with all these issues in the novel. But, after the publication of the novel *The Black Album*, the attitude of the native British towards the Muslim immigrants underwent a sea change, especially because of the two important events – the 9/11 terrorist attacks in America in 2001, and the 7/7 London bombings in 2005. These two terrorist attacks have created an atmosphere of fear and distrust in the British multicultural society, and in the aftermath of these two incidents, every Muslim immigrant is suspected as a terrorist. Kureishi, as a sensitive artist who is also a part of the British multi-cultural society, was fully aware of this dangerous shift in the attitude of the native British towards the Muslim immigrants. I would like to argue that he decided to examine this particular change in the socio-cultural dynamics of Britain after 7/7 by re-writing the novel *The Black Album* – which was an analysis of the relationship between Islam and Britian in the context of the fatwa against Rushdie – as a play. I would also like to argue that Kureishi decided to convert the novel into a play because the stage space in theatre is dynamic and allows a playwright to communicate his ideas directly to the audience and to have an interaction with them. Unlike a novel, which is privately consumed by a reader and therefore is open for any kind of interpretation, the effect of a play on the audience's mind is more penetrating and satisfying from the perspective of an author. I agree that a film can also leave a deep impact on the minds of the audience, but the production of a film involves different agencies which mediate the production and consumption of a film, and these mediating factors may dilute the impact of the film as desired by the screenplay writer. It is difficult for a screenplay writer also to have direct feedback from the audience. So, theatre is the most appropriate medium for directly communicating the playwright's ideas to the audience, and to have feedback on them. Therefore, Kureishi, by re-contextualizing the story of the novel, I argue, wrote the play *The Black Album* to motivate the audience to question the misconceptions about Islam and the British tendency of homogenizing the Muslims as fundamentalists and terrorists. This particular decision of Kureishi to write a play on unpalatable issues, at a time when he was at the peak of his career as a novelist and screenplay writer, is also noteworthy from another perspective. It proves that the forces operating within the literary market cannot always influence a sensitive and committed writer like Kureishi to stick to the populist mode of writing. A full time writer may write about popular subjects to earn his livelihood, but if a writer is committed to his community or race, then he is bound to respond to the issues that disturb him and he, like Kureishi, might produce works which may not have a good prospect in the market.

I would like to conclude by stating the need to seriously read the plays of Kureishi, especially *The Black Album* which apart from dealing with the issues related to racism and Islamic fundamentalism, also sheds light on the nexus between the publishing industry and creative writers. Popularity of any creative text is not the only criterion of judging the content value of a literary text, and this stands true for a writer like Kureishi. I do not mean to suggest that Kureishi's popular novels and screenplays are simply literary commodities – in fact, these novels and screenplays have given us Kureishi's insightful study of the problems of assimilation faced by the Muslim immigrants in Britain – having as such no literary value, but time is now ripe to engage ourselves with the plays of Kureishi which are more penetrating, incisive, and satirical than his novels or screenplays.

Notes

1. In the Faber and Faber official website a brief note of the publisher has been given to describe the nature of different works of Kureishi. The following note describes *Hanif Kureishi's Plays 1*, 'In 1981 Hanif Kureishi was voted 'Most Promising Playwright of the Year' by the

London Theatre Critics for his plays *Borderline* and *Outskirts*. Since then he has gone on to write best-selling fiction (*The Buddha of Suburbia*, Intimacy) and acclaimed screenplays (*My Beautiful Laundrette*, which received an Oscar nomination for Best Screenplay, and *Sammy and Rosie Get Laid*)'. In the cover design of Kureishi's novel *Something to Tell You* (2008) the tag line 'From the author of *The Buddha of Suburbia*' has been used to highlight the achievement of the author in the genre of fiction. In the 1991 Faber and Faber edition of Kureishi's famous novel *The Buddha of Suburbia*, the publisher has used the following highly enthusiastic review of the novel which appeared in *Sunday Times*: 'Brilliantly funny. A fresh, anarchic and deliciously unrestrained novel'. This apart, the cover design of *The Buddha of Suburbia* was changed thrice (once in 1991, and twice in 2009) by Faber and Faber to make it more appealing to the readers. This significant attention of the publisher is not only limited to the novels of Kureishi. In the cover design of the Kureishi's screenplay, *The Mother* (2003) Faber and Faber has mentioned the following comment of Allan Hunter (a film critic) to advertise the author's ability to write brilliant screenplays: 'Kureishi's screenplay is one of his most focused and engaging since *My Beautiful Laundrette*'. Faber and Faber has however not done much to advertise the plays of Kureishi. The 1999 cover of *Hanif Kureishi's Plays 1* (which has never been changed since its first production) looks less attractive than the covers of the novels and screenplays. Please refer to <www.faber.co.uk> for better understanding of this fact. Regarding the attention of the critics on the novels and screenplays of Kureishi please see the next note.

2. In fact, there are a few dissertations and quite a few number of essays and books on Kureishi which mostly deal with the films and novels of Kureishi. A brief overview of some of these works will help us understand this typical inclination of the critics and researchers towards the films and novels of Kureishi. In the thesis titled *Carnivalizing Conservatism: A Bakhtinian Analysis of Hanif Kureishi, Pat Barker and Zadie Smith in the Context of the Post-Thatcher Era* (2004), Heather Ann Joyce discusses Kureishi's novel *Gabriel's Gift* from the point of view of the Bakhtinian concept of carnivalesque asserting the fact that *Gabriel's Gift* is a 'uniquely dialogic novel' (16). Apart from this particular novel, there is no extensive discussion on any other work of Kureishi in this thesis. Trevor Douglas Smith in the thesis titled, '*A Funny Kind of Englishman': Hanif Kureishi's Representation of South Asians in British Cinema* (2004) makes an intensive analysis of Kureishi's screenplays which, according to Smith, represent 'the economic, political, domestic, and religious struggles faced by Pakistanis and Indians in Britain from 1970s to the 1980s with a

keen eye for contemporary political events' (4). Kureishi's screenplays, according to Smith, attempt to present the viewpoint of a writer like Kureishi who is an *'insider-outsider'* in Britain (Smith 4). In another interesting thesis, Amalie August Holland foregrounds the issues related to class, race, and ethnicity in the novels and screenplays of Kureishi. Holland in the thesis titled *Performers and Pretenders: Performance and 'Othering' in the Texts of the Victorian Social Explorers, George Orwell, and Hanif Kureishi* (2006) observes, 'Kureishi's characters identify themselves with and relate to the world around themselves largely in terms of class, rather than race and ethnicity', and she further notes that Kureishi attempts to redefine Englishness in post-imperial England (54). Kureishi's works have also been examined from the perspective of postmodern culture in Tracey K. Parker's dissertation titled *Pop Life: Images and Popular Culture in the Works of Hanif Kureishi and Zadie Smith* (2008). This dissertation aims to locate in the works of Kureishi the 'blurring cultural boundaries through performance that can negotiate power differentials between minorities and the white dominant culture of the UK, as well as within the white dominant culture' (31). Unlike the other dissertations which rarely discuss the plays of Kureishi, Parker's thesis significantly sheds light on the character of Susan in the play *Borderline* in which Susan as a British white journalist researcher fights for the rights of the minorities in England. Jonathan Tadashi Naito in the dissertation titled *The Postimperial Imagination: The Emergence of a Transnational Literary Space, from Samuel Beckett to Hanif Kureishi* (2008) studies *The Buddha of Suburbia* as a specimen of 'postimperial Bildungsroman' (180). Apart from these dissertations, there are several articles which separately deal with the different critical issues in the novels and screenplays of Kureishi. One article needs to be mentioned in this context because it primarily focuses on the novel *The Black Album*, and the author of this article, Donald Weber explores issues related to 'home', 'homelands', and 'belongings' in the novel *The Black Album* (121). Last but not the least, Frederick Luis Aldama's book *Postethnic Narrative Criticism: Magicorealism in Oscar 'Zeta' Acosta, Ana Castillo, Julie Dash, Hanif Kuresihi, and Salman Rushdie* (2003) is a significant contribution to the critical reception connected with Kureishi's films because his films, as Aldama analyses, invent 'magicoreels' (a term which Aldama adapts from magic realism) that, 'destabilize audiences' perception of reality and thereby denaturalize those networks of films that gel together and form a system of representation that primitivize the racial, gendered, and ethnic subject' (60).

Faber and Faber is a major publishing house in United Kingdom. Since its establishment in 1929, the company has focused mainly to publish the works of popular poets, playwrights, and novelists. In the early years of its publication, Faber and Faber published the works of the leading poets of the 1930s and 1940s. The poems of W.H. Auden, Stephen Spender, Ezra Pound, Marriane Moore, John Gould Fletcher, Roy Campbell, and Walter de la Mare were published by Faber and Faber. After World War II, Faber and Faber shifted its focus from poetry to plays and during this phase the works of leading playwrights were published. The plays of Samuel Beckett, John Osborne, Tom Stoppard and Harold Pinter were published by Faber and Faber. The reputation of Faber and Faber grew after the publication of the works of these renowned playwrights and poets. Since the 1980s, Faber and Faber started publishing the works of such novelists who have made their mark in the history of fiction writing. Kazuo Ishiguro, Peter Carey, Orhan Pamuk, and Barbara Kingslover are the names of few novelists whose works have been published by Faber and Faber (Source of this information on Faber and Faber is available in wikipedia.org).

3. Kureishi's screenplay *My Beautiful Laundrette* (1985) won the New York Film Critics Best Screenplay award, and it was also nominated for the Academy Award for the Best Screenplay. His first novel *The Buddha of Suburbia* (1990) got the Whitbread Award for the best first novel. The movie *Intimacy* (based on Kureishi's novel by the same name) received two Bears at the Berlin Film Festival: one Golden Bear for Best Film and the other Silver Bear for Best Actress. In 2006, Kureishi screenplay *Venus* received many awards at the Oscar, the BAFTA, the Screen Actors Guild, and the Broadcast Film Critics Association. This list of awards clearly indicates the popularity of his novels and screenplays.

References

Aldama, Frederick Luis. *Postethnic Narrative Criticism: Magicorealism in Oscar 'Zeta'Acosta, Ana Castillo, Julie Dash, Hanif Kureishi, and Salman Rushdie*. Austin: University of Texas Press, 2003.

Holland, Amalie August. *Performers and Pretenders: Performance and 'Othering' in the Texts of the Victorian Social Explorers, George Orwell, and Hanif Kureishi*. MA thesis. University of Arkansas, 2006. Ann Arbor: UMI, 2007.

Joyce, Heather Ann. *Carnivalizing Conservatism: A Bakhtinian Analysis of Hanif Kureishi, Pat Barker and Zädie Smith in the Context of Post-Thatcher Era*. MA thesis. University of Calgary, 2003.

Kar, Angshuman. 'Commodification of Post-Rushdie Indian Novels in English: Kunal Basu and the Politics of Decanonization'.

Postliberalization Indian Novels in English: Politics of Global Reception and Awards. (ed.) Aysha Iqbal Viswamohan. London: Anthem Press, 2013. 9–18.

Kureishi, Hanif. *The Black Album*. London: Faber and Faber, 2009.

MacCabe, Colin. 'Hanif Kureishi and London'. *AA Files* 49 (2003): 40–49.

Naito, Jonathan Tadashi. *The Postimperial Imagination: The Emergence of a Transnational Literary Space, from Samuel Beckett to Hanif Kureishi.* Diss. University of California, 2008. Ann Arbor: UMI, 2008.

Parker, Tracey K. *Images and Popular Culture in the Works of Hanif Kureishi and Zadie Smith*. Diss. University of Arkansas, 2008. Ann Arbor: UMI, 2008.

Smith, Trevor Douglas. '"A Funny Kind of Englishman": Hanif Kureishi's Representations of South Asians in British Cinema'. MA thesis. Simon Fraser University, 2004.

Chapter 14

Meena Alexander
A New Poetics of Dislocation

SUBODH SARKAR

'When she asks me what color she was when she was born, I am varnish now', she replies or sometimes she fixes herself a color change: 'peach'. And then continues: 'you are brown mama, papa is blond papa, and Adam is brown.' (*Fault Lines*)[1]

Meena Alexander's specific location is structured, restructured, and negotiated by the context of postcolonial Indian history, and her childhood Kerala which reached out for the realm of a transnational bi-polarity and finally arrived in the locus of a disgruntled self of angst and anxiety which can precisely be described as finding America and losing home. From the age of five, Alexander continues border-crossings. In *The Shock of Arrival*,[2] Alexander writes about her shock penetrating her subconscious of arriving at the centre of the new hegemony called America:

> And so the questions of colonialism bleed into an era of decolonization, into the complicated realms of American ethnicity. Then too, walking down a crowded sidewalk, descending the subway, there is always one's own body, which is marked as other in this country. Ethnicity can draw violence. And this is part of the postcolonial terrain, part of the sorrow and Knowledge of our senses. (72)

In her *Poetics of Dislocation* too Alexander creates a rich tapestry of dislocation as a resource of her basic experiences which provide a launching pad to reflect on the US profiling of South Asians and West Asians after 9/11. In fact, after a struggle with the difference between the place and placelessness for decades, Alexander now seems to have been settled in the US as an individual with an awareness of American and Indian identities coming together to build up a new consciousness of living in America.

Alexander's literary career began early, at the tender age of 10, when she began writing poetry, and while her poetry might be her best-known work, her works span a variety of literary genres. Her first book, a single lengthy poem, entitled *The Bird's Bright Wing*, was published in 1976 in Calcutta. Since then, Alexander has published seven volumes of poetry, including *River and Bridge*; two novels: *Nampally Road* (1991) and *Manhattan Music* (1997); a collection of both prose and poetry: *The Shock of Arrival: Reflections on Postcolonial Experience*; and her autobiography: *Fault Lines*.

No discussion on Alexander's poetry can begin without a reference to *Fault Lines*. This book is not only an unfolding of her past, it also reinforces the themes that recur in Alexander's poetry. As a result of her family's relocations, as a youth, Alexander struggles in *Fault Lines* to desperately arrive at a sense of identity, despite a past full of dislocated junctions and multiple fractures. Thus, this work revolves around the theme of establishing one's self, an identity independent of one's surroundings. Alexander writes: 'I am ... a woman cracked by multiple migrations. Uprooted so many times she can connect nothing with nothing' (*Fault Lines* 74). In fact, the title itself suggests a questioning of lines, boundaries, definitions of oneself. As Alexander writes, 'I am a poet writing in America. But American poet? .... An Asian-American poet then? ... . A woman poet, a woman poet of color, a South Indian woman who makes up lines in English ... . A Third World woman poet ... . ?' (173). The tension surrounding self-identification emerges in the book in a scene where Alexander's son, Adam, encounters a man who asks him: 'What are you?' Adam, of mixed heritage, chooses to identify himself as neither American nor Indian, but, rather, a Jedi knight (172). Alexander asks: 'What did my first-born wish for himself? Some nothingness, some transitory zone where dreams roamed, a border country without passport or language?' (173). Even choosing a cultural identity has its boundaries and borders by which to abide.

Poetry within Fault Lines

The images explored in *Fault Lines* abound in Alexander's poetry. Where and when boundaries melt into no man's land and borders blur into a 'void', there and then the agony and angst appear to be devastating for an immigrant like Meena Alexander. Let us re-examine one poem which was born out of this void:

> My back against barbed wire
> snagged and coiled to belly height
> on granite posts
> glittering to the moon
> No man's land
> no woman's either
> I stand in the middle of my life ...
> Out of earth's soft
> and turbulent core
> a drum sounds summoning ancestors. (*Fault Lines* 73)

Alexander struggles to develop her sense of identity in a culture still imprinted with the stamps of Britain. Alexander demonstrates in this autobiography both her triumph of will and her artistic lust for aesthetics of dislocation. In fact, *Fault Lines* has a mystery that connects the seismic discontinuities of Alexander's existence, linking them through the operation of her poetic gift. Her language, brilliantly precise and poignant, conveys the agony and ecstasy of the feel of her extreme sensitivity. Her description of giving birth captures that visceral moment more vividly than anything else:

> Sometimes I am torn apart by two sorts of memories, two opposing ways of being towards the past. The first makes whorls of skin and flesh, coruscating shells, glittering in moonlight. A life embedded in a life ... Rooms within rooms, each filled with its own scent: rosehips, neem leaves, dried hibiscus leaves that hold a cure, cow dung, human excrement, dried gobs of blood ... . Another memory invades me: flat, filled with the burning present, cut by existential choices. Composed of bits and pieces of the present, it renders the past suspect, cowardly, baseless. Place names litter it ... . Sometimes I think I could lift these scraps of space and much as an indigent dressmaker, cut them into shape. Stitch my days into a patchwork garment fit to wear. (29–30)

The pulls and pressures, joy and agony, madness and maneuver of a tradition have always been a central paradigm in South Asian women's experience spread over an embattled space fissured by multiple marginalizations. This process of mingling of two cultures, two ethnicities, two languages, and two geographies always seems to have been a difficult surgery on such an operation table that does not stand firm or grounded. There seems to be a perpetual conflict between inside and outside, between an adopted home in America and the invisible home being carried on back and this is worsened by 'an incessant struggle to surmount the obstacles to one's assimilation into a comfortable adaptation to the new environment' (Alexander, *Fault Lines* 131).

Gendered Identity in Postcolonial Societies

Meena Alexander's work examines her engagement with gender politics from the bag of mixed legacies of colonialism, cross border culture, transnational identity crisis and trauma. This is what remains like a surface in her Memoir *Fault Lines* and in her novels *Nampally Road* and *Manhattan Music*, as well as in many of her poems and reflections on the poetic process in *The Shock of Arrival*. For Alexander, feminism is not an inevitable inheritance of her western education. As Alice Walker searched for a new kind of feminism for the black women writers, so did Meena in her essay 'In Search of Sarojini Naidu', anthologized in her collection *The Shock of Arrival*. In this essay Meena embarks on precisely the task of relocating her literary foremothers. Like her literary foremothers, Antherjanam and Nalapat Balamaniamma, Alexander explores the issue of female sexuality in the newly emerging patriarchies of South Asian diasporic communities. But she does not stop merely with the recording of female bodily trauma. In *Nampally Road* and *Manhattan Music*, as well as in *Fault Lines*, Alexander suggests a path of recovery and healing through female solidarity and friendship. In this connection it is important to recognize the dichotomy of Indian versus American which goes deep down into the psyche of a woman to build up a gendered and sexualized paradigm. When the American media championed the 'model minority'[4] to be assimilated into the mainstream cultural hegemony, then it again rendered the women, who are the minority of the minority, as betrayed south Asians excluded and pushed to the corner, to appear as 'monolithic in public and even in private within the sanctity of the home' (Hand 103–104).

Amritjit Singh and Peter Schmidt in *Postcolonial Theory and the United States* have argued in favour of a more productive dialogue and mutual exchange between postcolonial and US ethnic studies. It is interesting to note that Meena Alexander and Trinh T. Minha have been clubbed together by Singh and Schmidt as examples of writers working at the intersection of the two cultural ethnicities: transnational and cosmopolitan. Alexander's work does not hesitate to crosscheck the problematic nature of racial politics within the US. In Minnesota she had a bad experience of racial slurs and verbal violence as a woman of colour, marked by a foreign accent. In negotiating her ethnic identity in the US, Alexander does not recuperate the idea of the US as a melting pot, into which ethnic minorities must relinquish their ethnic specificity to adopt an American identity. Alexander reconfirms to retain the particularities of her ethnic identity even when there is pressure to conform to a different standard. She walks down the Manhattan blocks with her sari on during her visits to the CUNY Graduate Center. However, the ever-present threat of violence in the aftermath of 9/11 forces her to wear western clothes on the street, changing into the sari in the ladies' room of the Graduate Center, where she teaches. This incident is captured in the poem 'Kabir Sings in a City of Burning Towers', anthologized in *Raw Silk*. The racialized otherness experienced earlier intensified during the racial profiling of South Asians and West Asians in the aftermath of 9/11. Alexander's work provides a launching pad to reflect and act on these problems of racial maneuvering and sexuality in US society. The other that has been exemplified in her skin and costume has also been stigmatized as a racialised matrix of sexuality.

In this connection Alexander's poem 'Rites of Sense' can be cited as an example of how she negotiates her fragile identity and her cultural in-betweeness. For Meena Alexander the question of freedom is a hard one. But of course it lies at the core of our existence in flux:

> Amma, I am dreaming myself into your body.
> It is the end of everything.
> Your pillow stained with white
> tosses as a wave might
> on our southern shore.
>
> Will you lay your cheek against mine?
> Bless my bent head?

> You washed me once, gave me suck,
> made me live in your father's house
> taught me to wake at dawn,
> sweep the threshold clean of blood red leaves.
> Showed me a patch of earth dug with your hands
> where sweet beans grow coiled and raw. ('Rites of Sense' 27)

The theme of the poem can be juxtaposed with her early novel *Nampally Road* of the monopoly of the modern nation-state is on the legitimacy of violence. It is not the external violence always, but it is the interiority of violence that renders her identity adrift in her travelling cultural space.

In *The Shock of Arrival*, among the American poetic figures that Alexander reflects on are Joy Harjo, Gloria Anzaldúa, Theresa Cha, Toni Morrison, Yusuf Komunyaaka, and Myung Mi Kim, among others. With Joy Harjo's poetry, Alexander arrives at a similar truth that colonialism has rendered them exiles in their own land. Alexander writes: 'And so the questions of colonialism bleed into an era of decolonization, into the complicated realms of American ethnicity' (*The Shock of Arrival* 5). Alexander thus makes an explicit connection between her own cultural inheritance of colonialism and Harjo's[5] distinct but comparable experiences of the loss of Native American culture and the survival of that culture, in spite of the genocide it has repeatedly encountered. She also finds a common theme of survival in the works of African-American writers like Morrison and Komunyaaka[6] that connect them to the theme of cultural loss and survival that emerges in Harjo's poetry. In Komunyaaka's poetry, Alexander witnesses the experiences of a black man growing up in segregated Louisiana and fighting in the Vietnam War, recording the irony of a person belonging to a racialized minority participating in an imperial war against a people of colour. Through her reflections on the works of these American writers, Alexander consciously creates a bridge between the experiences of a postcolonial Indian woman writer and the peculiar burdens of being a writer from a minority group within the US.

While creating these connections between the complex legacies of colonialism and the burdens of a racialized identity in the US, Alexander does not shy away from recording the horror and devastation of violent conflict in her poetry. In poems like 'San Andreas Fault' and 'Art of Pariahs', she crafts images of brutality with an almost journalistic commitment to veracity. Yet, these images of violence have a peculiar restraint and are held in a taut balance by Alexander's unswerving commitment to peace and love. The inspiration for Alexander for a fragile peace comes from her involvement with the tradition of medieval Bhakti and Sufi poetry. Her works are interspersed with a multitude of references to Rumi, Kabir, Mirabai, and Akkamahadevi. Although deeply condemnatory of the excesses of religious extremism in India, Alexander draws on this alternative tradition of mysticism, which is pluralistic and defiant of any one orthodox religion. Within this group, it is with the female mystical poets Akkamahadevi and Mirabai that Alexander feels the greatest affinity. In their steadfast devotion to their lords, both Mirabai and Akkamahadevi transgressed many of the established and accepted norms of feminine behaviour. Alexander identifies a connection between the bodily transgressions of these medieval Indian female mystics and the female poets of today. Their defiance of social standards and their love for their lords stand in contrast to the violent imposition of religious norms on societies. The mysticism of these women is a source for an alternative vision of the world, one based on love, tolerance, and joy. Alexander seizes this as a repository of hope in a world of suffering and despair.

Poetry as a Genre in Postcolonial Studies

Poetry in postcolonial scholarship has been badly ignored. How do we name the space for poetry within the postcolonial trajectory? Alexander uses a hyphen of Indian-American binary to negotiate an intercapillary void between prose and poetry. 'Post colonial poets have been marginalized in the discussion of post colonial literatures because the overarching paradigm for reading post colonial literature has been that of mimesis' (178) – observes Jahan Ramazani in his *The Hybrid Muse: Postcolonial Poetry in English*. He further elaborates his logic for the relative neglect of poetry in postcolonial studies for poetry is 'less favorable than other genres for curricular expeditions into the social history of the Third World: and consequently it is harder to annex as textual synecdoche for the social world of Nigeria, Trinidad, or India' (Ramazani 183). Foregrounding his arguments, Ramazani, rejecting the idea of Eurocentric homogenization of non-western literature, steps across the border to say that though the postcolonial poetry is a less transparent medium than the novel it ejects out a mosaic of a 'language of exceptional figural and formal density' (4) giving us deeper insights into postcolonial societies. Meena Alexander gets the entire support system from Ramzani's theory of postcolonial poetry in English. She is basically a poet of Indian origin, living in the US as a 'legal alien', confronting her own otherness in American society perpetually, tolerating her own hybridized self in a narrowly accessible manner, writing her own poetry as a bridge between Americanization and her postcolonial identity. She does exactly what the fiction writers do in their novels. In the aftermath of decolonization, Alexander is engaged with an on-going question in her poetry for the spillover of the colonialism into postcolonial oeuvre. 'Kabir Sings in a City of Burning Towers' from *Raw Silk*, is a poem that captures the aftermath of the 9/11. Similarly, she does not hesitate to ask Gandhi in another poem in the same anthology:

Mr Gandhi
Please say something
About the carnage in your home state. ('Raw Silk Mr Gandhi' 18)

Alexander juxtaposes two societies in flames of violence and trauma in a poetic way to ensure that the history of race is most captured in the clash of civilizations. Alexander's poetry is deeply engaged with the mixed legacies of violence, trauma, gender, race, and feminism. The gendered identity in a society replete with religious trauma and violence after 9/11 is a lonely traveller along the roads of multicultural transnationality. As a feminist, Alexander's mind is shaped by the intellectual legacy of the 1970s French and American feminism and by Indian women's struggles for social justice as well.

We can conclude by quoting Alexander's comment from *Poetics of Dislocation* on Joy Harjo who tolerated a total disappearance of her Native American land language and culture which were hijacked into a high power American cultural hegemony of modern time: 'colonialism has dispossessed her people, rendered them exiles in their own land, and Harjo is the griot of this forced exile, one who sings the body and soul that must survive passage' (23). Alexander has never been a forced exile in her own land; she chose her own destiny and destination by crossing the *kalapani* of the Indian Ocean, but she accepts grudgingly the idea of hyphenated identity put together from across the entire trajectory of the postcolonial hybridity.

Notes

1. Meena Alexander's *Fault Lines* as a book of autobiographical sketches was published in The Cross-Cultural Memoir Series. The book traces her development as a postcolonial writer from India to a much agitated adolescence in Sudan and then to England and New York City. It also closely examines Alexander's audacity and ambivalence of life as a South Asian American woman writer in a post 9/11 world.
2. In this autobiographical book Meena has told the story of her grandmother, her mother's mother, Elizabeth Kuruvila, a follower of Gandhi, the first woman member of the legislative assembly in Travancore who travelled widely all over India, to Europe and China. Meena must have inherited her gene for border-crossing from early childhood.
3. Jedi Knight in Star Wars is a symbol of hope in dark times. He is a fictitious knight at arms born in the imagination of Science fiction. The Jedi Knight stands for the legacy of the Jedi Order – more than 20,000 years of protecting the Republic and keeping the peace across the galaxy. Though Jedi Knights have served as generals, guerilla fighters, and warriors for generations, their legendary combat prowess faces its greatest test during this age. But Alexander digs up another meaning that Jedi is also an immigrant like South Asian aliens in America, he has his own culture from a distant planet, neither can he comprehend his new geography, nor can anyone understand him. Alexander's son is absolutely right to say that he is neither American, nor Indian, highlighting the dilemma and ambivalence of being an American of South Asian origin.
4. Model minority – South Asian immigrants became a sizable community in America with the immigration Act of 1965 which appeared to be non-racist and the law implemented was based on the preference for Indian professionals with high educational background, the Indians came to be regarded as model minority which categorically distinguished them as different from the early 20th century agrarian farmers in rural California. South Asians as exempt from unemployment and racism, the media myth of labeling the Indians as model minority has been internalized to a priority of becoming a stereotype expected to be living up to the standards of the model minority.
5. Native American woman poet Joy Harjo claims to be a poet of the lands that were stolen. Harjo never forgets her past, her origin, her

Native ways of life – but all these things are gone and lost and she enters into an imaginary world which truly existed once with a map buried deep in the heart.

6. Yusuf Komunyaaka, the first African-American male recipient of the Pulitzer Prize, had a difficult tenure of Military service during young adulthood which impacted his poetry enormously. Komunyaaka has been very prolific since his time at Irvine; he had published nine volumes of poetry. His third collection, *Copacetic* (1984), explored that after returning to Louisiana to show how the music of his home town was nuanced with racial issues of the time. The jazz music was not only a popular lifestyle in America but Komunyaaka realized that jazz was a platform for nursing the wounds caused by racial raptures and he transformed his poetry into a catharsis to heal the wounds.

References

Alexander, Meena. *Fault Lines*. New York: City University of New York, 1993.
——. *Night-Scene, The Garden*. New York: Red Dust, 1992.
——. *Poetics of Dislocation*. Ann Arbor: University of Michigan Press, 2009.
——. *Question of Home*. Poetry.org from the Academy of American Poets 2005. Web 5 April 2011.
——. *The Shock of Arrival: Reflections on Postcolonial Experience*. Boston: South End Press, 1996.
Hand, Felicity. "'The Old Rules are Not Always Right": An Analysis of Four Short Stories by Chitra Banerjee Divakaruni'. *Indian Women's Short Fiction*. (eds) Joel Kuortti and Rajeshwar Mittapalli. New Delhi: Atlantic, 2007. 103–104.
Ramazani, Jahan. *The Hybrid Muse: Postcolonial Poetry in English*. Chicago: Chicago University Press, 2001.
Singh, Arijit, and Peter Schmidt. *Postcolonial Theory and the United States*. Mississippi: University Press of Mississippi, 2000.

Appendix

Meena Alexander speaks and writes to Subodh Sarkar about her ambivalence between her Indian home and US ethnicity.*

Subodh Sarkar: Do you feel comfortable in the US when you wear sari or salwar kameez or any other Indian dress? Do you feel you are too much noticed, too much exposed as a legal alien?

MA: I do wear both, though much less so in winter. About being noticed? In New York there is such a mix of cultures, one sees all sorts of costumes on the subway and in the street. After 9/11 there was discomfort though, in case clothing brought too much notice. I have written about this in my poem 'Kabir Sings in the City of Burning Towers'.

SS: When you visit India, is your identity as an American citizen carried forward to your place of origin? When you went to the US, I am sure, you had an all-pervading obsession that you were carrying a home on your back. When you come to India do you feel you are carrying an extra-luggage? How do you settle this ambivalence?

MA: As a poet one is used to carrying conflicting worlds within, and the fluidity of self is what one longs for, a realm where the present is composed of all this richness. Are things hard sometimes, yes? Would I have it otherwise, I don't think so. This is my life, I write from it. When I walk in the street in Kerala, I really don't feel I am carrying extra baggage as you put it. But these are short visits home. What would it be

---

* This interview was born out of our several conversations over the years. I met Meena Alexander in New York and in New Delhi and we had discussions on Indian and American poets and poetry. I noticed in her a deep rooted search for Indian literature written in languages and also in the postcolonial write back generation. In India, she is not oblivious of America, and in America, she carries an invisible home on her back. None of her destinations is her final destiny, but it is the manifestation of her unique ambivalence that encourages her to participate in the melting pot of multiculturalism. This interview which was finally done electronically in 2009 was published in Sahitya Akademi's journal. See Meena Alexander in the editorial of *Indian Literature* September 2010 New Delhi.

like to live a very long time in India? I don't know. Perhaps one day it will happen or perhaps not.

SS: What is your idea of America? Is it really a mosaic of cultures as they gleefully claim? Or it is the vainglory of a totalitarian culture of a capitalist society? Some of the Indians of exceptional merit have been honored with positions in White House, Hollywood or NASA. These are only the bubbles of the upper class ethos and not the oxygen for all those who have migrated from India. Do you think the idea of America and the idea of India go together to give you a free zone of your own or you feel the transnational space for a writer is a hoax?

MA: For me the best idea of America is that of a great democratic continent that embraces the pulsing, various forms of life within. The truth? The truth is often bittersweet – there is poverty here, and injustice both economic and racial; there is also hope and exhilaration and wonderful thought and writing. The militarism of America is something I find very hard. There are people who resist it, but are their voices heard? I think of my friend Grace Paley the poet, who died not so long ago. All her life she was a member of the War Resister's League. I have an elegy I wrote for her, its on the web I believe: 'Nocturnal with Ghostly Landscape, on St Lucy's Day' – its in part about the war in Iraq.

SS: You have a new title now Poetics of Dislocation from University of Michigan. Congratulations. Your readers are aware of the fact that you are twice dislocated from the culture of one geography to the culture of another territory. How is your poetics of dislocation born?

MA: I really have no answer to this question, because all this is a mystery to me, part of survival.

SS:You were born in Allahabad, you were christened 'Mary Elizabeth' but you officially changed your name to Meena at the age of fifteen. This is also a sort of dislocation from one name to another. Your life began with a small dislocation but it entered in to a series, one leading to the other. Do you remember Mary Elizabeth?

MA: In a way it was not such a big change because I was always called Meena at home by my family. The formal name was for school and other such situations. Do I remember her? It's a good question. I see a girl in school in Sudan, a small girl with two plaits, struggling with a notebook.

SS: You went to Sudan with your family, then moved to England to receive your PhD, back to India to teach at Delhi University and you taught also at Hyderabad where you met your future husband, Now you are settled in New York as a writer, as a poet, as a professor. The story sounds like a romantic tale but it has its own angst and ennui. Is your poetry an oath against the oblivion and agony of dislocation?

MA: O my dear, I do not know what my poetry is. It is as much a part of me now as breathing and dreaming. Perhaps poetry is the dream that allows us to be real.

SS: One critic writes: 'With its restless crowds, cinemas, shops, temples, mango sellers, cobblers, cafes, and bars, Nampally Road becomes a metaphor for contemporary India. Alexander has given us an unsentimental, multifaceted portrait, thankfully remote from that of the British Raj. Her lyrical narrative has the eloquent economy that marks her best poetry ... . Alexander treads the waters of fiction lightly and gracefully' (Village Voice). Do you agree with this view? How do you recognize the metaphor for contemporary India? In what sense it is remote from that of the British Raj?

MA: If I remember correctly this was written about my first novel. It was set in Hyderabad where I lived and worked and where I am now returning for a month as a poet in residence at the University. Mercifully I was born after independence; I did not live during the British Raj.

SS: One Fault Lines, an exquisite work of autobiography you have written how you struggled to forge a sense of identity against a past replete with the memories of moves and changes. In this great book you have painfully tried to retain your identity like a snail carrying its home on its own back. You wrote: 'I am, a woman cracked by multiple migrations'. Do you still feel that you can connect nothing with nothing?

MA: Sometimes I do feel that. Perhaps a little less so than before.

SS: Does your Hyphenated identity hurt you in every moment of isolation and introspection?

MA: No, there is much else in life to think about.

SS: Do you think your autobiography is an extension of what you do in your poetry? When I write poems, I do feel I am writing my autobiography in disguise. I like your poems immensely. How do you transfer your prowess as a poet to the realm of prose?

MA: This is an excellent question and I do ask this myself, sometimes. I have not got to the bottom of this alchemical process. There are times when I do have to wait for form, the line becomes fluid, longer, and prose comes upon us. But in poems too, that leaps and trot of rhythm, its true can extend to prose. I do play with form a lot. I learn through this. Of course sometimes the poem comes, needing, requiring a particular shape, a particular clarity. I remember something the Malayalam poet Ayyappa Paniker once said to me: 'Meena let the poem come to you. The great poems will come, wanting to be written.' I do believe this.

SS: The Shock of Arrival: Reflections on Postcolonial Experience (1996) is another book I love to read again and again. I can feel the green wounds of a young woman of Indian origin badly negotiating her physical and metaphysical borders, accommodating the fears of interracial conflicts and tiptoeing on the threshold between entry and exit. Is that 'Shock' over now? Do you feel that you now contribute to the American Mosaic of multi-culturalism more comfortably than before?

MA: Thank you for your words. It was a hard book to write, but a necessary book for me. Now I have gone on, kept on writing, made a world with that.

New York City 24 December 2009

CHAPTER 15

Imtiaz Dharker's Responses to 9/11 and 7/7
A Study

SANJOY MALIK

Imtiaz Dharker is one of the few Muslim women poets from the Indian Diaspora. As a poet, Bruce King argues, she has multiple affiliations: she is a poet who is from a 'British Muslim Pakistani family' but has 'become an Indian poet' (280). In fact, Indian English poetry is no longer confined to India only. As Bruce King thinks, 'Indian poetry has become a global network of writers in many countries' (280). In such a network, Imtiaz Dharker has found her place as a new Indian woman poet along with other Indian Diaspora poets like Meena Alexander, Menka Shivdasani, Sujata Bhatt, and Chitra Banerjee Divakaruni. This essay, however, is neither an examination of the aesthetics of Indian diaspora poetry, nor is it an elaborate study of Dharker's poetry; it is rather an attempt to examine how Imtiaz Dharker responds to the ways in which the Western governments treat the Muslim immigrants in the wake of the terrorist attacks, particularly after 9/11 and 7/7.

In the history of America, 9/11 is a momentous event. The attacks not only destroyed the twin towers of the World Trade Center but killed thousands of people. The trauma the violent attacks of 9/11 produced left the entire nation stranded. These attacks exposed the myth of national security and individual freedom the US had prided itself on. After 9/11, a sense of insecurity gripped the US and the government initiated a military campaign known as the 'war on terror' to eliminate al-Qaeda, the perpetrators of the 9/11 attacks, and other militant organizations. The government also adopted stringent internal security measures in order to combat terrorism or to thwart any terrorist plans. In doing so, the US developed a high degree of scepticism towards Islam and Muslims. As Jocelyne Cesari puts it in his *When Islam and Democracy Meet: Muslims in Europe and in the United States*: 'For perhaps the first time in the United States, an entire religion is not only subjected to widespread public suspicion, but also to governmental surveillance of its activities and associations' (80). Europe, in fact, was also not spared from terrorist strikes. The London bombings of 7 July 2005 (also known as 7/7) that killed many people, destabilized the UK and made it suffer from a sense of utter insecurity. In the wake of the attacks, the European countries tightened up security measures and, like the US, they also began to suspect the immigrants. In doing so, they singled out Muslim immigrants and made them victims of various forms of discrimination and harassment. In his article 'The War on Terror and Muslims in the West', rightly does Mahmood Monshipouri point out: 'In Europe counterterrorism measures have led to discriminatory policies towards Muslim immigrants, especially in the case of nationality or citizenship tests, which tend to undermine the efforts of those Muslims who have sought to bridge their faith with Western values' (45–46). After 9/11 and 7/7, the countries in the West conceived of Islam in negative terms, considering it to be solely their enemy. They even went so far as to stereotype the Muslim immigrants as terrorists. They suspected Muslims of having links to terrorist outfits and having knowledge of terrorist plots, and, in the process, tried to rob them of their civil liberties. After 9/11, Louise Cainkar observes: 'Muslims were persons who, if not terrorists themselves, might be hiding terrorists or covering up the knowledge of brewing terrorist plots. So constructed, Arabs and Muslims in the US were symbolically reconstituted as people who were not really part of the American nation, they were the "them", and thus not fully eligible for its package of civil and constitutional rights' (184). In fact, many Indian diasporic writers have responded to the discriminatory policies and measures of the Western governments after 9/11 and 7/7. Whereas Meena Alexander, Chitra Banerjee Divakaruni, Jeet Thayil, among many others, have responded mainly to the aftermath of the terrorist attacks of 9/11,

Imtiaz Dharker has written about the terrorist attacks of both 9/11 and 7/7 and their aftermath.

Dharker addresses the hard times the Muslim immigrants face in the Western societies after 9/11 and 7/7 in her book *The Terrorist at My Table* (2007). In the section titled 'These are the times we live in', Dharker uses a number of collages to show how the British Muslims are suspected to be terrorists and, as a result, are robbed of their civil liberties as British citizens in the immediate aftermath of the 7/7 attacks. In the poem 'These are the times we live in I' written against the backdrop of the failed 21/7 attack,[1] Dharker captures the picture of a Muslim passenger being suspected and harassed by the British security agency in an airport:

> You hand over your passport. He
> looks at your face and starts
> reading you backwards from the last page.
> (...)
> You shrink to the size
> of the book in his hand. (1–3, 9–10)

The moment the security agent begins to closely examine the Muslim passenger, the latter begins to apprehend that he is going to be victimized as a terrorist. Imagining the disastrous life that a terror-suspect may face, he loses all his strength of mind. His entity begins to fall apart and inwardly he is reduced to 'the size of the book' held by the security agent. In the same poem Dharker further writes about how the security agent gets prejudiced against this Muslim passenger:

> You can see his mind working:
> Keep an eye on that name.
> It contains a Z, ... (11–13)

From the passport the security agent comes to know of the Muslim identity of the passenger. The Muslim name immediately evokes in his mind all the negative images that are associated with the Muslims in the common perception of the West. Once the security agent is confirmed that the name with a letter Z is a Muslim person's name, his suspicion increases. This suspicion seems to be impelled by the names, Ramzi Mohammed, one of the bombers of the abortive 21 terrorist attacks, and Shehzad Tanweer, one of the perpetrators of 7/7 terrorist attacks. Dharker shows that the security agent holds a very simplistic and essentialist view that any Muslim with the letter Z in his name could be a terrorist. So, the security agent frantically looks for discrepancies between the actual person and his photograph so as to detain the Muslim passenger. Dharker writes:

> In front of you
> he flicks to the photograph,
> and looks at you suspiciously. (20–22)

Non-availability of anything suspicious or any clues to the terrorist activities of the passenger leaves the security agent dissatisfied. Even after allowing the Muslim passenger in the flight, the security personnel continues to suspect him because of his (the security personnel's) anti-Muslim bias.

The act of harassing the Muslim passenger by the security personnel in the following manner amounts to torture and at the same time produces tactile sensations that make the passenger's own body alien to him:

> they changed your chin
> and redid your hair
> They scrubbed out your mouth
> and rubbed out your eyes.
> They made you over completely. (26–30)

When the governments have a little or almost no trust in the Muslim citizens, the Westerners take it for granted that they would keep harassing their fellow Muslim citizens. They indulge in acts like abusing, spitting, etc. Even Muslim women in the West are not spared. They are suspected either of being terrorists or the agents of terrorists and often become the victims of hate crimes. After 9/11, the racial prejudice against veiling on part of the Westerners becomes so intense that some of them go to the extent of pulling off the veils of the Muslim women publicly, thereby hurting their religious sentiments as is evident in Dharker's poem 'Its Face':

> This cloth belongs to my face.
> Who pulled it off?
> #
> That day I saw you
> as if a window had broken.

Sharp, with edges that could cut
through cloth and skin. (5-10)

The Westerners cannot tolerate the public display of the markers of Muslim identity, which, they believe, are nothing but anti-Modern and anti-West. In the face of this kind of intense anti-Muslim sentiment, the Muslim immigrants are miserably left coping with their religious identity. Tolerance for and recognition of difference in culture and ethnicity that are central to a multicultural society seem to disappear from the US during the post 9/11 period. It is not that the wearing of veils is not in consonance with the principles of American democracy which gives the freedom of religion. Despite this, many Muslim women who wear veils become victims of various forms of injustice in the US after 9/11.

Dharker is concerned about the Muslim identity in changed circumstances when she finds that Muslim immigrants are victims of the Western stereotypical assumption that they are terrorists. In the poem 'These are the times we live in II', Dharker emboldens the Muslim in the West to rise to the occasion and also prescribes him certain ways of tackling the situation:

Fight to get out of this.
Wrestle your way through.
Stop this thing
that is happening to you.
I'm nobody, you must say.
Don't point me out,
erase my photograph.
My name can't be on the list. (1-8)

When an innocent Muslim citizen is marked and photographed and his name is included in the list of the terror suspects, he apprehends that he is going to be under the surveillance of government agencies. He also apprehends that the normalcy of his life is going to be disrupted and even snatched away. The media will not lose the opportunity of stigmatizing him and making his life a hell. He is appalled at anticipating different forms of harassment and torture now and then. All these acts are likely to traumatize him. He finds not only his citizenship blatantly denied, but also his life utterly vulnerable because he is a Muslim. The Westerners have a prejudiced notion that Muslims are not compatible with the host societies. In the poem, Dharker, therefore, asks the Muslim to make a strong statement and teaches him what to say in his defence:

> I was not on that plane,
> That bus, that train
> I had left the building.
>
> I don't belong inside
> your cage of coverage.
> I'm not in the news. (9-14)

Here Dharker seems to ask the question: why should the Muslims be singled out? The poem shows that the suspected Muslim individual seeks to extricate himself from this painful life as he is captured inside the 'cage of coverage'. While he himself is innocent, having no links with any terrorist organizations, he is being suspected of being a terrorist and made to undergo various forms of harassment. He finds his movement being constantly watched and feels that he is a victim of unfair racial profiling. This is a kind of torture in the name of combating terrorism and ensuring the security of the country and it is nothing but a reflection of the racism entrenched in the West.

The American government officials are justifiably determined to ward off any potential terrorist attack. But in doing this, they are impelled by the assumption that terrorists are hiding among the Arab and Muslim Americans, who behave normally in the public space and wait for the opportune moment to attack the innocent Americans. The officials also hold a stereotypical belief that the Muslims have a proclivity to violence and terrorism and those who are not involved in such activities, at least support terrorism. Imtiaz Dharker seeks to subvert the Western stereotypical view that Muslims are a homogeneous group. In connection with this, it is important to mention what Tariq Modood in his article 'Muslims and the Politics of Difference' says. He observes:

> Muslims are ... not a homogeneous group. Some Muslims are devout but apolitical; some are political but do not see their politics as being 'Islamic', (indeed they may even be anti-Islamic). Some identify more with a nationality of origin such as Turkish; others with the nationality of settlement and perhaps with citizenship such as French. Some prioritize fundraising for mosques, others campaigns (sic) against discrimination, unemployment or Zionism. (193-194)

Imtiaz Dharker finds not only the Muslim identity at stake but also the existence of Muslim minorities at stake in a diasporic context and in this she finds no difference between the US and the UK governments, both of which homogenize the Muslims. Through one of the collages in *The Terrorist at My Table*, Dharker seems to highlight the non-homogeneity of the Muslims by stating the fact that after the 7/7 attacks many imams vehemently condemned the attacks as un-Islamic. This condemnation, however, failed to convince the British administration. Rather the administration, in the name of containing and eradicating terrorism, went on making life unbearable for the Muslims. The poem 'These are the times we live in III' brings out this crisis:

> They got an eraser as big as a house
> and they began to use it to delete your life,
> the names of your lanes and roads and streets,
> your stories and your histories,
> your lullabies. They rubbed
> out your truth, and they left in your lies. (1–6)

An 'eraser', a familiar thing, is presented here in the light of defamiliarization and hence, looks strange when the poet compares this small thing with a big one, a house – an unusual comparison, indeed. This house-like eraser has been portrayed as a tool of effacement. The host country like the UK has been so hostile towards its Muslim immigrants that it begins, with that kind of an eraser, to efface the names of the Muslim lanes, roads, streets in the UK and their stories, histories, and lullabies – the signs of attachment to their host society. Even the government officials snatch the 'family portraits' of the Muslims containing the lineage, and 'shot all over again with different people' as they are frantically looking for clues and trying to establish any possible links to terrorism or terrorist organizations. In the process, the officials, in the name of ensuring national security, not only intrude into the privacy of the family space of the Muslim immigrants, but also disrupt it in violent ways.

In an interview with Nandini Nair, Imtiaz Dharker says what the book *The Terrorist at My Table* is exactly about: 'The book is not about terrorism. It is more about how to deal with the constant doubt, suspicion.' In the book, she does not talk about what makes the terrorists. Nor does she talk about whether the terrorists striking the Western societies are justified or not. Dharker is rather highly critical of the ways in which the Western governments single out the Muslim immigrants and suspect them to be terrorists. The police and military often intrude into the personal lives of the Muslim immigrants. They ask them, for example, to open their emails so as to trace the possible terrorist links and if a Muslim immigrant fails to remember the password for the email id, s/he is highly suspected. In this context, it is important to mention that in the UK, a law, known as the 'British Anti-terrorism, Crime, and Security Bill', was passed on 13 November 2001 and this law greatly enhanced the power of the police and military to demand financial records, email, postal communication, and transportation records of anybody who is suspected as a terrorist (Monshipouri 54). The fact that the immigrant Muslim is an American citizen or a British citizen does not carry any meaning if s/he fails to provide, for example, email details. Such an immigrant is immediately ordered to leave the host country. In the poem 'Password', Imtiaz Dharker quite effectively brings out this predicament a Muslim immigrant finds himself in:

> You have to remember the Password.
> [...]
> Give it to me.
> Right now.
> Wrong!
> You don't have the Password.
> That was your last try. Sorry.
> Pack up. Move on. Goodbye. (1, 13–18)

This kind of treatment that the Muslim immigrants receive is nothing but a legacy of the neo-Orientalist attitude of the West that sees the Muslims as the other. Islamophobia often prompts the Westerners to develop certain prejudices against the Muslims. Dharker seems to have contested such prejudices when she uses Abdul Rehman Malik's article 'Hear the True Voices of Islam' as an illustration in *The Terrorist at My Table*. This article highlights the meeting between the Prime Minister Tony Blair and the 'moderate' Muslim leaders in the wake of the 7/7 London bombings. In this meeting, when the 'moderate' leaders, thought to be the representatives of the British Muslims, agree to the creation of a task force for tackling the 'evil ideology' of militant Islam; they, perhaps, make it clear that those terrorists who have perpetrated this violence are

Islamist militants rather than true Muslims. By using Abdul Rehman Malik's article as an illustration in her book, Dharker seems to foreground Malik's view that Islam has become an 'aberrant theology' in the hands of the terrorists and that all Muslims cannot be suspected to be terrorists. In this context, one can refer to Jane I. Smith who, in the article 'Islam in America', says: 'Muslims themselves are suffering from the pain of seeing a few of their co-religionists act in extremist ways that they strongly disavow, some even saying that they feel true Islam has been hijacked by those who do violence in the name of the faith' (40). In a similar vein, Dharker seems to have suggested that very few Muslims are terrorists and this is a fact which cannot be generalized. A handful of Muslims are perpetrating violence in the name of Islam but Islam does not condone any act of violence or terrorism.

Dharker also seeks to debunk the neo-Orientalist view that Islam and terrorism are inseparable. Mahmood Mamdani, in his very famous *Good Muslim Bad Muslim: Islam, the USA, and the Global War against Terror*, too believes that religion has nothing to do with terrorism and says: 'Terrorism is not a necessary effect of religious tendencies – whether fundamentalist or secular. Rather terrorism is born of a political encounter. When it harnesses one or another aspect of tradition and culture, terrorism needs to be understood as a modern political movement at the service of a modern power' (61–62). Louise Archer, in his article 'Race, "Face" and Masculinity: The Identities and Local Geographies of Muslim Boys' tells us about how the British doubt the loyalty of their fellow Muslim citizens. He says that British Muslim youngmen 'are popularly feared as the archetypal "outsiders within" – those who cannot be trusted and whose loyalty to the nation-state, and to the values and ideology of "Britishness", cannot be counted upon' (74). The Europeans predominantly believe that the harmony between Islam and Europe is almost impossible. In this context, Dharker's poem 'Still here' seems to be very interesting in which she writes:

Its (sic) just to reassure yourself
you are still in place

Still here. (11–13)

This is interesting to note that in spite of facing all kinds of hostility, in the poem Dharker shows that the Muslims still do not lose their sense of belonging and their loyalty to the host countries.

In the wake of different terrorist attacks, the Western societies tend to perceive the Muslim immigrants only in terms of their religious identity; the ethnic identity of the Muslims now seems to have relegated to the background. Imtiaz Dharker in her poetry collection *The Terrorist at My Table* (2007), written after the 9/11 and the 7/7 terrorist attacks, challenges the Western stereotypical construction of Muslim identity which believes that Muslims are a homogeneous group of terrorists. She, therefore, protests against the harassment of the law-abiding 'good' Muslims in the name of war against terrorism. She also seeks to dispel the Westerners' misconception that Islam condones terrorism and instead tries to convince them that Islam actually condemns terrorism. Only a few Muslims who are terrorists misrepresent Islam, thereby tarnishing its true image. *The Terrorist at My Table*, in fact, seems to make a plea for a true understanding of the Muslims and the Islam in the West.

Note

1. On 21 July 2005 six terrorists, who intended to cause a large-scale loss of life in London, failed in their attempts because the bombs they used did not explode. Only the detonators of the bombs exploded, thereby causing minor injury, but no fatality.

References

Archer, Louise. 'Race, 'Face' and Masculinity: The Identities and Local Geographies of Muslim Boys'. *Muslims in Britain: Race, Place and Identities*. (eds) Peter Hopkins and Richard Gale. Edinburgh: Edinburgh University Press, 2009. 74–94.
Cainkar, Louise. 'American Muslims at the Dawn of the 21st Century: Hope and Pessimism in the Drive for Civic and Political Inclusion'. *Muslims in the West after 9/11: Religion, Politics and Law*. London and New York: Routledge, 2010. 176–197.
Cesari, Jocelyne. *When Islam and Democracy Meet: Muslims in Europe and in the United States*. New York: Palgrave Macmillan, 2004.
Dharker, Imtiaz. 'In Verse and Visuals'. Interview by Nandini Nair. *The Hindu*. 19 May 2007: n.p. Web 21 June 2014. <http://www.thehindu.com/todays-paper/tp-features/tp-metroplus/in-verse-and-visuals/article2256747.ece>.
——. 'Its Face'. *The Terrorist at My Table*. New Delhi: Penguin Books, 2007. 21.

———. 'Password'. *The Terrorist at My Table*. New Delhi: Penguin Books, 2007. 51.

———. 'Still Here'. *The Terrorist at My Table*. New Delhi: Penguin Books, 2007. 53.

———. 'These are the times we live in I'. *The Terrorist at My Table*. New Delhi: Penguin Books, 2007. 45.

———. 'These are the times we live in II'. *The Terrorist at My Table*. New Delhi: Penguin Books, 2007. 47.

———. 'These are the times we live in III'. *The Terrorist at My Table*. New Delhi: Penguin Books, 2007. 49.

King, Bruce. *Modern Indian Poetry in English*. Oxford: Oxford University Press, 2001.

Malik, Abdul Rehman. 'Hear the True Voices of Islam'. *The Observer*. 24 July 2005. Web 7 September 2013. <www.theguardian.com/uk/2005/jul/24/july7.religion>.

Mamdani, Mahmood. *Good Muslim Bad Muslim: Islam, the USA, and the Global War against Terror*. New Delhi: Permanent Black, 2005.

Modood, Tariq. 'Muslims and the Politics of Difference'. *Muslims in Britain: Race, Place and Identities*. (eds) Peter Hopkins and Richard Gale. Edinburgh: Edinburgh University Press, 2009. 193–209.

Monshipouri, Mahmood. 'The War on Terror and Muslims in the West'. *Muslims in the West after 9/11: Religion, Politics, and Law*. (ed.) Jocelyne Cesari. London: Routledge, 2010. 45–66.

Smith, I. Jane. 'Islam in America'. *Muslims in the West after 9/11: Religion, Politics, and Law*. (ed.) Jocelyne Cesari. London: Routledge, 2010. 28–42.

Index

Acculturation, 5
Ahmed, Aijaz, 107
Alexander, Meena, 7, 29, 33, 213–220, 223–228
Ali, Kazim, 96
Ali, Monica, 68, 113, 125, 132
Amnesia, 17
Anderson, Benedict, 58
Appadurai, Arjun, 30, 46
Arnold, William, 14
Ashcroft, Bill, 104
Asian-African Heritage Exhibition, 84
Awaaz, 85

Babri Masjid, 93
Basu, Kunal, 75, 140
Benjamin, Walter, 74
Bhabha, Homi K., 17, 29, 31, 68
Bhasha literatures, 8
Bhasha writer, 8

Bhatt, Sujata, 33, 227
Bissoondath, Neil, 7, 13, 19, 23–24
Brah, Avtar, 91
Braziel, Jana Evans, 3, 4
Bush, George W., 90

Chadha, Gurinder, 164, 170, 171, 175–177, 185, 187
Chakrabarty, Dipesh, 17, 72
Chatterjee, Partha, 72
Chaudhury, Amit, 113
Clifford, J., 1
Cosmopolitanism, 129
Cyber Communication, 30
Cyber Space, 2

Dabag, Mihran, 1
Dabydeen, Cyril, 13, 23, 24
Das, Kamala, 35
Dasgupta, Alokeranjan, 8

Index

de Man, Paul, 74
Derrida, J., 17
Desai, Anita, 33, 186
Desai, Kiran, 68, 193
Deshachars, 144
Devi, Mahasweta, 22
Dharker, Imtiaz, 227, 229–236
Diaspora studies, 6
Diasporic writing, 6
Divakaruni, Chitra Banerjee, 75, 94–95, 227–228
Dukawallah, 82–83, 86
Durant, Sam, 17

émigrés, 68
Espinet, Ramabai, 13, 23
Expatriate Writer, 7

Faber and Faber, 202–203
F.D.I., 56
Finance Capital, 3
Foucault, Michel, 118
Freud, Sigmund, 18, 20, 23, 25
Frye, Northrope, 73, 76

Ghare Baire, 41
Ghetto, 37
Ghosh, Amitav, 8, 70, 72, 75
Gilroy, Paul, 17, 69
Globalization, 43–50, 53, 59, 60, 67, 71, 139, 144, 170
Govender, Ronnie, 15
Gupta, Sunetra, 94, 113

Hall, Stuart, 17, 113, 159, 175, 186
Hassim, Aziz, 95
Husain, M.F., 15

Imaginative Realism, 73, 78
Impossible Mourning, 17
Indentured labourers, 13
Indianness, 33, 42, 158, 188
International Monetary Fund, 49
International Organization for Migration, 47
Ishigura, Kazuo, 16
Islamophobia, 234
Iyer, Pico, 15–16

Jahazi Bhai, 18, 53

Kalapani, 220
Kar, Angshuman, 201
Kargil War, 58
Khair, Tabish, 75
King, Bruce, 227
Krishna, Srinivas, 140, 148, 151, 153–154
Kureishi, Hanif, 113, 125, 132, 140–141, 173 –174, 199–203, 205–208

Lacan, J., 20, 127
Lahiri, Jhumpa, 33, 94, 102–103, 113, 118, 124, 140, 143, 186
Lal, Brij V., 4
Lefebvre, Henri, 123

Mamdani, Mahmood, 235
Mannur, Anita, 3, 4, 94
Markandaya, Kamala, 33, 96
Mathur, Anurag, 7, 94
Minha, Trinh T., 218
Mishra, Sudesh, 17, 19
Mishra, Vijay, 14, 17, 19–20, 124, 127
Mistry, Rohinton, 19, 115
Modood, Tariq, 93, 232
Morrison, Toni, 74
Mukherjee, Bharati, 19, 22, 33, 68, 75, 113
Mukherjee, Meenakshi, 42, 103
Multiculturalism, 94, 117, 121, 139–140, 152–153, 158, 168

Naficy, Hamid, 141–147, 148, 151, 154–155
Naik, Panna, 29, 33
Naipaul, V.S. 7, 23, 189
Nair, Mira, 143, 144–145, 154
Namjoshi, Suniti, 33, 181
Naxalbari movement, 102, 104–106, 110
Nelson, Emmanuel S., 31
9/11, 5, 90–92, 104, 207, 213, 217, 220, 227–231, 236
Non-Resident Indians, 55, 147

Obama, Barack, 103
OCI, 69

Pandey, Mangal, 125–126, 133

Parameswaran, Uma, 15, 94, 96
Pardesh, 144
Parmar, Pratibha, 178–182
Phillips, Caryl, 18
PIO Card, 56, 59
Platt, Kristin, 1
Postcolonialism, 33, 219, 221
Pravasi Bharatiya Divas, 8, 56, 57

Rao, Raja 7, 93
Rath, Sura P., 31
Ray, Satyajit, 142
Ricoeur, Paul, 18
Rushdie, Salman, 19, 68, 71–72, 125, 140, 200, 203–205, 207

Safran, William, 1–2, 43–44, 51, 68
Scapes, 46
Sen, Amartya, 32, 51, 95
Sepoy Mutiny, 125
7/7, 207, 227–229, 233–234, 236
Siddiqi, Jameela, 86
Sidhwa, Bapsi, 140
Skype, 68
Smith, Zadie, 113, 116–118, 120–121, 125, 128, 131–132
Spivak, Gayatri Chakraborty, 22, 32
Srinivasan, Shiva Kumar, 17, 20–21
Submigrants, 68
Sunder Rajan, Rajeswari, 42
Syal, Meera, 163, 167, 186–191, 193–194

Tagore, Rabindranath, 41–42
Thatcher, Margaret, 121, 173, 206
Thiong'O, Ngugi wa, 83
Tinker, Hugh, 53
Tololyan, Khachig, 1, 45, 68
Transculturalism, 67, 111
Transmigrants, 68
Transnational constellation, 2
Transnationalism, 3, 44, 47–48, 50, 67

Trishanku, 31, 161

Vassanji, M.G., 76, 86, 95, 124
Verto Vec Steven, 45

Washington Post, 81
Weil, Simone, 16
World Bank, 49
World Trade Organization, 49

Zizek, Slavoj, 20, 153

6060101